on track ...

Gong

every album, every song

Kevan Furbank

sonicbondpublishing.com

Sonicbond Publishing Limited
www.sonicbondpublishing.co.uk
Email: info@sonicbondpublishing.co.uk

First Published in the United Kingdom 2021
First Published in the United States 2021
This edition 2025.

British Library Cataloguing in Publication Data:
A Catalogue record for this book is available from the British Library

ISBN 978-1-78952-340-9

Typeset in ITC Garamond Std & ITC Avant Garde Gothic
Printed and bound in England

Graphic design and typesetting: Full Moon Media

Thanks to ...

I want to give my gushing, heartfelt thanks to a number of Gong people who very generously contributed their time, memories and general wisdom towards the production of this book.

In particular, I want to give three cheers and a tiger to: the current magnificent Gong lineup of Kavus Torabi, Dave Sturt, Fabio Golfetti, Ian East and the mysterious Cheb Nettles; the bass legend and producer Mike Howlett; the tall and handsome Josh Pollock; Gongmaison, Shapeshifter and Magick Brother violinist Graham Clark; Jonny Greene of www.planetgong.co.uk; Harry Williamson; Brian Abbott; Keith 'Missile Bass' Bailey; and Trilogy synth wizard Tim Blake. Without their assistance, this book would be an awful lot thinner.

I want to thank Stephen Lambe of Sonicbond Publishing for his encouragement, guidance and support.

And, last but definitely not least, thanks to my wife Liz and daughters Sarah and Emily for being my Pot Head Pixies.

on track ...

Gong

Contents

Introduction

In the late 1970s I visited a friend studying at the Imperial College, London. He was a Mike Oldfield fan and had found, lurking in the college music library, an album by Pierre Moerlen's Gong that featured the *Tubular Bells* guitarist on the title track, 'Downwind'. He investigated further and discovered another Gong album that sported on its cover a large, green cartoon teapot.

He described the two albums to me thus: 'This,' he said, holding up *Downwind*, 'is great. But this,' holding up *Flying Teapot*, 'is a load of rubbish.'

Intrigued, I listened to both albums on his portable record player (a primitive music reproduction device, kiddies. Look it up on Wikipedia) and discovered he was half right. *Downwind* was, indeed, great. But *Flying Teapot* was wonderful!

How to describe the aural delights that burst from those innocent-looking microgrooves? It is said that writing about music is like dancing about architecture. In which case, writing about Gong music must be like dancing about architecture while stoned and dressed as a pixie.

Silly yet serious. Apparently random yet carefully constructed. Sometimes angry but frequently bathed in love. Musically daring and unpredictable yet played with consummate skill, with bass and drums interlocked like the pieces of a Rubik's Cube. With Gong, you never know what is coming next. But you know it will be life-affirming, genre-crushing and ear-tickling. It will be like nothing you have ever heard before.

But there is more to Gong than, er, Gong. Its family tree has grown and spread like a particularly virulent Japanese knotweed, creating an entire forest of wonder. Pierre Moerlen's Gong, Mother Gong, Gongmaison, New York Gong, Planet Gong, The University of Errors, Brainville, Hadouk, the Invisibles – all have ploughed their own unique furrow yet added to and enriched the Gong musical landscape.

So much so that Gong have been able to continue and develop despite key members escaping their earthbound existences. Daevid Allen – who planted the seed and nurtured the family tree – sadly left us in 2015. Yet Gong goes on under new leader Kavus Torabi, who wasn't even born when the band's first two albums were released.

This book is a celebration of Gong music, track by track, with some history and mystery thrown in. It also covers most of the offshoots and spin-offs but steers clear of solo work – that would really demand a book in itself. Fans will hopefully find something new and interesting within the pages – at the very least, the book may encourage you to go back and listen to all those wonderful albums all over again.

For those who are intrigued but unfamiliar with the world they are about to explore, I suggest you sit down with a cup of tea, book in hand, first album on the turntable or on the *Spotify* playlist and your ears – and mind – set to open.

A Pot Head History

He knew what he wanted to do for the rest of his life at the age of seven. A bunch of Irish-Australian gipsies hit town 'in a cloud of dust, leapt out of this old van and started playing the most fantastic music I had ever heard'. What impressed young Christopher David Allen – born 1938 in Melbourne – was not just the sounds produced by these itinerant troubadours but also the fact that it was a family affair. Even children aged three and four were making a contribution. He thought: 'That's what I want to do. No doubt about it.' So he bought himself a ukulele, which was soon replaced by a guitar.

It is unlikely his father had the same career trajectory in mind. Walter Allen was a director of an upmarket department store in Melbourne, Australia, and got his wayward son a job there. But, being very tall, Christopher saw further than most people, and what he discovered was this: A flourishing of art, music and protest taking place on the other side of the world.

He saw people emerging from the monochrome, post-war world into a new, colourful era of experimentation and revolution; he saw the Beat Generation authors of the late 1950s, rejecting conventional society and expanding the horizons of literature by writing about freedom and exploration; he saw music without boundaries, such as the free jazz of Sun Ra and Ornette Coleman; he saw the surreal humour of The Goons and French theories of anarchy. And young Christopher wanted to be part of it all.

So he left his home and travelled to Europe, arriving in London in early 1961, where he immersed himself in poetry and jazz. Looking for somewhere to live, he rented a room at the fourteen-room Georgian home of sixteen-year-old Robert Wyatt-Ellidge – later just plain Wyatt – and his bohemian, left-wing parents near Dover. Wellington House was a meeting place for local musicians and poets, including pianist Mike Ratledge, guitarist and bass-player Hugh Hopper and self-confessed 'musical ignoramus' Kevin Ayers.

Christopher had, it seemed, a profound influence on some of the dissatisfied youth in and around Canterbury, with his freewheeling attitude to life and a collection of more than 100 jazz records. But he was soon forced to leave for London after deep, philosophical discussions led to Robert attempting suicide. With then-girlfriend Kay Calvert, he moved to Paris, staying at a hotel famed for its popularity among the 'beat' fraternity and collaborating with experimental composers such as Terry Riley.

During this time Christopher and Kay married, living on a houseboat on the Seine bought from an English poet and teacher called Gillian Mary Smyth. Sadly for Kay and the marriage, Allen saw a kindred spirit in Gilli, born 1933 in London, who worked at Paris's university, the Sorbonne. She said in *Gong: Politico Historico Spirito*, that they shared 'similar visions of the purpose of what they were doing, a passion for poetry, an absurd sense of humour and a desire to push back the barriers in life and art'. By 1963 Daevid and Kay's marriage was over and he and Gilli were an item.

Returning to London at the end of 1962, he met up again with Hugh and Robert and formed a group to perform jazz and poetry – the Christopher Allen Trio sounded a little straight and boring for a guitar-toting, verse-spouting beatnik, so he decided instead to go by his middle name, David, but jazz it up a bit with an extra 'e'. Thus, the Daevid Allen Trio was born.

During its brief existence, the trio had a four-night tenure at the Establishment Club in London's Soho, run by comedian Peter Cook, followed by performances at the Marquee Club in Oxford Street. But gigs were hard to come by, not helped by their uncompromising approach to performance and Allen disappearing off to Morocco or Ibiza. They met up again in Deya, Majorca, where Allen supplied Wyatt with his first proper drum kit. But there was more happening back in Canterbury, where Hugh and his brother Brian formed The Wilde Flowers, soon joined by Wyatt and Ayers.

As The Wilde Flowers – precursors of Caravan and other bands within the so-called Canterbury Scene – slowly gained in popularity and musical experience, Daevid and Gilli were still living and performing in Deya. By this time, thanks to Kevin Ayers, he had heard The Yardbirds' 'Still I'm Sad' and was particularly mesmerised by the guitar-playing of Jeff Beck. He realised the way forward was to deliver his philosophical and political ideas through pop music dusted with his own brand of whimsy and weirdness. As he said in his foreword to Graham Bennett's book *Soft Machine: Out-Bloody-Rageous*: 'We might also make some money!'

A chance meeting with wealthy Texan businessman Wes Brunson, who believed God wanted him to invest money in spreading new-age beliefs, resulted in an immediate return to Canterbury and the formation of Mister Head, with Allen on bass, Kevin and Larry Nowlin on guitars and Robert on drums. By 1966 Mike Ratledge had joined on keyboards and, with a radically new sound, a change of name was required. Kevin suggested one inspired by another Burroughs book, The Soft Machine, so Allen was deputised to go off to Paris to get the great man's blessing. When Nowlin left, Allen and Ayers swapped instruments, and the Softs recorded some demos that remained in the cupboard until 1971 due to a financial dispute. They even released a single on Polydor; the frantic 'Love Makes Sweet Music' backed with 'Feelin' Reelin' Squeelin'', in 1967. Pop stardom beckoned. Then it said, erm, no, that's okay.

Coming back from France after a tour of Europe Allen was stopped from re-entering the UK because he had outstayed his visa – he was labelled 'unsuitable, penniless' – so he wandered to Paris with Gilli. Together they created an early version of Gong – referred to years later as Protogong by Allen – with Ziska Baum on vocals, Loren Standlee on flute and Daniel Laloux hitting things. It was the vocal interplay between Ziska and Gilli that evolved into the 'space whisper' alongside Daevid's glissando guitar, and those early, frequently unrehearsed, performances attracted attention from the likes of Yoko Ono and Ornette Coleman. Gigs included one at the

Museum of Modern Art in Stockholm, performing with US jazz trumpeter Don Cherry in front of a backdrop of giant cornflake packets.

But these experiments were interrupted by the student riots in May 1968 – Daevid and Gilli had to flee the country to avoid arrest after trying to hand out teddy bears to the very sensitive French police. In her book *Gong: Politico Historico Spirito*, Gilli wrote:

> Suddenly, it was war. There were pitched battles in the streets and long lines of Darth Vader-attired, and enraged, police ... Authority came marching in black jackboots over political ideals and aspirations, and the bloodied face of the 15-year-old schoolboy staring from the cover of *Paris Match*. The first victim killed by the police, poignantly symbolised an impossible revolution.

In fact, Daevid and Gilli got out just in time – the day after fleeing their tiny loft in the Rue Beaubourg police turned up to raid the premises, breaking the legs of an American staying there at the time. Arriving in Deya, Majorca, again they found Didier Antonin Georges Malherbe, a rather wonderful Paris-born sax and flute player, living in a goat herder's cave on the side of a mountain in writer Robert Graves's back garden (Graves was a friend of the Wyatt family). Didier, born in January 1943, took up the saxophone after hearing Charlie Parker's composition 'Bloomdido', then studied flute in India before meeting Allen.

Returning secretly to France a few months later – living in a rundown mill house near the Alps bought from enterprising flea market antique dealer Bob Benamou (who became Gong's first manager) with some financial help from Allen's father – they recorded demos under the name of the Banana Moon Band with Patrick Fontaine on bass and Marc Blanc on drums. These tracks, made at Studio CBE in Paris and released on CD in 1992 under the title *Je Ne Fum' Pas De Bananes*, included compositions that were to pop up on various albums over the next 25 years, including Gong's debut, *Magick Brother*.

Allen was beginning to stir up interest from record companies – he had become a bit of a cult figure in France thanks to the popularity there of Soft Machine plus some supportive newspaper articles – but turned down every deal he was offered until approached by entrepreneur Jean Georgakarakos – aka Karakos – boss of fledgeling anti-establishment record company BYG and described by Gilli as 'a kind of gipsy ringmaster to the circus of avant-garde'. He suggested Daevid sign a three-year recording contract without hearing a note of music – it's the kind of thing that used to happen in the 1960s – so Allen quickly put together the first proper Gong band for a live appearance at the Amougies Festival in Belgium on 27 October 1969.

And so the magick begins...

Magick Brother (1970)

Personnel
Daevid Allen: guitar, bass, vocals
Gilli Smyth: space whisper
Didier Malherbe: flute, soprano saxophone
Rachid Houari: drums, percussion
Additional personnel
Barre Phillips: contrabass on 'Rational Anthem (Change The World)' and 'Princess Dreaming'
Earl Freeman: contrabass on 'Ego', piano on 'Gong Song'
Burton Greene: piano on 'Ego'
Dieter Gewissler: contrabass on 'Mystic Sister, Magick Brother' and 'Gong Song'
Tamsin Smyth: voices on 'Mystic Sister, Magick Brother' and 'Princess Dreaming'
Recorded September and October 1969 at Studio Eta and Studio Europa Sonor, Paris
Producers: Jean Georgakarakos, Jean Luc Young
Executive Producer: Pierre Lattes
Engineers: Dominique Blanc-Francard (Studio ETA), Jean Francois Baudet (Studio Europa Sonor)
Label: BYG Actuel
Released: March 1970
Highest chart positions: Uncharted
Running time: 43:52
Current edition: Snapper SNAP199CD (2004)

What's interesting about Gong's debut album is that it arrived with virtually all the band mythology intact. According to the Planet Gong website, Allen had a vision back in 1966 in which he believed he was ...

> ... an experiment being supervised by intelligences far beyond his normal level of awareness, that he is later to call the Octave Doctors, seeing himself on stage in front of a large rock festival audience and experiencing a connection with them that had the quality of intense LOVE, while at the same time being surrounded by an enormous cone of etheric light…

The Soft Machine was his first attempt to create a band that could fulfil his aims, but Daevid thought it lacked spiritual integrity – Gong would be his own creation that would reconnect him with his original vision. But he was also canny enough to realise that taking the whole thing too seriously would be a career-limiting mistake, that his philosophical and political points might be better received coated with liberal helpings of whimsy and absurdity.

As well as being a poet and musician, Allen was also a talented artist – the Pot Head Pixies, with little propellers twirling about on top of their pointy heads, came out of cartoon sketches he and Gilli had made. Other ideas came from philosophy and religion – the Flying Teapot a clear reference to the argument by philosopher Bertrand Russell against people making unfalsifiable claims; the 'search for self-understanding' part of many spiritual beliefs. Tea is, of course, a slang word for marijuana but, in Allen's whimsical world, also meant tea.

Much has been made about the influence of Pink Floyd's original frontman and main composer Syd Barrett and there are indeed some similarities, not least in their raw but inventive guitar work and the fact that Syd was singing about gnomes in 1967, creating fairy tale and nursery-rhyme images with psychedelic wordplay. Allen did that too but, unlike Barrett, he always made sure there was meaning behind the madness.

The mythology really only makes one musical appearance on 'Magick Brother' but is more prevalent in Allen's entertaining and extensive illustrations in the gatefold sleeve. There you will find the pixies, Captain Capricorn, Fred the Fish (the one with the chip on his shoulder) and much cosmic explanation of Gong wisdom. Even if you are not a vinyl junkie, it's worth seeking out the original gatefold for the artwork alone (although be prepared to fork out up to £150!).

Magick Brother is pretty much a Daevid and Gilli production with a bit of help from Didier Malherbe, the sax and flute playing hermit from Majorca, and Rachid Houari, a mad Moroccan drummer from the backing band of French pop star Claude Francois, who co-wrote the original French lyrics of 'My Way'. Bassist Christian Tritsch, another Francois band member, was also recruited but didn't join the sessions in time so Allen plays all the bass parts. The sound was fleshed out with help from three musicians who were also recording for the BYG label, plus occasional Gong collaborator Dieter Gewissler and Gilli's daughter Tamsin from her first marriage.

The material consists of songs Daevid and Gilli had been working on during their stay in Deya but are all credited to Gilli, apparently for legal reasons. It is very clear they are mainly Allen compositions – Gilli's contribution was probably mostly lyrical. Many of them have a simple structure with words that are pretty standard for protest songs at the time, with attacks on 'big, bad' businessmen and exhortations to change the world. They include a track originally recorded as a demo by the Banana Moon Band, the somewhat politically incorrect 'Pretty Miss Titty'.

Contrary to popular belief, the album wasn't recorded on the sound channel of a movie camera – Gong used proper studios in Paris with eight-track equipment – but there is certainly a lo-fi feel, aided and abetted by a guitar sound that's a bit hollow and, occasionally, not quite in tune! The same can be said for some of Gewissler's double bass bowing, while Daevid's playing on both bass and guitar is fairly rudimentary, to say the least.

Indeed, there's a rather primitive feel throughout the album, which lacks some of the musical elements one usually associates with Gong – there's no spacey synthesiser wash and precious little electric lead guitar, the bass takes a modest back seat and the drumming is there as a garnish rather than a main ingredient. But we do get Gilli's space whisper that opens the album and Didier's playful, lyrical sax and flute, although there's not nearly enough of it. You will also hear Allen's glissando, made by stroking the strings of his guitar with the handle of a gynaecological instrument as he tried to reproduce Syd Barrett's slide guitar experiments with Pink Floyd.

The result is a lighter, poppier album than its successors, which has more in common with Allen's late-1970s solo work than the material he would produce under the Gong name. But it has a naive, anarchic charm – there are some interesting songs that bounce along happily, and a sense of random spontaneity in the sound effects and performances. Allen's voice is unique and charming, and the whole thing feels as if the musicians are thoroughly enjoying themselves without getting too hung up on performance or recording quality.

The cover for the original release was printed before the track listing was decided so the liner notes split 'Mystic Sister: Magick Brother' into two tracks and transpose 'Glad To Sad To Say' and 'Rational Anthem', an error that continues through to this day in some digital downloads. It also divided the songs into an 'Early Morning Side' and a 'Late Night Side', although the tracks don't seem to match the concepts. The original release gives Daevid and Gilli as much credit on the cover as the band, no doubt in the belief that their names would be more of a selling point (and BYG's contract was with Daevid, not Gong). That seems to have done the trick as it was chosen as album of the week on a French radio station and the band was able to get a few months of gigs on the back of it.

Some critics regard *Magick Brother* as Gong's finest album, being more raw, spontaneous and revolutionary. But most would follow the opinion of *Allmusic*: Interesting but not typical Gong.

'Mystic Sister: Magick Brother' (Credited to Gilli Smyth but really Daevid Allen & Gilli Smyth)

The first Gong song opens with, suitably, a gong. Then Gilli's space whisper, put through various echo and tape effects backed with Allen's Pink Floydian guitar noises, Dieter's bowed bass, and Didier's indistinct flute, soars out of the speakers for about two minutes. That's the 'Mystic Sister' section. Daevid enters with some swiftly but gently-strummed acoustic guitar in a slightly flat D major and you realise it's a folk song really, with lyrics that are part nursery rhyme, part love song and part cosmic tribute to oneness and Krishna. 'You are my Magick Brother/You are the one I love/You are my Mystic Sister/You are the one in love/Welcome to the Aquarian Age', he gently croons. Didier plays virtually non-stop throughout on flute, with some added sax sounds, while the drums are fairly laid-back and unobtrusive. Sadly, someone let Dieter stroke his double bass – it is frequently horribly out of tune, moaning and groaning like a centenarian with severe constipation. Daevid's voice is mostly double-tracked throughout with additional, almost indistinct, vocals from Gilli's daughter Tamsin (by her first marriage to 'a guy with a good job'). After nearly six minutes the song ends on Dieter's double bass and Didier's flute, with gentle tabla drumming and a few random bass notes from Daevid.

On the lines 'Maybe we'll all find out/Just what it's all about' Daevid moves from D to Ab (it's a flattened fifth, in case you're asked). It's the first appearance of a common musical device in his compositions: the so-called Devil's Interval, a chord sequence that's supposed to sound so uncomfortable and disconcerting that it was known as 'diabolus in musica'. Now, in this song, it's quite gently done on acoustic guitar, so the discomfort level isn't particularly high. If you want to really hear the 'devil in music' listen to the classical composer Holst or a bit of Black Sabbath. It would reappear in songs such as 'You Can't Kill Me', 'You Never Blow Yr Trip Forever' and 'Shapeshifter'.

As an opening song, it works to introduce Allen's particular brand of benign, upbeat, hippy-dippy wisdom and hints strongly at the random weirdness that's about to follow.

'Rational Anthem [aka Change The World]' (Credits as above)
A chopping guitar intro in C leads to a repetitive cycle of four chords – B, F sharp, A and E – for the chorus of 'Yes we are, we're gonna change the world', with a loping, slightly swinging rhythm. Lyrically, as the chorus suggests, it's standard 'save the world' fare, with the occasionally pointed remark that 'money never gets paid' – no doubt a little dig at concert promoters! Barre Phillips makes occasional whale noises on contrabass while Gilli attempts some just-about-there backing vocals and a few gentle oohs and whoops. Daevid also overdubs his own harmonies. The song ends on the chopping chords intro with spoken words from an unidentified man who may be Brahmanananda, who ran a retreat in the grounds of Bob Benamou's house and was later immortalised by Allen as Banana Ananda. 'We've waited too long for peace and love,' he intones, 'But I'm happy to say that we have already won ...' Some squeaks on contrabass bring the song to a close.

'Glad To Sad To Say' (Credits as above)
Things slow down now with some gentle but slightly disturbing plucking of electric guitar in E minor with an added ninth (the recording has been slowed down, so it's actually in E flat minor). There's a B in there that goes to C and then C sharp – think of the intro to Monty Norman's 'James Bond Theme' – and Allen sings over weird, low buzzing sounds that may have been produced by Didier as they have a breathy, wind-produced quality, then overdubs his own moanings and groanings. 'Goodbye to all the wisdom in the world,' he croons in a gently sad voice, before a sudden lurch into some chopping guitar chords similar to those used in 'Rational Anthem'. We're soon back into the gentle E minor sequence for more spooky sadness, then briefly into slow major chords before everything slows to a stop in Em again. It's an

atmospheric, affecting little number with no drums, no Gilli and sparse bass. It's not played terrifically well – Allen's plucked notes on his electric guitar have a lot of fret buzz – but that seems to add to the disturbing effect.

'Chainstore Chant/Pretty Miss Titty' (Credits as above)
We open with a louder but equally disturbing little section in which Allen repeats the chilling phrase 'pockets full of blood!', echoed by Gilli, while distorted electric guitar mirrors his bluesy vocal line. Allen speaks the line 'the bloody pockets, mate!' and then we're into a song originally demoed by the Banana Moon Band in 1968 and later released on the compilation album *Je Ne Fume Pas De Bananes*. In fact, the demo is superior to this one – it's at the correct speed and in the right key of D minor, and the electric guitar is in tune! This version is slightly slowed down, as are all the tracks here, so it's in D flat minor and Allen's tuning is a little suspect. It's another plucked-guitar song, slightly faster than 'Glad To Sad To Say', with a descending note going from D to D flat to C to B (at least, it would do if it was at the correct speed). Allen sings about the unfortunately-named 'Pretty Miss Titty' who works in the city bashing a typewriter. Apparently, 'they don't love or hate her, just masturbate her potato', which is the first time I've heard of that particular use for the humble spud. Other verses touch on Old Mother Hubbard and Millie, Molly, Mad the Maid, who apparently has been entertaining Old Father Time. The chorus addresses the aforementioned 'big, bad businessman', asking him if he has any love. I suspect it's a rhetorical question, and the answer is 'no'.

The song drives along nicely in the chorus, with gentle phasing on rhythm guitar, some indistinct lead guitar work and Rachid drumming with unexpected power. It slows to an end on the plucked D minor notes.

'Fable Of A Fredfish: Hope You Feel OK' (Credits as above)
Another segue that opens our first introduction to Fredfish, who turns up later on Allen's first solo album 'Banana Moon' as 'Fred The Fish & The Chip On His Shoulder'. The title is announced, there's a brief burst of what sounds like a recording of a Gilbert and Sullivan song, then some swiftly-approaching feet before a breathless Allen delivers a short nonsense poem. Then some heavily-phased guitar notes played high up on the fretboard introduce an upbeat ballad full of positive sentiments – 'And it feels like morning/And the sun is shining/If it's today tomorrow/There'll be no time for sorrow/You find that you always knew/The things to do'. Ahh, nice. It's not only Allen's guitar that has the phaser setting up to 11 – it's all over his multi-tracked voice, too. The result sounds a bit woolly and muffled, quite heavy on the bass, and Allen's voice is sometimes a little indistinct during the verses. But he produces some lovely harmonies here and it's nice to end side one with something less strident than the politically-themed tracks. It's in F sharp, which is an unusual choice for a guitarist. Bearing in mind the question marks over some of the tunings on the album, it could well have been in F or G originally.

'Ego' (Credits as above)
The original side two opens with a rollicking singalong in three-quarter time. Burton Green plays joyous honky-tonk-style piano while Gilli goes 'Oom, taa!' and there's plenty of high-pitched giggling and squeaking as if the entire thing is taking place in a pub full of drunken pixies. Earl Freeman is supposedly playing contrabass here but, if so, it's mixed low down and exists more as a feeling than a sound. Musically, 'Ego' is surprisingly intricate given its basic 'oompah' rhythm – it opens in D major and there's an F minor thrown in before it settles down in B major. Just when you think it's getting a bit contemplative on you, it dives back into its 'oompah' rhythm and the pixies have another pint. The lyrics are simple and sparse, with Allen cunningly rhyming 'go' with, er, 'go', and the whole thing descends into random piano tinkling and squeaking. Sounds mad but there is more to it than meets the ear and is actually a very cleverly-constructed little song that benefits from the ramshackle, anything-goes approach.

'Gong Song' (Credits as above)
As mentioned above, most of the Planet Gong mythology accompanying this album is confined to the liner art. 'Gong Song' is, as the title suggests, the first time it spills into Allen's songwriting and is a sign of things to come. Originally demoed in 1967 as a sort of 'why can't we just all kinda get along' polemic, it opens with an introductory poem that puts the sentiments into the mouth of a Pothead Pixie tourist. In fact, this song has such an important place in the development of Allen's later work that the introduction deserves to be quoted in full. Here it is:

> You know ... once upon a time from a far-off planet/Was a little green man who came down by comet/When I first met him in a London taxi/he told me his name was Pot Head Pixie/He told me he came from a planet called Gong/Sang me this small, green song.

So what does the pixie have to say to the many travellers on our little blue and green world? Basically, stop your whining, be happy with what you are and what you have because, as the chorus suggests, you never know just where you really, really come from. You could have pixie DNA.

It could all be a little preachy and sanctimonious. Indeed, the demo version comes very close. But the lyrics are allied to a simple, pretty little verse and a bouncy, chirpy chorus based on a four-chord sequence of D, G, C and with a bit of wah-wah on Allen's guitar. There's a heavier, harder middle-eight in F sharp, during which Rachid has a good old bash, before it calms down again for the verse and the chorus, ending with Allen's guitar chords bouncing between D and E flat before degenerating into a bit of a free-for-all of drums, bass and piano, with Allen muttering nonsense underneath. Earl Freeman is on piano and Dieter Gewissler on contrabass, although you don't really notice them until the end. Oh, and Didier plays merry sax throughout.

'Princess Dreaming' (Credits as above)
A very Gilli piece opening with cacophonous tape loops repeating what sounds like someone standing on the tail of a cat with a sore throat – someone (possibly Tamsin) appears to be meowing in the background, too. After about a minute or so it merges into Gilli gently intoning a poem about a girl going to sleep – the princess in the title we assume – while Didier gives us some swooping, bird-like flute and Barre Phillips bows some deep contrabass. Finally, monk-like chanting dissolves into a low chuckle that leads straight into…

'5 & 20 Schoolgirls' (Credits as above)
Lots of descending notes here as Daevid sings a slightly menacing verse about '5 & 20 schoolgirls lost in the fog/Nobody can find them, not even with a dog', his voice and Didier's sax moving down a semi-tone each half a bar until they hit D major for the line 'They got a big brass clock that goes tick-tock'. Then it's into the chorus over the descending chords of G, F, E flat and D, with Allen repeating the word 'waiting' as his guitar and bass jump about between D and E flat (just like the end of 'Gong Song'). There's a middle-eight about 'Mothers in a coma, drinking too much soda' before we go back into the verse and chorus.

Out of all the songs on the album, this most strongly suggests the direction Allen would go on 'Camembert Electrique' – it's tight and tough, with some magnificent sax improvisation from Didier, and its use of hypnotic and repetitive single guitar notes heralds the likes of Selene.

'Cos You Got Green Hair' (Credits as above)
The album ends with a soft, atmospheric piece featuring monk-like chanting, Allen's glissando guitar, eastern-influenced flute from Didier and mysterious lyrics about a lady with exotic hair colouring. It's more of a slow chant than a song, washing over you like gentle waves of contemplative sound, mostly in E but shifting almost imperceptibly between major and minor (there's an A in there too) before gently drifting away after five minutes. It is a lovely, peaceful way to end the album.

Camembert Electrique (1971)

Personnel:
Blumdido Bad De Grass (Didier Malherbe): saxophones and flute
Submarine Captain Christian Tritsch: bass guitar, lead guitar on 'And You Tried So Hard'
Pip Pyle: drums, tables, chairs and breakage
Bert Camembert (Daevid Allen): guitars & aluminium croon, lewd guitar, bass guitar on 'And You Tried So Hard'
Shakti Yoni (Gilli Smyth): space whisper & lady voice
Venux De Luxe (Francis Linon, sometimes miscredited as Lindon): switch doctor & mix master
Additional personnel:
Eddy Louiss: organ on 'I've Been Stoned Before'
Constantin Simonovitch: phased piano on 'Dynamite'
Recorded during full moons of May, June & September 1971, at Strawberry Studios ('Honky Chateau'), Herouville, Normandy, France
Producers: Jean Georgakarakos, Jean Luc Young & Pierre Lattes
Engineer: Gilles Salle
Label: BYG Records in France, Virgin Records in UK
Released: October 1971 (France), June 1974 (UK)
Highest chart positions: Uncharted
Running time: 39:36
Current edition: Charly X 680 (2015)

For many Gong fans, this is where it all really begins. Everything comes together on *Camembert Electrique* – the writing, the performances, the whole unrestrained joy of it all, the feeling of a commune of like-minded souls exploring uncharted musical territory while pleasantly out of their heads on plant material. This is the album that turned many British listeners on to Gong because it was released in the UK in 1974 by Virgin Records for 59p, an astonishingly-cheap price even nearly 50 years ago. Crazy yet confident, anarchic yet tight as a drum, *Camembert Electrique* is sometimes overshadowed by the Planet Gong trilogy that followed but shouldn't be – it is a classic in its own right, and spawned some of Gong's most-loved tracks: 'And You Tried So Hard', 'Dynamite', 'Tropical Fish/ Selene', the medley of 'I've Been Stoned Before: Mister Long Shanks: O Mother' and, most of all, the gloriously-defiant 'You Can't Kill Me', a call to arms if ever there was one (Thank you, Kavus!).

Had it been recorded directly after *Magick Brother* we would be applauding the band's swift development from Daevid Allen's faltering first steps as Gong leader to this musically-adept collaborative unit. But two years had passed between them and a lot of changes had taken place. For a start, this wasn't the second album Allen recorded – it was the fifth, with his solo album *Banana Moon*, the soundtrack to the film *Continental Circus* and Dashiell Hedayat's *Obsolete* in between.

Secondly, Christian Tritsch had arrived, and we should not underestimate the impact he had on Allen's songwriting and general state of wellbeing. Tritsch was not only his musical foil and sounding board, he also wrote some of the best songs on both this and *Banana Moon*. Part of the reason why Allen almost dissolved the band during the making of *Flying Teapot* in 1973 was because Tritsch had quit.

Meanwhile, drummer Rachid Houari left the band in July 1971 – Allen said on the *Planet Gong* website: 'In the end, he was playing quieter and quieter until one day he just wasn't there any more.' His replacement was Pip Pyle, and it came about thus: Allen owed BYG a solo album as part of the original contract, and one stipulation was that it included at least one other ex-Soft Machine member. Robert Wyatt was available to drum on the sessions, which took place in January and February 1970 at Marquee Studios in London. But he wasn't quite as available as he thought, so he asked pal Pip Pyle to take his place on one of the tracks, the Christian Tritsch album opener 'It's The Time Of Your Life'. Born in Sawbridgeworth, Hertfordshire, in 1950, Pip formed Delivery with childhood pal Phil Miller but left after a row with the band's singer, Carol Grimes. Allen invited him to join Gong after Houari had finally disappeared.

Before he vanished, Houari drummed on a single credited to both the band and Daevid Allen. 'Est-ce Que Je Suis (Garcon Ou Fille)', backed with 'Hyp Hypnotise You', were rehearsed in December 1969 at Chateau du Thiel in Normandy, the allegedly haunted ancestral home of young and precocious French film-maker Jerome Laperrousaz, then recorded in the spring of 1970 at Studio Blanc-Francard. Allen and the band also provided suitably 'out there' music for Laperrousaz's celluloid efforts, including his 1972 movie about motorcycle road racing, *Continental Circus*.

In January 1971 Allen, Smyth and Tritsch went to the UK to make Banana Moon. The band's final commitment before recording *Camembert* was to be the backing group for Dashiell Hedayat, a French musician and author whose real name was Daniel Theron but also went by the names Jack-Alain Leger, Eve Saint-Roch, Paul Small and Melmoth.

Finally, sessions for Gong's second album release started in September 1971 at the 18th-century Chateau d'Herouville in Val-d'Oise, France, which had been turned into a recording studio by French film composer Michel Magne.

Much of *Camembert* was written and rehearsed at a hunting lodge in Voisines, south-west of Paris, where the band lived a 'hippy' commune lifestyle, although the seeds of 'Dynamite' and 'Selene' were planted further back in 1968 when Daevid and Gilli were rehearsing with the Banana Moon Band in Montaulieu. The collaborative nature of Gong is shown in the joint credits for many of the songs, and even those written solely by Allen were arranged by 'everybody at once', according to the extensive artwork and notes included in the original 1971 release.

Musically, this is a magnificent melange of psychedelia, space rock, free jazz, experimental tape loops and punk rock five years before its time. Allen's guitar sound is more muscular and confident, Tritsch and Pip are a driving force in the rhythm section and Didier is as inspired as ever on various blowy things. From whimsical, hippie fool on *Magick Brother*, Allen has developed a 'f*** you' attitude – still silly, still mischievous but also angry and defiant when required – and Gilli gets more opportunities to take centre-stage and channel her cosmic cries.

There's also the suggestion of a storyline here – a device that would, of course, become more fully developed over subsequent albums – and the conceit is this is a direct transmission from the Planet Gong, broadcasting by Invisible Radio Gnome. In an interview with *Melody Maker* around the time of the album's release, Allen said it was driven by 'the idea of the unexpected. As soon as something seems to be going along in one way, change it. Throw in the banana, do something absurd, something completely opposite. Anything'.

Why *Camembert Electrique* which, I believe, translates as Electric Camembert? For a start, the band was in Normandy, home of the moist, soft, creamy cheese named after the town of Camembert, known as 'the largest small village in France'. It has also been suggested by people who know about these things that cheese equals LSD, just as tea equals pot. So when the song 'Wet Cheese Delirium' asks in French 'Do you want a camembert?' it is really asking if you would wish to share in some lysergic acid diethylamide. The cheese also found its way into the work of surrealist artist Salvador Dali – in his painting Persistence of Memory the dripping, flexible watches were inspired by runny cooked camembert.

We also find Allen adopting the name Bert Camembert as a nom de plume – he also called himself Dingo Virgin and the Divided Alien – perhaps as a dig at the ultra-cheesy German orchestra leader Bert Kaempfert, who was still unaccountably popular in 1971. Other silly names used or bestowed upon various members of the group include Shakti Yoni for Gilli Smyth, a reference to the goddess Shakti and yoni, a Sanskrit word for the womb. Christian Tritsch dubbed himself The Submarine Captain, a name later bestowed upon Steve Hillage, while sound engineer Francis Linon became Venux De Luxe. And, of course, there's Bloomdido Bad De Grass (spelt Blumdido in this album's liner notes), a combination of a jazz standard written by sax genius Charlie Parker and an almost-literal English translation of Didier Malherbe's surname.

Allen's liner art and notes are, as usual, wonderfully-drawn in his ramshackle but delightful way, and the cover art is a striking and unmistakable labour of love. The 2015 remastered CD reproduces all the artwork in a 24-page booklet, but this is an album you will want on vinyl, simply for the cover.

Nearly 50 years on, *Camembert Electrique* is still strong and streamin' mate!

'Radio Gnome' (Daevid Allen)

On some releases this is retitled 'Radio Gnome Prediction', to differentiate from 'Radio Gnome Invisible' on 1973's 'Flying Teapot, although it's hard to mix up the two. 'Radio Gnome' is a 26-second sound collage, with Allen's Pixie-lated voice intoning 'Bon Soir! C'est une emission Planete Gong par Radio Gnome Invisible direct de la Planete Gong! La Planete Gong!' over repetitive creaky and bouncy sound effects. This is the Pothead Pixie himself introducing Radio Gnome to your head, leading into what sounds like crowd noise at a gig as Allen plays the intro riff to…

'You Can't Kill Me' (Allen)

When I dubbed 'You Can't Kill Me' a call to arms, I was actually quoting current Gong frontman Kavus Torabi, who introduced it as such on stage in Aylesbury before launching into the fastest, most vicious and head-pounding version I had ever heard. It didn't come across as a song from half a century ago – it sounded like an up-to-the-minute blast of defiance from a 'yellow vest' protest. In fact, some of the 'gilets jaunes' who staged day-glo demos in France at the end of 2018 used the song as their anthem. As protest songs go, it's somewhat ineffective – you can kill my father, son, children and family, it says. Even my family tree. That's a lot of successful killing there. But here's the punchline: 'You can kill my body baby, but you can't kill me.' You can destroy the mortal remains, but you can't destroy the movement that has been created, the spirit of rebellion that has been sparked or the words and music that inspire.

Allen opens with a great little wah-wah'd heavy rock riff in E, throwing in a B flat 'diabolus in musica' that we discussed in the previous chapter. He sings the verse lyrics, which Gilli echoes in her high-pitched space whisper. Then in comes Didier with some great sax improv, followed by the defiant repetition of 'You can do what you want'. The opening riff returns but transforms into a fast, repetitive riff in B major, overlaid by Allen's howling guitar lead and glissando washes. More magnificent riffs follow, with Allen repeating 'I'll be seeing you again', driving the phrase time and time and time again into your brain until you are ready to beg for mercy.

Then, just when you think you can't possibly take any more, a fast drum flourish by Pip takes us back into verse one again and, finally, we stagger to a halt after a repeat of the 'You can do what you want' section.

Phew! Just listening to it again is an exhausting but exhilarating experience, and three things stand out: Allen's guitar playing is infinitely better here than on *Magick Brother*, Pip's drumming powers things along in ways that Rachid could have only dreamed of and the almost infinite repetition is a powerful musical tool.

'I've Been Stoned Before: Mister Long Shanks: O Mother' (Allen)

'Then all of a sudden we find ourselves at the funeral listening to the rational anselm [sic] of the Pot Head Pixies, sung by Dingo from the other side,' say the liner notes. Allen calls for attention, and then guest musician Eddy Louiss plays a cheesy A major chord on church organ for the opening lines. Eddy was a French jazz organist who played in Stan Getz's band before going solo in 1977, dying in 2015 aged 74.

Allen's highly-amusing lyrics talk of being stoned in St John's Wood crematorium in London, in The Hague in Amsterdam and in Prague, Czechoslovakia, sung to portentous organ backing, sounding very much like a cross between a hymn and a very slowed-down 'Knees-up Mother Brown' cockney singalong. As the singer apparently collapses stoned, the organ descends down discordant chords, Gilli space whispers and Didier plays random sax over pounding drums from Pip.

Then Didier picks up a little repetitive nursery rhyme tune, first used by Gong on 'Hip Hypnotise You' on the flipside of the 1970 single 'Est-Ce Que Je Suis'. Bass and guitar provide a mischievous little backing, alternating between the chords of F and F sharp, picking up speed as we go before Daevid comes in with a little ditty about an 'O! RTF girl'. ORTF was Office de Radiodiffusion Television Francaise, the French state broadcaster, founded in 1964 and then split up into five separate organisations a decade later. Gong wrote a theme tune for ORTF News during their time at the haunted chateau, which helped to provide much-needed finance.

Daevid's ditty leads immediately into a brief chorus of 'Mister Long Shanks', followed by the almost-as-short 'O Mother', an upbeat little song full of repetitive lines over deceptively-tricky time signatures and including the endearing lyrics 'Yer bum titty bum Pompidou, who's yer father and mind how you go'. After going through the chorus and verse twice it comes to a sudden stop, ending four and a half minutes of the most bizarre music to have come out of Allen's head. So far.

'I Am Your Fantasy' (Words: Gilli Smyth, Music: Christian Tritsch)
On some versions of the album 'I've Been Stoned Before' stands on its own and this is the third part of the medley with 'Mister Long Shanks' and 'O Mother'. But originally this was a standalone track four, a poem gently intoned by Gilli over Tritsch's bass playing ascending lines that alternate between the major chords of A and D, with a bit of glissando filling it out and Gilli space whispering. 'I am the dream that gets into your bed,' intones Gilli, the night shadow that loves you.' And then, rather obliquely: 'I am your knee.' After the frantic, disjointed nature of the preceding track, 'I Am Your Fantasy' is a welcome gentle interlude.

'Dynamite: I Am Your Animal' (Tritsch/Smyth, possibly Allen too)
Christian Tritsch joined Gong in time for the band's debut live appearance at the Amougies Festival in October 1969 and immediately made his presence felt not only as a bass player but also as a composer. He penned 'It's The Time Of Your Life', which was rehearsed by Gong but ended up on Allen's first solo album, and 'Dynamite: Goldilocks', originally credited to just Tritsch and Gilli. According to the liner notes on the compilation album 'Camembert Eclectique',

the birthplace of 'Dynamite' was a communal fire pit by a river in the Montaulieu valley in south-east France, which dates it to before December 1969 when the band decamped to the haunted chateau in Normandy. Live, the band would sometimes sing 'Bamboule' instead of 'Dynamite', a reference to an itinerant French 'India freak' who cooked chapatis and char tea over the fire pit.

The earliest existing recordings show the structure of 'Dynamite' is pretty much set in stone: a first section in which the word 'Dynamite' is yelled about 26 times, with Didier providing little saxophone licks between stabs of sound from the band; a second featuring Gilli's 'I Am Your Animal' poem over a fast, repetitive bass run in 6/8 from Tritsch, with Allen harmonising on guitar (and Gilli repeating the word 'f**k' quite a bit); and a third that returns to the original 'Dynamite' section (in early versions the band sang 'Goldilocks').

It ends with the first appearance on the album of the 'Ya sunne, wicked old target' coda, a bit of nonsense poetry the Daevid Allen Trio used to perform as far back as 1963. Here it is combined with various mutterings, cries and croons underneath, followed by 'Ya finger at the trigger and ya body burnin' up, Camembert Electrique' sung very fast, with vocal melody doubled up on guitar. There is a short pause before we end side one with...

'Wet Cheese Delirium' (Allen)

A tape loop featuring Didier asking if you would like some Camembert over various spacey noises, ending most abruptly after 29 seconds.

'Squeezing Sponges Over Policemen's Heads' (Allen)

The shortest sound collage at 13 seconds, this pretty much carries on from where 'Wet Cheese Delirium' leaves off. A voice repeats 'Gong', there's brief laughter and, faintly, Didier repeating his offer of cheese. Then we crash into ...

'Fohat Digs Holes In Space' (Allen, Smyth)

If Shakti represents female reproductive potency, then Fohat is the male. The 19th-century theosophist Helena Petrovna Blavatsky described it as 'The essence of cosmic electricity. An occult Tibetan term for *Daiviprakriti*, primordial light: and in the universe of manifestation the ever-present electrical energy and ceaseless destructive and formative power. Esoterically, it is the same, Fohat being the universal propelling Vital Force, at once the propeller and the resultant.' So there.

More light is shed by Pestonji Temulji Pavri, who writes that a spirit or force 'formed within the aether an incalculable number of tiny, spherical bubbles, spoken of in The Secret Doctrine as the holes which Fohat digs in space'. And that is how the Solar System was born.

Allen calls the tune 'a ryvmick glissando wif Bert the Bert and his aluminium ork and Yoni 'pon the broomstick'. It's a sequence of clashing chords utilising the ol' Devil's Interval again, driven by pounding drums from Pip, Didier's muscular saxophone and Allen providing shimmering glissando.

Opening in E minor it slides down to B flat, then up to D flat, then down a bit to B, down a bit more to B flat, and down a bit further to G. Then the whole sequence starts up again. Not a 12-bar blues, then. It settles into an E minor glissando sequence with Tritsch's bass bubbling away playing E notes an octave apart.

After nearly four minutes of driving musical Solar System-building, Didier takes up a perky little repetitive tune that finally leads into a vocal section over the rising chords of E minor, G, A and B. Allen sings four verses that end each time with a question – 'Where am I, babe? What's happenin' man? Who are you, babe? Wot's freedom, babe?' – and each time the band responds with a high-pitched and gleeful 'You don't know!'. The tune moves up a semitone into F minor for a Didier sax solo, then into D minor for a surprisingly accomplished bit of distorted lead guitar from Allen before the whole thing collapses into a brief rendition of the Irish child's nursery rhyme 'Oh Can You Wash Your Father's Shirt', played by Tritsch on the bass and sung by Allen with these choice words: 'I gone and got me dirty Bert a-hangin' on the line…'. When he was young, his family used to gather around a piano to sing Irish songs, and this is one that no doubt stuck in his mind.

The music suggests constant movement and, unsurprisingly, it was originally composed for the soundtrack of *Continental Circus*.

'And You Tried So Hard [aka Tried So Hard]' (Tritsch, Allen)
Gong meet The Byrds via Jefferson Airplane in what is by far the most commercial track on the album and one that arguably would have made a better single than the defiantly eccentric 'Est-ce-que Je Suis'. Written mostly by Tritsch, Allen provided lyrics and Gilli an uncredited poem in the middle. Based around the chord of D major and its sustained fourth – you just put your little finger on the third fret of top E – Tritsch strums guitar just like on a late 1960s Byrds number, with Allen playing some high bass notes before settling down into a steady rhythm driven by Pip's slightly-too-busy drumming. The band provide some lovely harmonies on the opening chorus before things get a bit heavier in a second section in A, in which Allen rather dubiously suggests the way to 'make the big time' is to 'lay the lady at the right time'.

A pretty third section follows based on the chord sequence of D, C, G and A, with high-pitched flute that, for me, smacks of early Jefferson Airplane, then a quieter fourth section in which Tritsch provides effective finger-picked electric guitar while Gilli talks about a wise brown frog giving princely advice while trembling by a waterfall. Then we are back into the 'And you tried so hard to get there' chorus that once again builds up into a final guitar flourish in D major.

This is a superb slice of pop psychedelia, full of catchy melodies and musical hooks, beautifully put together and performed, with Tritsch clearly leading the way. It doesn't attempt to fit itself into Allen's loose Gong story

– in fact, the reference to 'drinken all the sky wine' suggests to me a nod to 'Clarence In Wonderland', a song by Allen's former Soft Machine colleague Kevin Ayers that appeared on his first solo album *Joy Of A Toy* in 1970 and was performed live by Gong. Ayers spent time with Allen in Ibiza after quitting Soft Machine and was virtually a member of the band for the first tour of the UK in 1971. One could argue that Ayers tried so hard to make the big time as a solo artist but frequently sabotaged his own career by scurrying off to the Balearic islands to immerse himself in vino, so it's no stretch of the imagination to suggest he is the subject of this track.

'Tropical Fish: Selene' (Allen)

'All the way from Oz ... writ & all by Dingo', boast the liner notes. In fact, like 'Dynamite', 'Tropical Fish' and 'Selene' date back to the Cafe Montaulieu stay in late 1969. They may well have been written in time for *Magick Brother* but probably required Tritsch's presence to really do them justice as they require some pretty fast interlocking guitar, bass and vocal riffs. They were certainly available for Allen to include on his solo album *Banana Moon* but somehow don't quite fit with that record's loose, home-made feel. In fact, out of all the tracks on *Camembert Electrique*, this medley points the way towards the more spacey, jazzy sound of *Flying Teapot*, especially in the instrumental sections in which Didier plays mystical sax over Allen's glissando guitar and Gilli's space whisper, while Tritsch keeps a bubbly bass riff going.

'Tropical Fish' itself opens with indistinct mumbling before a fanfare of sorts starts proceedings, with guitar, bass and sax repeating the notes E, F, E and E flat. Then Allen's vocal comes in, shadowing a fast guitar and bass riff. 'Well shady lady – what's your problem? Trying to buy a brand new husband?' he sings. Is this a reference to Gilli, who had left one husband behind her in London, the father of her daughter Tamsin? Further evidence is provided by the chorus, which opens with 'She seems like a typical witch to me' – a reference, perhaps, to Gilli's witch persona, developed further on later recordings. A repeat of the line 'Stranger and stranger, why do you do it?' leads the band into what Allen calls a 'sax guitar dubble bubble duet' followed by glissando and space whisper, a section that bears some resemblance to later instrumentals on *Angel's Egg* and *You*.

A similar fanfare but with slightly different chords ends the 'Tropical Fish' section and brings the music virtually to a halt while we enter the 'Selene' half – in Greek mythology, Selene was goddess of the moon and drove the chariot that carried the celestial body across the sky. Allen croons a long, lingering 'Seleeeeeennnnee' over rich glissando, then his guitar begins a steady chug in A major and Gilli whispers the lyrics, repeated by Allen as a mystical chant, almost like a call to prayer. 'Selene' ends with a repeat of the 'Ya sunne, wicked old target' section first used at the end of 'Dynamite: I Am Your Animal'.

And that is the end of the album, apart from a very brief ...

'Gnome The Second' (Allen)

A 27-second tape loop opens with the bong of a gong and various sound effects as a pixie-lated voice pronounces the name of the planet and points out, in a voice which quickly becomes virtually indistinct, that this has been a 'Radio Gnome Invisible direct emission de la Planet Gong'. And that's all, folks.

Continental Circus (1972)

Personnel:
Daevid Allen: guitar & vocals
Gilli Smyth: space whisper
Didier Malherbe: sax, flute
Christian Tritsch: bass
Pip Pyle: drums
Recorded April 1971, at Chateau d'Herouville, Normandy, France
Producers: Unknown
Engineer: Unknown
Original Label: Phillips
Released: April 1972
Highest chart positions: Uncharted
Running time: 34:13
Current edition: Mantra 089 remastered edition, released 1994. Other 'unofficial' releases are available.

Daevid Allen met young film-maker Jerome Laperrousaz in early 1968 as the Banana Moon Band played at various locations in and around Paris, and he filmed them performing for *Nightmares Of Mr Respectable,* a movie about the clashes between students and the police in France. He also captured the Amougies concert, the first proper Gong live appearance, before offering the band his ancestral home, the supposedly haunted Chateau du Thiel in Normandy, as 'winter quarters'. Here Gong created and recorded the 'Est-ce que Je Suis' single, plus their most lucrative composition so far, the theme tune for ORTF News.

Fast forward to early 1971 and Laperrousaz was working on a documentary about Australian Grand Prix motorcycle road racer Cyril John Findlay – known as Jack – and focusing on his 1968 season when he came second in the 500cc class to Italian world champion Giacomo Agostini, riding a British Matchless bike. Laperrousaz called on Allen to provide some suitably powerful, driving music to accompany the breathtaking scenes of high-speed motorcycle racing, and the band recorded three tracks for the film in May that year, followed by sessions for Dashiell Hedayat's *Obsolete.*

Released a year later to coincide with the film, *Continental Circus* really only contains one new song, 'Blues For Findlay', credited to Gilli Smyth and Laperrousaz (who clearly provided the lyrics as an instrumental version is credited to Gilli alone). The second track, 'What Do You Want?' is an early version of 'Fohat Digs Holes In Space'.

The album is credited to 'Gong avec Daevid Allen' – the record label clearly believed his name still had more commercial clout than Gong's in France, although it could well have been pressed and printed before *Camembert Electrique* had been released. No album producers or engineers are listed, but we can be pretty sure that Laperrousaz himself took a close interest in what the band was recording and the final result may have been shaped by the movie's sound mixer Paul Bertault. It was released through the Dutch label Philips Records, which at the time was known for championing psychedelic music.

Released after *Camembert Electrique* it is a bit of a throwback to the looser, more improvised style Allen displays on his solo album *Banana Moon*, especially on the long track '... And His Adventures In The Land Of Flip'. Had the album been released shortly after it was recorded, it would be seen as an important musical stepping stone from *Magick Brother* through to *Camembert Electrique*, as Allen's songwriting becomes more intricate and structured. But there is still plenty here to enjoy, with the 11-minute 'Blues For Findlay' showcasing the band's ability to drive hard, repetitive guitar riffs into your brain before soothing everything with a layer of glissando and space whisper.

The cover shows a strangely psychedelic, pixelated shot of Findlay crouched over his bike with a kangaroo emblem on his helmet, shot by Bruno Leys, while the back contains stills from the film showing Findlay apparently sliding upside down on his head along the track.

'Blues For Findlay' (Gilli Smyth/Gilli Smyth & Jerome Laperrousaz)
The opening track crashes in with a repetitive four-note riff in B major on phased guitar, building in intensity before stepping up to E minor, now utilising a repetitive eight-note riff that goes up from E to G then steadily back down through G flat and F. Allen sings the lyrics, printed on the reverse of the original album sleeve, about the 'greatest private rider in the world', with a chorus of sorts that repeats 'Can't you see me Agostini?' and 'Comin' up behind ya' while playing random but inspired lead guitar over Pip's busy drumming and Tritsch's rock-solid bass.

After about three and a half minutes of this, the song heads back into the eight-note riff and verse two, which pretty much repeats the sentiments expressed in the first verse, only now the trees are going past fast and 'the world is coming at me, the world is coming at me'. We're now at six minutes, about halfway through the song, and there are washes of strange psychedelic sound before a brief middle-eight over staccato drums in which Allen sings 'Watch out factory man/Bidin' my time/I'm comin' up behind you/Gonna leave you behind/I'm eatin' up the track/And I'm all alone/Rich man, I ain't accident-prone'. For me, that section sounds like pure Allen, as does the section almost straight after in which he intones 'Time is your life/ Time is your wife'.

By this time, the relentless four-beats-to-a-bar rhythm that has driven this song for the last seven and a half minutes begins to stutter and break down. Allen plays rich glissando guitar followed by some high-pitched notes that eventually lead back into the eight-note riff again, a repeat of the 'Watch out factory man' section before fading out on some languid power chords.

It is a remarkably powerful piece of music that hammers its point home through almost endless repetition while staying at all times within the minor blues triad of E, A and B, and captures Findlay's relentless nature as he stuck on Agostini's tail throughout the 1968 Grand Prix season.

'Continental Circus World' (Gilli Smyth & Jerome Laperrousaz)
Four minutes of extracts from the movie soundtrack, featuring announcements in French, the throaty buzz of roaring motorcycles and some brass band marching music. Some of the racers introduce themselves over the tannoy system, with excerpts from 'Blues For Findlay' playing underneath them. There's a bit of echoey tape loopiness towards the end before the track ends with the buzz of a motorcycle roaring off into the distance.

'What Do You Want?' (Gilli Smyth)
An early version of 'Fohat Digs Holes In Space', the track begins about a third of the way through the version on *Camembert Electrique* when Tritsch plays a simple, repetitive riff in E on bass, Allen provides glissando guitar and there's some distant space whispering from Gilli. After nearly six minutes, Allen repeatedly sings the line 'Takes a little time to know you, got to know you well' to the tune Didier plays on the *Camembert* version. Then we go into the ascending chords, over which Allen sings 'Well, what do you want, what do you really really want?'. The song changes key and Didier plays sax – followed by some screaming lead guitar from Allen that leads into the 'Oh Can You Wash Your Father's Shirt' nursery rhyme.

'Blues For Findlay – Instrumental' (Gilli Smyth)
As the title suggests, it's an instrumental version of 'Blues For Findlay' but with enough differences in structure and performance to show it's not just the backing track shorn of the vocals. It opens with the four-note motif in B major and quickly goes into the psychedelic glissando section, pretty much staying on the same chord for about eight minutes before finally moving into the eight-note sequence in E minor. Didier gets to play this time, and there's a menacing minute of sax and bass playing in unison before a final, discordant flourish.

Flying Teapot (1973)

Personnel (translated from the original liner notes!):
Daevid Allen (alias Dingo Virgin): vocals, guitar
Gilli Smyth (The Good Witch Yoni): space whisper
Tim Blake (Hi T Moonweed the favourite): synthesizer, vocals
Didier Malherbe (The Good Count Bloomdido Bad De Grasse): saxes, flute
Steve Hillage (Stevie Hillside): guitar
Christian Tritsch (The Submarine Captain): guitar
Francis Moze (Francis Bacon): pianos, bass
Laurie Allan (Lawrence the alien): drums
Rachid Houari (Rachid Whoarewe the Treeclimber): congas
Additional personnel:
Lady June: vocals on 'Radio Gnome Premix – Story Narration'
Recorded January 1973 at The Manor Studios, Oxford, UK
Producer: Giorgio Gomelsky
Engineer: Simon Heyworth, aided by Tom Newman
Original Label: Virgin records (BYG Actuel in France and Japan)
Released: May 1973 in the UK, later in the year in France and Japan
Highest chart positions: Uncharted
Running time: 39:45
Current edition: UMC/Virgin 7714150 2019 2CD remaster with bonus tracks and selections from live concert at Le Bataclan, Paris, 1973.

Sometimes the greatest art comes out of chaos. That's true of so many musical performers and particularly pertinent when it comes to the ever-changing, shapeshifting entity known as Gong. The Radio Gnome Invisible trilogy of *Flying Teapot, Angels Egg* and *You* sound as if they were part of a grand plan drawn up by Daevid Allen and executed by his dedicated team of merry minstrels. But in reality, the recordings came out of a period of radical change for the band, with more departures and arrivals than Heathrow airport. There were rows, legal battles, a steady turnover in drummers and, apparently, a huge pudding fight involving Richard Branson.

What Daevid Allen did have was a story concerning one Zero the Hero who, in the words of his creator on the *Planet Gong* website, was:

> A sort of hippy prodigal son who would leave his familiar surroundings for a trip to an unknown planet in a mythical universe. On his return, he would find himself radically changed and would thus try to encourage similar adventurism among other earthlings. Although I had created several skeleton song structures for the album, the substance and arrangements of the actual music would be as much as possible born out of spontaneous group improvisation.

After the cheese fixation of *Camembert Electrique*, Allen fully embraced tea as his inspiration of choice, and we see the use of the teapot as both flying machine and the source of the telepathic pirate radio that transmits the Gong sound to the Earthlings. His flights of fancy reach their peak here, with a cast of characters including Mista T Being, a pig-farming Egyptologist who invented the telescope through which one can see the Planet Gong, The Cock Pot Pixie, chief pilot of the flying teapot, and The Good Witch Yoni, who soars across the sky on a vacuum cleaner of unknown make.

Every member of the band plus roadies, producers and management receive gloriously silly names, the new additions including Stevie Hillside, Francis Bacon, Lawrence the alien, Hi T Moonweed and Simon Sandwich. Allen himself is no longer Bert Camembert but now a fully-fledged Dingo Virgin – a name that led some to believe he was one of the owners of the Virgin company, a misapprehension that Daevid and the rest of the band fully enjoyed encouraging.

But first, some comings and goings. *Camembert Electrique* heralded a 'crisis of splittingness', according to Allen. The album wasn't even in the record shops before drummer Pip Pyle announced his intention to return to England, where he would eventually join his old Delivery chums in the quintessential Canterbury band, Hatfield And The North. While touring in the UK Gong tried out Allen's old Soft Machine pal Robert Wyatt, but he was keen to start his own band, Matching Mole, and instead recommended Laurie Allan.

Born in London in 1943, Laurie first met Daevid back in 1968 while a member of the Gunter Hampel Trio with guitar wizard John McLaughlin before replacing Pip Pyle, who had gone off to Gong, in Canterbury-esque prog blues band Delivery. Now he was once again filling Pip's empty drum seat, arriving in France in December 1971.

Allan was, in the words of the other Allen (on the *Calyx* website):

> One of the most interesting drummers we ever played with. He would play differently every night, and when he couldn't think of a different way to approach it, he would leave the band. He was wonderful to play with, very sensitive ... and also very paranoid; he would always play with his back to the wall, he was scared that somebody had to kill him ...

In fact, Laurie quit Gong after just three months, leaving the band to try out various replacement drummers including Mac Poole from heavy rockers Warhorse, Charles Hayward from Phil Manzanera's Quiet Sun project, and Rob Tait from Vinegar Joe and Arthur Brown's Kingdom Come. Eventually, Laurie returned in December 1972 in time for the *Flying Teapot* sessions, along with *Magick Brother*'s drummer Rachid Houari on congas.

It was also time to say goodbye to Kevin Ayers, who had been touring with Gong since August 1971 but wasn't really a proper member of the band. He left in early 1972 before work started on *Flying Teapot*. But it was hello to Tim Blake, who joined as the band's synthesizer player in November 1972. Blake, born in London in 1952, was the sound engineer at Marquee Studios while Daevid Allen recorded his first solo album there, *Banana Moon*. Allen invited Blake to become Gong's sound engineer, but it wasn't until more than a year later that he arrived with his synthesizer.

There was yet another new face in bassist Francis Moze, born in France in 1946. Christian Tritsch wanted to move to guitar, so Giorgio Gomelsky recommended former Magma bassist Moze as a suitable replacement – although, by all accounts, he didn't intend to stay beyond the making of *Flying Teapot*.

Another addition to the lineup came too late to make much of a contribution to the album but would play a pivotal part in subsequent recordings before embarking on a long and successful career of his own – Chingford boy Stephen Simpson Hillage. Born in August 1951, he formed Uriel with school pals Dave Stewart and Mont Campbell, followed by Khan while at the University of Kent in Canterbury. By December 1972 Hillage was in Kevin Ayers' band Decadence – Gong saw them at a gig in Fontainebleau and Didier Malherbe jammed with them on stage, his saxophone blending with Hillage's guitar in a most mystical, magical way. He was invited to join the *Flying Teapot* sessions but arrived too late to make much of a contribution beyond some rhythm guitar and adding spacey sounds to the title track. Of course, he was to make his presence felt soon after! In fact, Hillage had already played an important part in the band's fortunes by persuading Allen to keep going after the latter felt the urge to pack it all in. In a 1975 interview with Clive Williamson, Allen said: 'This was the guy I was supposed to meet. It was pretty obvious the boys on Planet Gong really wanted me to take off and do something else.'

By the end of 1972 Gong were an eight-piece, and most of the songs that would make up *Flying Teapot* were being tried out in the band's live set. Their French record company, BYG, had booked them into Richard Branson's new Manor Studios – set up a year earlier to record albums for the entrepreneur's Virgin record label – and, according to Tim Blake, they turned up in the UK on New Year's Eve 1972 to be met by Virgin directors squirting champagne out of water pistols. A dinner that evening with Branson turned into a massive pudding fight.

There are conflicting reports about the recording sessions, which started on 2 January 1973, with Simon Heyworth producing. Steve Hillage said, in the liner notes for *Love From The Planet Gong* boxset: 'There were some moments of chaos but also some moments of great hilarity.' Tim Blake concurred: 'It was an exciting time recording *Teapot*, albeit a weird one.' But there are reports of the sessions occasionally being very tense, with clashes between the two Alle/ans and between Francis Moze and virtually everyone. Hillage also felt uncomfortable because the guitarist he was supposedly replacing, Christian Tritsch, was still there.

One further spanner hurled itself headlong into the works – BYG had got into financial difficulties, leaving the band signed but skint. Luckily, there was Virgin Records ready, willing and able to take Gong on. Allen believed the

BYG contract only applied to France, so he was free to sign a new contract covering the UK – a notion BYG challenged when the label suddenly popped its head up again. In the event, BYG and Virgin agreed to go 50:50 on the deal, with the former releasing the album in France with different cover art later in the year.

How to describe *Flying Teapot*? It's gentler than *Camembert Electrique*, spacier, more whimsical, more fun, with all the songs serving the storyline. Guitars are more muted, and everything has a hazy synthesizer wash from Tim. Most of the tracks are generally less complicated than on *Camembert*, although the title track clocks in at a mighty 11:53 on the CD versions – 12:30 on the original album. But they are all utterly brilliant – catchy, melodic, surprising, funny, exciting and played with precision and joy. Didier's sax darts around everywhere, making this as much a jazz album as it is prog or space-rock, and it is a tribute to the strength of these compositions that practically all of them became much-loved parts of the band's repertoire, played time and time again over the next four decades.

The original gatefold sleeve is, as usual, immense fun to pore over and read, from the colourful giant teapot on the cover, through Allen's quirky little etchings and wordplay on the inside, to the grinning mountain range on the reverse. The inside cover includes a short précis of the story – elaborated on later for the 2019 boxset *Love From The Planet Gong* – and advertises a booklet called The Pocket History Of The Planet Gong (actually named A Pocket Introduction To The Planet Gong) that added further to the mythology but was a little out of date, naming Pip Pyle as the drummer and Kevin Ayers as a member, and inaccurately listing *Banana Moon* as a Gong album.

The 2CD remastered version released at the same time as the boxset contains some additional studio tracks and is the one I am listing here.

Flying Teapot may not be the best of the trilogy – and I'll fight anyone who disagrees that it's *Angels Egg* – but it holds a special place in the hearts of all fans as the beginning of the classic Gong period.

'Radio Gnome Invisible' (Daevid Allen)

Not to be confused with 'Radio Gnome' on *Camembert Electrique*, this is a fully-fledged 5:31 song that opens the three-album story. A pig farmer in Norway called Mista T Being meets Hi T Moonweed in the market, who proceeds to sell him a gold (or silver) ring that, when slipped into the left earlobe, picks up a strange gnomic voice that burbles away almost indistinctly – 'radio to radio, brain to brain' – before guitar, bass and drums commence a clip-clopping rhythm that's part cosmic twitch, part Roy Rogers and Trigger. A weirdly weird sax tune leads into a crashing of chords when we learn that this is Radio Gnome Invisible, ha. Then we are into a faster section based on alternating major chords of B and A flat as we are 'receiving, perceiving your telepathic powers', with amusing use of a car horn to punctuate the lines. Up we go into D flat for a mystical Eastern section set down in the Persian market, then D and E for 'What's that in the sky now? Teapots that can fly now?', followed by a circular round of seemingly disconnected chords – F sharp, B flat, D major, A flat, then repeat – as the band chants 'banana, nirvana, manana'. There's a second excursion into the D to E segment with different lyrics and the song appears to come to an end.

But no! With a chant of 'Pot Head Pixies' the band go through the entire sequence again, this time adding words to Didier's quirky little opening sax tune. We end with a gentle burbling of sound and voices, slowly fading out of sight. And that, according to Allen in the *Flying Teapot* booklet, 'was how T Being and Fred the Fish by virtue of this crystal earring received a telepathic message from the Planet Gong and set off for Tibet to observe the first landing of a Flying Teapot and to meet the Pot Head Pixies whom they were to walk about with'. And that was how *Flying Teapot* opened, with one of the most bizarre songs ever committed to tape. A little disjointed perhaps – live, the band would frequently just play the first half – but an indication that we are in for a very wild ride.

'Flying Teapot' (Allen, Francis Moze)

Ghostly glissando fades into view, as a distant light edges closer to Mr T Being and Fred the Fish as they clamber over the smiling peaks of the Himalayas and join the Great Yogi Beer, Banana Ananda, as he sits in deep contemplation, waiting for the first landing of the Flying Teapot. There's a deep, gnomic rumble and high-pitched saxophone wanderings before Moze's bass starts a funky rhythm of bubbling notes, followed by a steady drum rhythm. Then the voices of the tall, green propeller-headed pixies begin their chant with 'If you feel belief – Hi Pete – I got a story to tell you' – Pete being a Gong band roadie, who is also mentioned in 'The Pot Head Pixies'.

After about four minutes of relentless rhythm in A minor – lead guitar now doubling the bass riff – we move into E and several other chords for a slice of gorgeous Didier, with Hillage providing wah-wah guitar before the whole song seems to break down on a flourish of piano notes played by Moze at about six minutes But it's only a brief interlude as the song bounces back into action and the pixies repeatedly exhort us to 'Have a cup of tea, have another one'. On a shout of 'Right!' we're into an E minor funky section, driven by Moze's superbly-nimble bass-playing and glissando guitar from Allen. The vocals repeat 'High in the sky, what do you see/Come down to earth, a cup of tea/ Flying saucer, flying teacup/From outer space, flying teapot'. This continues for three more minutes before rising chords take us into a brief bit of mad piano (played by an apparently very grumpy Moze), followed by silly voices and noises from Didier and some random tickling on the cymbals and banging on drums. Finally, drum and bass climb the scales to the final sudden ending.

Tim Blake has claimed ownership of the chord sequence under Didier's sax solo – in the information contained in the *Love From The Planet Gong* box set, he writes:

> Didier had qualms about playing a sax solo on a one-chord piece, as the 'Flying Teapot' track seemed to be. It was a unique and fascinating experience for me, the electronics player (only three years out of school) to be able to score a break full of chord changes to give Bloom something to bite on.

Sprawling and unpredictable, yet jam-packed full of tight playing and superb performances, 'Flying Teapot' is the anarchic, beating heart of the album, as much of a jazz tour-de-force as a progressive rock epic.

'The Pot Head Pixies' (Allen)

We've met a Pot Head Pixie once before, in 'Gong Song' on *Magick Brother*. At the time, the little alien being with a propeller on the top of his pointy head seemed a little worried about our mental health: 'Why do you feel so good?' he asked, then 'Why do you feel so bad?' This time round, the pixies are embracing craziness almost as some kind of health benefit. 'I am, you are, we are crazy!' they sing joyously, as if insanity is a perfect state of mind. They also insist 'Somebody somewhere has got to be high', equating this utopian state of insanity with being stoned.

It should come as no surprise to any reader that Allen was an enthusiastic dope smoker, almost evangelical in his belief that one could reach some sort of personal nirvana through pot. In an interview with Jimmy James in 1998, published on *Perfect Sound Forever* online music magazine, Kevin Ayers recalled meeting Allen thus: 'I was just out of an English private school, and suddenly I encountered this exotic person who said, 'F**k this, f**k that, smoke pot, read this'. All these people who had just come out of school were sort of wandering around in the job market thinking, 'what do I do now?' – suddenly, Daevid Allen's going, 'smoke pot now, peace, love and f**k your neighbour'.' But Allen always stressed he wasn't controlled by drugs, adding, in *Celebrating Daevid Allen: The Gong Father* by Raul Da Gama in May 2017: 'Dope is a great route to discovery, but you've got to use your own energy to chase it up.'

The essentially harmless, mischievous nature of the Pot Head Pixies is emphasised by the upbeat, pop-rock nature of the song, which began life as 'Big City Cat' – a live recording from November 1972 shows the structure of the song already in place, including the whimsical middle-eightish from Didier and the falling and rising chords at the end.

Opening with the aforementioned statement of mutual craziness, the recorded version once again mentions Pete the roadie, exhorting him to meet the titular aliens, and fills in some vital information about their origins and lifestyle – they come from the planet of love and they ride in a flying teapot. Two verses of silliness are punctuated by a slower section in three-quarter time in which Didier, in a rich French accent and as the voice of the pixie, mentions that he can be contacted through Radio Gnome. Then we are back into a third verse that ends with someone making a popping noise with their mouth before saying 'Good afternoon'.

It's a cracking little pop song that perfectly encapsulates the sense of humour and mild mischief embodied by Allen's little pixie creations.

'The Octave Doctors And The Crystal Machine' (Tim Blake)
American engineer Robert Moog is credited with developing the first synthesizer, which he debuted in 1964. Bands such as The Beatles – and albums including 1968's *Switched-On Bach* – helped make the electronic instruments part of popular music production. Blake's interest was piqued by his involvement with Hawkwind, and he bought a synth from Electronic Music Studios, using it to set up his own Crystal Machine project that produced a demo tape of his own compositions. When he joined Gong in 1972, he was one of the first musicians to bring the synth out of the studio and onto the live stage.

For this brief musical interlude, Blake eschewed the state of the art studio and instead set up a 'time-lag accumulator' in his bedroom at the Manor, recording it there. Waves of cascading, pulsating and overlapping notes buzz up and down for just under two minutes, creating a transcendent and hypnotic instrumental break before merging into the following track.

In Allen's Gong mythology, the Octave Doctors are 'gong gurus and benevolent all-wise and loving advisors of the phps and protectors of the planet. They appear as a giant radiant eye which hovers inside an upturned cone which is set inside a luminous egg-shaped aura', and the Switch Doctor – at that time Venux de Luxe (or Francis Linon) – is the resident Octave Doctor on Planet Earth.

'Zero The Hero And The Witch's Spell' (Allen, Christian Tritsch)
Repeated E and B harmonic guitar notes introduce the second-longest track on the album and one that contains several distinct sections. The first is a slow, dramatic ballad with crashing E minor and C major chords as Zero the Hero professes his love for the Pot Head Pixie. Didier plays mournful flute while Tritsch adds slide guitar. Then, at about 1:40, Rachid's congas introduce a bit of rapping gibberish mouth music from Allen before alternating A flat, A and B guitar chords bring in some sprightly Didier sax jazz.

Allen sings a swift, four-line verse before we suddenly pause and enter a brief section of Gilli's echoing space whisper. Alternating A flat and A notes from the bass pick things back up again, and there's a smattering of percussive bangs and taps from Laurie before the song enters a slow, dramatic and powerful section in A flat minor with Didier's sax soaring over glissando guitar. Gradually, a little six-note sax motif starts up, is echoed by bass and guitar, and we suddenly plunge into the last track on the album.

Steve Hillage also contributes spacey sounds to the track, which the band knew as 'Tic Toc' because of the rhythmic ticking effect provided by the guitar notes in the intro. It is called 'Tic Toc' on the Live Au Bataclan album, recorded in Paris in May 1973 but not released until 1990.

'Witch's Song/I Am Your Pussy' (Gilli Smyth, Allen)
Zero the Hero tries to 'make' the Good Witch Yoni, but she finds it quite offensive and sings a song that, according to Allen's liner notes, could be Women's Lib, a movement that started in the US in the late 1960s and soon gained momentum across Europe. 'Don't want to f**k you,' space whispers Gilli in her opening poem, as the band play a perky, uptempo little tune beneath her, 'just hear you rap.' In fact, the Good Witch Yoni comes across as quite sinister here, using her sexuality to draw Zero into her trap before flying away on her broomstick accompanied by some maniacal cackling over descending and ascending chords.

He, meanwhile, only wishes to feed her fish and chips in a delightful middle eight – the chords are A, C and F – that's played first as an instrumental by Didier on sax, and second with lyrics sung by Allen. It's one of Gilli's most effective pieces – she couldn't really sing, but her spooky spoken word pieces work beautifully against Allen's bouncy, pop-jazz music. The song – and original album – ends with slowly descending chords.

Bonus Tracks
'Radio Gnome Invisible – Rough Mix' (Allen)
There are some conflicting reports about who mixed the album. According to the liner notes on *Love From The Planet Gong*, Daevid Allen did it at the Manor at the end of February during a three-month sabbatical from the band while he and Gilli 'contemplated the future'. But Allen himself said it was mixed partly at the Manor by Giorgio Gomelsky and partly at Beatles producer George Martin's Air Studios in Montserrat through late January and early February.

He also reports on the *Planet Gong* website, how engineer Simon Heyworth was 'practically driven to a nervous breakdown by the Gong group production method. Everybody in the control room trying to mix their bit audibly. Finally, the band was banned and Simon mixed alone'.

The early mixes included in the 2CD deluxe release remastered by Heyworth do not differ much from the final released tracks. This rough mix of 'Radio Gnome Invisible', for example, is notable for having a lot of heavy echo on Allen's voice at various points and being about nineteen seconds shorter.

'Radio Gnome Premix – Story Narration (Allen)
A more interesting bonus track is this out-take from the sessions, which seems to have originally been intended as a linking piece from 'Radio Gnome Invisible' to 'Flying Teapot'. Opening with a clash of voices over bubbling sound effects, it settles into Allen narrating some of the story with glissando washes beneath him. You will recognise some bits and pieces that have turned up elsewhere on later albums or used as intros for live performances. It also features the voice of painter, poet and musician June Campbell Cramer, known as Lady June. She met Allen while modelling in Majorca in the 1960s

before moving to London where she hosted parties for way-out rock musicians, including one for Gilli's birthday during which Robert Wyatt fell out of her window and broke his back.

'Flying Teapot – Mix 21' (Allen, Moze)
Shorn of the original's first two minutes, this mix starts with Moze's funky bass and the 'If you feel belief' vocals, cutting off at the conclusion of the piano freak-out. Beyond that, I can't spot any major differences.

'The Pot Head Pixies – Second To Last Mix' (Allen)
As this is the second to last mix, you would think it's pretty spot-on. And it is. The only real difference is it's about two seconds shorter. And, er, that's it.

'Flying Teapot – Rough Mix' (Allen, Moze)
Slightly longer than 'Mix 21', this starts at the same point as the original but again ends at the piano freak-out.

Angels Egg (1973)

Personnel (translated from the original liner notes!):
Didier Malherbe (Bloomdido Bad De Grasse): saxes, flute, vocals
Gilli Smyth (Shakti Yoni): space whisper
Mike Howlett (T. Being Esq.): bass
Steve Hillage (Submarine Capt Hillage): guitar
Tim Blake (Hi T Moonweed the favourite): synthesizer, vocals
Pierre Moerlen (Pierre de Strasbourg): drums, vibes, marimba
Mirielle Bauer (Mirielle de Strasbourg): glockenspiel
Daevid Allen (Dingo Virgin): vocals, guitar
Recorded by Manor Mobile at Pavilion du Hay in France at full moon August 1973.
Producer: Gong under direction of Giorgio Gomelsky
Engineer: Simon Heyworth
Original label: Virgin Records
Released: December 1973
Highest chart positions: Uncharted
Running time: 45:14
Current edition: UMC/Virgin 7714151 2019 2CD remaster with bonus tracks and selections from live concert at Club Arc En Ciel, Roanne, 1973.

It's almost as if *Flying Teapot* and *Angels Egg* (the original release had no apostrophe) were recorded by two different bands. Gone were Christian Tritsch, Laurie Allen and Francis Moze. But Planet Gong drew Mike Howlett, Pierre Moerlen and Mirielle Bauer into its orbit – and this is when Steve Hillage really came into his own. What happened between the end of January 1973 and the beginning of August when Gong started recording sessions in their new home in Voisines, near Sens, south-east of Paris?

As mentioned in the last chapter, the *Flying Teapot* sessions almost ground to a halt thanks to Gong's record company BYG suffering financial difficulties. In the liner notes for *Love From The Planet Gong*, Hillage says:

> Daevid was loudly proclaiming he had had enough and was planning to retire. Other band members were announcing they would be leaving, and it was becoming apparent that this fantastic band that I was about to become a full member of was disintegrating before my eyes. It was a strange moment.

First to go was Tritsch, just days after the *Flying Teapot* recordings were completed, later saying in a Facebook post in 2020 he wanted to have a try 'in the normal world'. He was swiftly followed by Moze who, according to Allen, in a quote from 'The Making Of Flying Teapot', by Fred Dellar, published in *Mojo* magazine in 2002, 'blew up at me and resigned but sensibly made sure he had recorded all of his tracks'. Then Laurie Allan decided to jump ship, joining a new short-lived lineup of Delivery (he would pop back occasionally to fill the drummer's stool for some of Moerlen's frequent disappearances). By this stage Daevid and Gilli had decided they needed a break, returning to Deya in Majorca to spend time with new baby boy Taliesin.

This left the ever-loyal switch doctor Venux De Luxe, Didier Malherbe, Tim Blake and new boy Hillage with live dates in February but no drummer or bassist. The first vacancy was filled pretty quickly when Pierre Moerlen turned up, having seen the band perform a few days before and hearing they needed a new boy in the engine room. Moerlen, born in Colmar, France, in October 1952, was a classically-trained percussionist with previous experience in French rock and jazz bands and was welcomed with open arms. Allen later said: 'Pierre famously walked up at a gig in Lyons and declared: 'I am your new drummer!' Nobody told me for a week.'

He brought with him his then-girlfriend, percussionist Mirielle Bauer, born August 1951 in Alsace, France. The low notes were provided by Didier Thibault from Moving Gelatine Plates. Together, this five-piece fulfilled the February gig dates in France, performing a setlist that included Kevin Ayers's 'Why Are We Sleeping?' and an early version of 'I Never Glid Before'.

Meanwhile, Daevid had been tipped off about bass player Mike Howlett and turned up to see him play in London while en route to meeting Gilli in Deya. Liking what he heard, he said 'You're perfect mate! Just go!', sending him off to the Pavillon du Hay – things had not really worked out with Thibault. Howlett – born in Lautoka, Fiji, in April 1950 – spent his teenage years in Sydney playing in bands from the age of 12, covering 1960s music from Hendrix to Motown and Stax. When he joined Gong, he was into funk and soul, and also Herbie Hancock, Miles Davis and Weather Report. He brought a funky groove thing that helped give many of the *Angels Egg* tracks a pace and swing that made them almost danceable.

This second lineup of what has been dubbed 'Paragong' (although never actually billed as such) gigged through March and April, gradually building up material that would form most of *Angels Egg* – 20 minutes of the band's live set was captured during this time but not released until 1995. This period helped bond them together while providing opportunities to improvise and compose as a single unit. Mike said, in an interview with the author for this book:

> Didier, Steve, Tim and Pierre all seemed to be happy that I had arrived and solved the 'bass player' problem. I was not aware at that time that, apart from Didier, they were relatively new to Gong too. I simply accepted that we were all there to do something great and mystical – that's what it felt like. We were all very capable players, and the Paragong gigs were, I thought, a way for us to play live and work out new material as well as old material. We were all good improvisers too, and we built into those gigs a lot of space for improvisation.

Refreshed and rejuvenated, Daevid and Gilli returned in May and led the band through a tour to support the *Flying Teapot* album. This included gigs in the

UK, during which Gong went back into Manor Studios to cut an abortive single, the rather clumsily-titled 'Ooby Scooby Doomsday Or The D-Day DJ's Got The DDT Blues', and Hillage and Moerlen took part in a live premiere of Mike Oldfield's 'Tubular Bells' at London's Queen Elizabeth Hall. Then, on August 3, it was back to Pavillon du Hay with the Manor Mobile to make *Angels Egg*.

Daevid and Gilli had been unhappy leaving the French countryside to record in England, so insisted the big house they were living in, set in 100 hectares of forest, should be wired up so everyone could perform their individual parts in any room – or patch of wood – they desired. Mike Howlett recalls in an interview with the author:

> Didier asked the engineers from the Manor Mobile if he could be recorded in the forest, which he thought would have a nice ambience for his flute and saxes. The guys were very accommodating and ran cables out for microphones and headphones. Gilli thought that was a great idea and would suit her Mother Goddess nature spirit sort of thing, albeit most of her sound was generated by a Binson Echorec electronic echo unit. Again, the guys were happy to oblige. Then Tim thought he should also be in the forest, because, obviously, his synthesiser, which he put through his own mini-PA system with two large Altec Lansing speakers, would undoubtedly be enhanced by such an environment. To complete the ensemble, Daevid wanted to be recorded sitting cross-legged in his 'meditation chamber' in the top of the house. Remarkably, this all worked and this is how the album was recorded!

The 'other-wordly' nature of the recording somehow transmitted itself to the vinyl grooves, creating an album that is both spacey but earthy at the same time. With nearly three times the number of tracks that *Flying Teapot* possessed, it comes across a little bit like a vaudeville show, with every member of the band taking a turn in the spotlight: Tim Blake with his synthesizer opener 'Other Side Of The Sky', Hillage with his spacey guitar piece 'Castle In The Clouds', Gilli with her unforgettable 'Prostitute Poem', Didier with his juicy plateful of 'Flute Salad' and Moerlen with his percussion interlude 'Percolations'. Holding it together like an impish hippy music hall compère is Allen, with his delightfully silly lyrics and suitably barmy storyline as Zero the Hero delved further into the mysteries of Planet Gong, assisted by the Pot Head Pixies and copious amounts of 'tea'.

The pairing of Pierre Moerlen's crisp, inventive drumming and Mike Howlett's powerful, dancing bass created a rock-solid rhythm section that allowed the rest of the band to improvise over the top, leading to the creation of extended instrumental jams that reached their peak on the next album, *You*.

The cover art – drawn once again by Allen – shows scenes from the songs as Zero feeds fish and chips to Yoni, drinks tea with her and then receives some delicate female pampering while the Moon Goddess Selene reclines rather revealingly near the album title (some copies had a sticker placed over this saucy image). The original gatefold sleeve had little inside except gold pencil drawings on a blue background, while the back cover contained the latest instalment of the story alongside visual interpretations of the tracks. The first pressing of the album also contained the so-called 'Blue Book' of Gong lore and lyrics.

Some members of the band have been a little critical of a few of the songwriting credits on the album and feel they made important contributions that were unfairly overlooked – not to mention the fact that the names of both Mike Howlett and Pierre Moerlen are spelt incorrectly! To solve the eternal discussion about who wrote what that exists in every band, even idealist hippy ones, it was agreed that all future compositions after *Angels Egg* would be credited to all the band members equally.

The version of the album to get, if it's still available, is the remastered 2CD 2019 release that includes selections from a concert in Roanne, France, in August 1973, as well as some bonus tracks, which will be the one reviewed below.

Some of the band consider *Angels Egg* to be Gong's finest moment. Nearly 50 years later, Mike told the author: 'I think it stands the test of time. It has an atmosphere that pervades throughout and perhaps this is, in part, because there was no tension or rancour – we all seemed to just embrace the moment and perform to the best of our abilities.' Tim Blake said in the *Love From Planet Gong* box set liner notes: 'I would say to this day that *Angels Egg* was the best recording of my time at the heart of the Gong band. If I ever hear it I close my eyes and am taken straight back to that marvellous house near Sens.'

'Other Side Of The Sky' (Tim Blake, Daevid Allen)

At the end of *Flying Teapot* we left Zero the Hero feeding fish and chips to the Good Witch Yoni's pussy. But *Angels Egg* doesn't open with the sound of a cat digging into some battered cod. Instead, we start with Gilli intoning 'She is the mother of everything ... and you are her egggggg' before Tim Blake cranks up the Crystal Machine and some gentle electronic throbbing fades in under Gilli's space whisper and Didier's plaintive sax.

This is one of the compositions worked up by Blake – he believes during the first tour of the 'Paragong' lineup with Didier Thibault on bass – although Allen added some cosmic lines about passing beyond 'countless worlds, the eternal wheel, the ceaseless tide of selves' and sparse, chanting vocals buried deep in Blake's synthesizer soundscape. Drums and bass enter, the whole thing builds up nicely, with Hillage providing some ethereal lead guitar. As everything comes to a climax, Allen sings 'Hare, hare supermarket! Hare, hare London bus! Hare, hare ladies' lavatory!' before the track fades out on the echoed repeat of 'Hare, hare, hare…'. Tim Blake told the author: 'When we recorded 'Other Side Of The Sky', Daevid burst into improvised vocaling all over it! Ladies' lavatories indeed!'

It fades directly into the opening of …

'Sold To The Highest Buddha' (Mike Howlett, Allen)
A slightly swinging drum rhythm and Howlett's (misspelled 'Howlitt' on the original album's back cover) simple rising and falling bass line of E, F sharp and G (and back again) bring in a catchy little song as Zero tries to make contact with a rocket contraption piloted by Captain Capricorn. Howlett came up with the bass riffs while driving the group's minibus on the UK tour in June 1973. He also provided the 'hang on to your head' chorus line and the punning title.

Allen composed and sings the lyrics for the verses, melodically complex lines that play against the gentle rhythm of the track, with Hillage sometimes double-tracking his voice with lead guitar, sometimes leaping off into atonal little riffs. Then we are into the powerful chorus of 'Look out, we're being invaded', followed by the repeat of the line 'Hang on to your head' over a deceptively tricky time signature of, I think, 7/4. The whole song comes to a halt before Pierre on hi-hat takes things back to the beginning again.

After a second rendition of the chorus and the 'hang on to your head' chant, the track moves into a section known as '6/8' (Allen's illustrations on the back cover mistakenly put this in the middle of 'Buddha' instead of at the end), one of the compositions created by the 'Paragong' lineup and originally played live as a standalone track – technically, it should really be credited to Blake, Howlett, Hillage, Malherbe and Moerlen.

As the title strongly suggests, it's in 6/8 and features Didier letting loose with some bebop lines on his sax while Hillage plays intricate jazz chords beneath him and Pierre swings along with busy, almost freeform drumming in one of the jazziest moments on the album.

'Castle In The Clouds' (Steve Hillage)
Steve says Allen asked him to make a short, spacey piece that evoked a castle in the clouds, and Hillage obliged with passages of lead guitar, swamped with echo, over bubbling synth. Hillage liked it so much he later used it in live concerts as the intro to his cover of Donovan's 'Hurdy Gurdy Man'.

'Prostitute Poem' (Gilli Smyth, Hillage)
Hillage plays a large part in this composition, too, dating from the return of Daevid and Gilli to the band. The latter had a freeform poem written in a mixture of French and English from the point of view of a prostitute old with experience and full of ambivalence about her chosen profession – 'I want your body/I do not want your body'. Gilli asked Hillage to find a way of evoking 1950s Paris with the music, and he came up with a mournful saxophone tune in three-quarter time, punctuated by arpeggios in C major. Opening with 'it is night' the words are the prostitute's thoughts during a sexual encounter – 'I kiss your lips' she says, 'You die', a possible reference to 'la petite mort' or 'a little death', a description of sexual orgasm.

'Givin' My Love To You' (Allen)
According to the liner note, we 'finish up in an old French cafe with pocket billiards barflies in glorious Saturday night high camp parlour parody for fun', although this sounds more like a 'Knees Up Mother Brown' type Cockney croon, with overstrung piano and drunken sing-along vocals with general pub chatter accompaniment. The lyrics even go so far as to say 'give a dog a bone', from the children's counting song 'This Old Man'. Giving a dog a bone is, of course, a rather coarse euphemism of British origin for sexual intercourse, which was taking place in the preceding song.

'Selene' (Allen)
This is the second song Allen has written about the Moon Goddess in Greek mythology – the first was the penultimate track on the *Camembert Electrique* album. That was a drone-like chant – this time round, the Goddess is celebrated with a slow, stately ballad driven by Howlett's bass. Moerlen plays tinkling tuned percussion, Hillage some tasteful guitar arpeggios, while Allen's double-tracked voice creates a hymn-like quality. It ends with what sounds like the many voices of Allen performing an adhan, an Islamic call to prayer. 'Selene shines in the prostitute, the prostitute shines in Selene,' say the somewhat politically-incorrect liner notes as we end side one, the side of the Goddess.

'Flute Salad/Oily Way' (Didier Malherbe/Allen, Malherbe)
Listed as 7a and 7b on the original album, the opening to side two, combined with 'Outer Temple' and 'Inner Temple', represents quintessential Gong for many, combining all the elements of jazz, humour and glissed-out space-rock that make the band so unique. The sequence became a staple of the Daevid Allen-led live set, apart from when Gong were forced to use a drummer who couldn't even attempt 'Oily Way'.

Interestingly, all four tracks were mainly composed before Daevid and Gilli returned to the band from their Majorca break. 'Flute Salad' started life as an interlude in the 'Paragong' set during which Didier would improvise with echo, building up complex polyrhythms and harmonies. There's a chunky five-minute version on the *Live au Bataclan* recording, along with an early attempt at 'Oily Way' with slightly different lyrics and a missing middle eight. Malherbe uses various effects devices to build up layers of flute, rising and falling through Eastern scales, with judicious use of warm synthesizer to back it up. After about two minutes of what sounds like the wind blowing harmoniously across the Sahara, we reach the distinctive 'up and down' flute motif that heralds the start of the 'Oily Way' section. Didier plays it three times, then Hillage provides a harmony on guitar while the flute plays the tune an octave higher. The result is exquisitely mysterious.

'Oily Way' was another composition from the Paragong team, credited mostly to Didier who came up with the chorus line and the title. When Allen arrived, he rewrote some of the lyrics then added a middle-eight section – well, more of a middle-sixteen – based on the intro flute motif. The verse chord sequence is a strange, atonal beast, something like (to my naive ears) C sharp minor, E, G and B flat – mounting minor third jumps that Howlett believes Steve Hillage came up with, while the joyful chorus slips into F major. There are stops and starts all over the place but keeping it all together is Howlett's rock-solid bass and Moerlen's inspired drumming – listen to how he uses the full range of his kit to propel the song along, and marvel at his inspired fills that plug the various gaps.

Like Didier's other main composition on the album, 'Eat That Phone Book Coda', the lyrics don't really push Allen's story any further. Instead, they are more of an overview of the Gong landscape – the album sleeve says 'Oily Way' is where the Pot Head Pixies explain to Zero the intricate workings of flying teapots and how they ride an invisible big dipper through time.

After the final chorus we go straight into...

'Outer Temple' (Blake, Hillage)

Zero has an 'oriental' cup of char here, provided by the Hubba Gubba Tea Company of Tibet, with a two-minute tune composed by Hillage playing gentle, rhythmic arpeggios in C#m, occasionally popping up to D major. Over a hypnotic chant of 'have a cup of tea, luverly cup of tea', Blake provides bubbly synth sounds while Malherbe's sax rises and falls in a suitably mystical fashion. Slowly, the whole thing builds up to a crescendo of drums, bass, sax and tea chanting before a Hillage-penned semi-tone climb leads us into...

'Inner Temple' (Allen, Malherbe)

Credited as you can see, to Daevid and Didier but it is Mike Howlett's repetitive, funky bass line that anchors the piece, a steady, four to a bar glissando-swamped instrumental that also gives Malherbe a chance to shine on saxophone. Gilli adds space-whisper for a hypnotic, spacey two-and-a-half minutes, during which, according to Allen, Zero is introduced to 'the iridescent Angels Egg, the 32 Octave Doctors in one, the secrets of life and death cycles of the PHPs'. Live, this would stretch to double the length, and is a precursor to *You*'s 'Isle Of Everywhere', another Howlett-inspired composition.

Both Temples were originally created by the Paragong lineup before Daevid and Gilli returned from Deia to add their parts. Mike said: 'When Daevid returned he worked out the glissando guitar part, which is actually a very significant component, creating complex harmonies around the basic riff that Didier could use to inspire his improvised solo.'

'Percolations' (Pierre Moerlen)

After what has been essentially a medley clocking in at nearly 10 minutes, we need a little pause for breath, and this is provided by Moerlen. 'Percolations' is 46 seconds of seemingly random percussion, with background sounds of slapping and the occasional scream! Pierre came from a very musical family – his younger brother Benoit will make an appearance in this book a bit later – and was taught percussion by Jean Batigne, founder of Les Percussions de Strasbourg. He had a foot in both the rock and classical camps, and the schizophrenic nature of his career was reflected in his frequent absences from Gong as he tried to concentrate on being a more 'serious' musician.

'Percolations' falls into the camp of 'serious modern classical music' – it is difficult to believe that the slapping and screaming were Moerlen's idea – and gave its title to a later composition released under the Gong name that is more structured and composed. It leads almost imperceptibly into ...

'Love Is How Y Make It' (Moerlen, Allen)

What a beautiful little song this is, a gentle, contemplative piece led by Moerlen's vibes and marimba, with Mirielle on marimba and percussion, and delightful lyrics from Allen. Pierre and Mirielle were teen sweethearts and her cousin by marriage was a founder of Les Percussions de Strasbourg. Here, the Pot Head Pixies are imitating the destructive tendencies of human beings but Zero stops them in their tracks with a song about love – 'ringing bells and singing tales of how this world could be if only we could learn to melt together'. Love is, indeed, how you make it, take it, give it and live it, and Zero's manifesto here could be a guide to us all. Allen also nails his romantic colours to the mast, saying 'That is why I sing this song, and why there is a band called Gong'. This is Mireille's only contribution to the album and her parts were written out by Pierre – she was also classically-trained as a percussionist and Moerlen was very specific about what he wanted.

Drums come in and the percussion is faster and more furious as Allen repeats the title. At the end the percussion drops down into a different, slightly more menacing key as Allen chants 'give a little wink, give a little think, give a little drink' before a very sudden ending. 'Love Is How Y Make It' foreshadows Moerlen's later approach to Gong compositions, relying heavily on repetitive, overlaying tuned percussion in a tricky-dicky time signature.

'I Never Glid Before' (Hillage)

Hillage's masterpiece on this album was one of the earliest tracks to be written when 'Paragong' were touring with Didier Thibault on bass. Things didn't work out with that particular Didier, and this song really does rely on a pumping bass line to keep things going, which Mike Howlett does superbly well. He told the author: '[Hillage] was surprised but pleased when I played it, as it was not something he would have considered at all, being from the more prog rock-ish Canterbury school.' Not only that, guitar and bass manage to mirror Allen's vocal in the verse, which has a quaver dropped at the end of the second bar, which makes it feel rather oddly-timed.

The whole thing is based on Hillage's eight-note riff that goes up, comes down and then takes a cheeky little leap at the end. Drums and bass open things up with a busy, almost military rhythm before guitar and sax play the riff in unison. As said before, the verses really do their own thing, creating a sense of impending collapse in the song before it dives back into the riff again. We go up from B to C# for the chorus of 'Oooookay, you're Mr Illuuuuusion', before the stuttering, staccato mention of the title – 'No I never, no I never ever glid before-a, I never, oh no'.

Then we're back into a short rendition of the riff before Hillage leaps off into the stratosphere with blistering lead guitar – at least two of them, actually. There's a slow section of short vocal lines – 'Last warning, tide turning, moon burning, slow-motion' – that serves as a middle-eight of sorts until a brief Howlett bass solo takes us back into a slower version of the riff that drops down a tone and a half to the original starting chord of B major. Then another change as vocalist and guitar sing and play in a kind of stepping rhythm before Allen repeats the title over the riff, which speeds up ... and up ... and up ... with Didier playing screeching sax over the top. Suddenly everything comes to a stop with the lines 'that's another story – now's the time to go and find the cuppa tea, see. Bomp.'

Phew! Only Gong could manage to take something with so many parts to it, in so many different keys and tempos, and create something that sounds as if they always belonged together. 'I Never Glid Before' shows how well Hillage and Allen blended their talents – Daevid takes no credit for the lyrics, yet they could easily have come from his wacky pen, and Hillage's melody lines mirror Allen's almost scattish style of singing.

There's a frantic urgency to the song that mirrors the subject matter – 'glidding' is how the flying teapots move, dontcha know – that helps to end the album's story on a high. But there's one more track to go ....

'Eat That Phone Book Coda' (Malherbe)

Actually, it's not so much of a coda – a passage that brings a piece or movement to an end – but a summation of what has gone before, a restatement of general Gong themes in which Bloomdido Bad de Grasse 'takes his magick hooverhorn and drops hints about how he changed from Pot Head Pixie to human bean'.

Let's talk for a moment about Didier. Probably the most accomplished musician in Gong, he also seemed to personify the band's impish, mischievous spirit with big, darting eyes, a seemingly never-ending parade of hats and endearing on-stage antics, such as his attempts to 'reel in' members of the audience with an invisible fishing rod.

And his playing! Apart from the sheer variety of wind-driven instruments he mastered, there was his innate ability to come up with simple yet delightful melodies, to create almost whole songs out of his improvisations. His influence is all over *Angels Egg*, as it would be over *You*, and he probably had a hand in many more tracks here than he was credited for.

The opening few seconds of 'Eat That Phone Book Coda' display his sheer mastery of the saxophone as he soars into the air before crashing to earth in a blast of sound. Then there's that bluesy refrain, played alongside Allen's vocal, with Pierre playing busily along on drums before a mysterious 6/8 section as Daevid sings 'the planet was, I realised, one of the spots before my eyes'. After that, a playful nursery-rhyme motif goes with Allen's 'O mamy maya, I pray for a banana', repeated by Mike on bass and Steve on guitar. There's laughter and crowd noise before a triumphant fanfare of sax takes us into the last few lines of the album – 'At the end of the day, when there's nothing left to play, and you're all alone except for Radio Gnome, here's your Angels Egg for breakfast in the morning'.

Here ends one of the best – if not THE best – albums Gong ever made. Bye bye.

Bonus Tracks

'Ooby-Scooby Doomsday Or The D-Day DJ's Got The DDT Blues'

(Allen, Blake)

By Daevid Allen's own admission, he was never very good at identifying – or, indeed, composing – music with commercial potential. He was one of the first to hear Mike Oldfield's *Tubular Bells*, Virgin Records' debut release, and pronounced it far too esoteric for popular consumption. And when Virgin asked Gong for a single, he suggested 'Ooby-Scooby Doomsday' and was laughed out of the office.

That's not to say there is anything wrong with it – it's a great Gong track that remained unfairly hidden from our ears until it turned up on the *Live Etc* album, issued in 1977. But 'Una Paloma Blanca' it ain't. For a start, the title takes longer to say than some Beatles singles actually last (it originally had Blake's single-word title 'Revolution' but Allen changed it). Secondly, it's more than five minutes long, which would test the attention span of most Radio 1 listeners. Thirdly, it's unashamedly political, calling out for 'Revolution!' and lambasting politicians, and also includes drug references, enough to make the BBC get its knickers in a twist. And, fourthly, it is so defiantly quirky and disjointed that it would blow the minds of any Bay City Rollers fans.

It was the first track to be recorded by the *Angels Egg* lineup – and the only one taped at Manor Studios in Oxfordshire – during a tour of the UK in June 1973, a week before Hillage and Moerlen took part in the live premiere of 'Tubular Bells' at the Queen Elizabeth Hall. If it was indeed written by Allen and Blake – and I think we've already established that some of the song credits during this time are a little suspect – then it had to be during the six weeks from the beginning of May when Daevid and Gilli returned to the band.

What influences can we identify for the lyrical content? There are some clues in the title. 'Ooby-Scooby Doomsday' is clearly a reference to the US animated TV series Scooby-Doo, which had been running on CBS since 1969.

But Doomsday? Well, in 1973 it was reported on Australian TV that a computer simulation had predicted the end of the world in 2040. We don't know if Allen saw that, but it would explain the apocalyptic nature of the lyrics, as politicians' actions file up behind them. Then there is a reference to DDT, the insecticide first made widely available in the US in 1945. By 1973 a series of hearings had been held on its health dangers and a US court ruled it should be banned.

And, of course, there was general unease about nuclear weapons – serious protests against their existence broke out in 1971 and, by 1973, were in full swing in many parts of the world including Allen's home of Australia.

Musically 'OSDOTDDGTDDTB' – to give it an abbreviated title – is a multi-sectioned beast that opens with military drumming from Pierre, a saxophone reveille, then cries of 'Revolution! Bad vibrations! Manifestations!' before we hear part of the title sung over lurching chords. This is followed by a quicker section of rising chords, reminiscent of the second half of 'Fohat Digs Holes In Space,' which slows down for 'Oh my papa's got money' and 'He has fun with bombs and guns'. Back we go into the verse, in which Allen reveals his own political confusion – 'You talk about the left-wing, you talk about the right-wing, being nothing's getting pretty frightening' and another rendition of the slow section before the whole thing goes through again from Pierre's drum intro.

We then enter what could be a kind of middle-eight of heavy power chords as Allen reveals 'I don't want no ugly revolution, I just wanna get high' – which, let's face it, is a pretty succinct description of Gong's political manifesto. And now a section that's bizarre even by Gong's standards – punctuated by mad saxophone blowing and random guitar, Allen recites, in a cockney accent, 'Fee fi fo fum, I smell the blood of an Englishman' and, as the song seems to break down into chaos, suggests 'Let's all go to church and be good-looking'.

It all ends with about 20 seconds of complete and utter musical mayhem that leads into a long, drawn-out ... sneeze. Yes, really. It is utterly mad, delightfully entertaining and about as commercial as ... well, Gong.

'Love Is How Y Make It – 1973 Vocal Mix' (Moerlen, Allen)
So far as I can tell, this is identical to the original album except for some slightly more prevalent harmony vocals. It adds very little to our knowledge and understanding of the track.

'Eat That Phone Book Coda – Early Version' (Malherbe)
Again, you won't find much here that's different to the final recorded version except for minor changes to Didier's sax intro, a bit more chuckling and laughing in the background and a bit of hesitancy in Allen's vocals at the end.

You (1974)

Personnel:
Mike Howlett: bass guitar
Pierre Moerlen: percussion with Mirielle and Benoit
Steve Hillage: lead guitar
Bloomdido Glad de Brass (Didier Malherbe): wind instruments and vocals
Hi T Moonweed (Tim Blake): Moog and EMS synthesisers and mellowdrone
Dingo Virgin (Daevid Allen): vocal locust and glissando guitar
Shakti Yoni (Gilli Smyth): poems and space whisper
Bambaloni Yoni (Miquette Giraudy): wee voices and chorousings
Recorded at the Manor, Oxfordshire, Summer 1974.
Producer: Simon Heyworth and Gong under the universal influence of C.O.I.T
Engineer: Simon Heyworth
Side one mixed at Pye, Marble Arch. Side two mixed at the Manor
Original label: Virgin Records
Released: October 1974
Highest chart positions: Uncharted
Running time: 44:38
Current edition: UMC/Virgin 7714152 2019 2CD remaster with bonus track and selections from live concert at Hyde Park, London, 1974.

For the first time in Gong's long and convoluted history, a second album was recorded by virtually the same lineup – the only change was the addition of Pierre Moerlen's brother Benoit. But the band's sixth release – and the last in what was originally supposed to be a trilogy – was not without its own birth pangs. Even before *Angels Egg* was released, Pierre quit to tour with Les Percussions de Strasbourg, with ex-Battered Ornaments drummer Rob Tait replacing him until the following March. Gilli Smyth also took a break – she was having pregnancy difficulties with her third child Orlando and gave birth at the end of January. She was replaced briefly by US-born singer and percussionist Diane Stewart-Bond, second wife of sax player and notorious occultist Graham Bond. Both the newcomers appear on four live tracks recorded in January 1974 and released on the *Live Etc* album in 1977.

Then in October 1973, Gong were unceremoniously turfed out of their idyllic forest home and forced to live with friends while touring the UK before eventually moving to Middlefield Farm in Witney, Oxfordshire. Pierre came back in March the following year, and Diane was replaced by Steve Hillage's girlfriend, Miquette Giraudy. Born in Nice in February 1953, Miquette had a short-lived film career before meeting Steve, working with him as his musical and life partner ever since. The band then rented a cottage in Little Bedwyn, Wiltshire, where material for *You* was written and rehearsed.

Throughout this time Gong toured almost incessantly, on average doing a gig every two and a half days. They were particularly frequent visitors to the

UK, completing a three-month tour there at the end of 1973 and returning in the middle of 1974, and were one of the acts on the bill of a free open-air concert in Hyde Park, London, on 29 June. At the same time, *Camembert Electrique* had been released by Virgin for the price of a single, helping to spread their music across the land. Unfortunately, Gong's new high profile also brought them to the attention of the local constabulary, who raided the farm in Witney and arrested Daevid Allen on suspected drug charges. Ironically, he had just decided to give up smoking dope.

All the tracks on *You* are credited to Gong on the reverse of the record sleeve – on the labels they are the work of COIT, Compagnie d'Opera Invisible de Thibet, an alternative collective name for the band. The decision to share the glory, no matter who actually wrote the songs, may have come out of dissatisfaction among some members at the rather random nature of the credits on the *Angels Egg* album. Most of *Angels Egg* had been written without Daevid Allen – on *You* he was there at the start of the creative process and the music came from an intense period of collaboration.

On the Planet Gong website Allen explained:

> The creation of *You* was very different to *Angel's Egg*. We had come to the conclusion that, because I was contributing a lot of the material, it was too much my original creation. It was time we created something completely together, so we booked up a cottage in England, and we lived there for a week, we saved up some wonderful acid and we took this acid together as a group. And this was one occasion where there was no paranoia, it was just a wonderful, wonderful trip and we all played and played and played. And we connected so strongly together out of the improvisations, we just improvised and recorded it and then at the end of the day, we would listen to the recordings and take the pieces out that we wanted to learn.

However, Mike Howlett recalls he, Tim, Steve and Didier were the prime instigators for the change.

Some of the tracks slipped into the setlist from April 1974 – interestingly, they included an early version of Steve Hillage's 'Solar Musick Suite' that was destined for his first solo album. It seems likely, however, that few of the new *You* tracks had lyrics at that stage as Allen didn't write them until May that year. Then in July, the band went into the Manor studios to make an album that was eventually to tear Gong apart.

You is a different animal to *Angels Egg*. There are just eight tracks instead of thirteen and fewer 'party pieces' from individual members. This is truly a collaborative effort, with the album dominated by four big beasts – 'Master Builder', 'A Sprinkling Of Clouds', 'The Isle Of Everywhere' and 'You Never Blow Yr Trip Forever' – created out of the swirl of musical ideas emanating from every member of the band. The emphasis is on soundscapes and grooves and it is a much more serious album with fewer vocals and less humour. In fact, it is no surprise that Daevid Allen quit the band after this as it is the least Allen-esque recording in his career.

The cover sports none of Allen's whimsical cartoons and playful notes – instead, Tim Blake and Brigitte Perron designed the front, a Mayan pyramid seemingly floating in space, while Allen drew a large mandala eye for the back under the words 'Gong is one and one is you', If you bought the first pressing of the album you were also treated to an insert that contained the third part of the adventures of Zero the Hero, plus the lyrics and who sang them. After that, however, you were on your own.

The album was named one of Rolling Stone magazine's 50 Greatest Prog Rock Albums Of All Time, and its influence in the five decades since its release has stretched beyond progressive rock into the worlds of ambient, techno and trance music. In 1997 it was released as a double album remixed by the likes of The Orb, The Shamen, Astralasia, Youth and System 7. For many fans it is the pinnacle of Gong's art – it is certainly a big, bold album that has lost none of its impact.

'Thought For Naught' (C.O.I.T.)

A gentle little opener, based on a sinuous, Eastern-influenced Didier flute tune, 'Thought For Naught' is just one and a half minutes long and is a meditation on the meaning of life – Zero has returned from the Planet Gong to find himself in bed, and has to do some serious thinking. Didier does most of the singing, coming in the second you drop the needle on the record (or however you consume your music) with no intro or fanfare. Gilli interjects a few lines while Pierre doubles up the flute with gentle tuned percussion and Blake adds bubbly noises underneath. The title is perhaps inspired by 19th-century authors James and Horace Smith, who said 'Thinking is but an idle waste of thought, and naught is everything, and everything is naught'.

'A PHP's Advice' (C.O.I.T.)

Another short song originally conjured up by Didier but with a bit more spirit to it as Allen's lyrics do what it says in the title – dispense advice from a Pot Head Pixie. The melody is not unlike 'Thought For Naught', with a whimsical, nursery-rhyme feel but speeded up somewhat with added clip-clops, boinging noises and comedy clarinet licks. Tuned percussion plays throughout and the whole thing rattles along happily for under two minutes. It leads directly into…

'Magick Mother Invocation' (C.O.I.T)

Two minutes of deep, mystic 'ommmming', with added space whisper and swirly, buzzy synth that goes almost imperceptibly into…

'Master Builder' (C.O.I.T)

Steve Hillage woke up one morning with a riff in his head. Rushing down to the cottage in Little Bedwyn – about 45 minutes from the farm where they were staying – he tried it out on guitar, with Mike Howlett on bass. Steve said on the *Love From Planet Gong* box set notes: 'We loved it! After a day of jamming around, we had pretty much the whole arrangement, including the melody at the end to which Daevid later added the 'Master Builder' lyrics. We thought this was one of Gong's finest moments!' So good, in fact, that Steve also recycled it for his 1978 album *Green* as 'The Glorious Om Riff'.

Divided into three sections on the lyric sheet, it opens with the Mystic Mister Invocation – a chant by the band that emerges from the 'oms' of the previous track, backed by Tim's synths, rising in volume and intensity. They sing 'iao za-i za-o', representing sexuality; 'ma-i ma-o', representing the mother force; and 'ta-i ta-o now' representing the light force. The melody consists of just two alternating notes, G and G sharp. Pierre's drums build up in intensity until the whole thing explodes into Didier's saxophone solo over Steve's guitar riff. Then, after a few brief key changes, everything suddenly stops and there is a brief moment of silence apart from the sound of birds twittering before Allen's vocal comes in for section two, in which Zero seeks to bring his vision from Gong down to Earth. 'Maybe you know' says Allen, as the band jump in and out of earshot, punctuated by strange discordant sounds on Hillage's guitar. Then we leap back into the chants, with frantic, piercing lead guitar from Steve.

After about five and a half minutes, we enter section three in which Zero asks Hiram the Builder how to structure his vision. The answer comes in Allen's 'Master Builder' lyric – 'Master Builder, tell me how you make a temple? Tools and moonstones, you don't really need them you know' – as the song's key rises up ... and up... before coming to a sudden and unexpected stop.

A Sprinkling Of Clouds' (C.O.I.T)

Tim composed the twinkling synth part in his room at the farm – Mike Howlett remembers he had a fairly large space above what were originally cowsheds with his synth studio dominating most of the area. He told the author:

> It was a beautiful piece built on arpeggios with a very long tape echo so the harmonies all built on each other and slowly revolved. I thought it took a lot of inspiration from Terry Riley, who was a long time friend of Daevid and Didier. I brought the two riffs to the piece, the first half being constructed with four bars of 5/8 and one bar of 4/8, adding up to 24 quavers.

Mike plays a nice little bass solo at about three minutes in, there's warm glissando underneath and the whole thing feels like you are drifting through the clouds. Restrained drums in 4/4 – just some cymbals and rimshots – come in at about the two-minute mark as everything begins to build up in volume and intensity. Blake's keyboard flourishes become more pronounced before, at about five and a half minutes, everything kicks into top gear, with Howlett contributing a tricky, driving bass pattern and Hillage's lead guitar crashing in, playing discordant, apparently random notes before settling into a riff that's reminiscent of section three of 'Master Builder'. Didier comes in with a sax solo at seven minutes, the drums are now pounding away and the music is almost literally taking the tops of our heads off and sending them into orbit. Finally, we have a slow winding down and the tune ends on Didier's bamboo flute and Blake's synth. In an album packed full of wonderful musical moments, this is almost – but not quite – the highpoint.

'Perfect Mystery' (C.O.I.T)

Daevid Allen was criticised by some members of the band for having little to offer the *You* recording sessions apart from stuff dating back to 1970. But Steve Hillage said he wanted an old song to link the new material with the earlier Gong sound. 'Perfect Mystery' certainly dates back to at least January 5, 1971, when it was performed for French TV and released on an 'unofficial' CD of *Continental Circus* in Sweden in 2011 under the title 'Excerpt from Camembert Electrique' (although it doesn't actually appear on that album).

It opens with four piercing notes on guitar followed by a tune Allen had already used a few times in the past – the Irish song 'Oh, Can You Wash Your Father's Shirt', a pretty nursery rhythm-style piano practice piece using just the black notes. Then comes the first verse, which has the same lyrics as the 1971 version, including the amusing and slightly paranoiac couplet 'Cops at the door! No cops at the door…' A short, gentle interlude of Gilli talking over minor chords picked out on guitar leads us back into the four-note intro again and another rendition of the Irish nursery rhyme.

The second verse has clearly been freshly-written for *You* as it references the track that is about to follow, 'The Isle of Everywhere', and takes Allen's Zero the Hero story a little further – he has set off for the island in search of illumination. It ends with Gilli intoning: 'What a surprise – she looked around for Zero, but he's lost his eyes in a fruitcake'!

Like 'Thought For Naught' and 'A PHP's Advice', 'Perfect Mystery' is short and sweet, with a charmingly child-like melody, whimsical sax from Didier and Pierre's tune percussion playing unobtrusively beneath.

'The Isle Of Everywhere' (C.O.I.T.)

If one were to identify the composition that most fully represents Gong in all its groovy, space-rock glory, it would probably be this. It's not the longest recording in the trilogy – that's 'Flying Teapot', which originally clocked in at more than twelve minutes – but this is still nearly 10 and a half minutes of pounding, funky, glissando-drenched wonderment, with inspired soloing from Steve and Didier, nimble and inventive drumming from Pierre and a funky bassline from Mike that holds everything together.

In fact, one can look on this and 'You Never Blow Yr Trip Forever' as one continuous 22-minute track, if you like, as it was recorded in a single live take, solos included, with only a few minor overdubs and Allen's vocals added later. Bearing in mind the many changes of chords, timings and pace involved, that is an astonishing feat and could only be achieved by a group of musicians who were at the very top of their games.

According to the original lyric sheet included with the first pressing of the album, there are three sections to 'The Isle Of Everywhere'. The first, called 'The Melting Feast Of Freaks', was devised by Mike Howlett, who came up with the bouncing bass riff and the continuous cycle of three semi-tone key changes, similar to the verse chords in 'Oily Way'. He told the author: 'My intention was to create a structure for improvisation that would allow us to roam freely wherever the music took us but to have a base to return to so that it was not aimless.' The band discovered the bass riff worked in a number of different timings, including 7/8 and 3/4. Didier and Steve both solo over the cycle of chords, Daevid adds glissando guitar and Tim supports with warm synth pads.

Section two, entitled 'Get It Inner', was written mostly by Didier and consists of the sax player making mischievous pixie sounds before engaging in a bizarre, barely-audible little dialogue with Zero over Pierre's steady, no-frills drumming and various squeaks and pops of musical sound from Tim. Finally, section three – called 'Peace of Mind Or Piece Of Cake Or Zero Goofs Again' is Tim's synth wash under Allen singing 'Zero ... where are you ...' as the band begin to play the chords for the following track, and Didier provides swooping flute.

Mike says: 'Everyone brought something to the piece because of the improvised solos – Gilli's magical space whisper on the intro, Didier's beautiful solo cycle and, of course, Steve really kicking it up a level for his final cycle. Daevid's glissando guitar creates wonderful and strange harmonic frameworks that shift the tonal sense around as well as being a big part of the illusion of constantly rising throughout. I think that combination of ingredients, including Tim's special synth bubbling and swoops, was just about the most perfect instance of Gong's unique sound.'

'You Never Blow Yr Trip Forever' (C.O.I.T)

Here, then, is a perfect mystery. According to the lyric sheet, the final track on the album begins with the band playing the 'Devil's Interval' chords – in this case, A major to E flat; how Satanic is that! – with Allen singing 'Maybe you're here for the giggle'. But on every version I own, 'Trip' actually opens with part two of 'The Isle Of Everywhere'. And that's clearly wrong because 'Get It Inner' is and always has been part of track seven on the album, so there. Not that it makes a huge amount of difference as virtually most of the album B-side was recorded in one take, as mentioned above. But this book is nothing if not an exercise in pedantry.

Anyway, the last of the four big pieces on the album is, once again, a multi-sectioned beast with riffs and musical ideas both old and new. Most of it came from Steve and Daevid; some of it originated during the rehearsals in Little Bedwyn, one part dates back to 1969. The 'devil's interval' chords I mentioned earlier were one of Allen's favourite musical devices – go back to 'Magick Brother, Mystic Sister' for a fuller explanation of why Beelzebub claims this particular sequence of notes. In 'Trip' things start slowly but quickly burst into life with Hillage playing the powerful, disturbing riff, accompanied by some apparently random time signatures between Allen's lyrics. 'Maybe you're here for the giggle, maybe you're into the puzzle,' Allen sings, addressing the listener as much as any of the characters in his story.

There's a chorus of sorts in the 'more you know the more you know you don't know' stanza that ends with a statement of the song title, although this particular musical sequence is repeated twice more without the title making another appearance. Then we enter the oldest section of the song, the 'hole in the morning', originally part of a composition called 'Mama Maya Mantram' from 1969 – a short snippet appeared on a limited edition tape from the Gong Appreciation Society, and sharp-eared listeners will also hear the roots of 'Allez Ali Baba Black Sheep Have You Any Bullshit: Mama Maya Mantram' from the Planet Gong live album.

We are now about halfway through, with Allen scatting along to Hillage's lead guitar as the band plays a steady, pulsing three-quarter time rhythm that builds up in volume and power before seemingly falling apart into the final sequence of 'Why don't you try?' and 'You are I and I am you'. Didier's flute, Gilli's space whisper and Daevid's ghostly chanting takes us into the final few minutes that, live, would be a chance for the entire audience to join in the final lines and express their 'oneness' with the band, winning over even the most cynical listener. The sound fades ... slowly ... to silence.

Mike says about the marathon recording: 'I remember it being a very special night, partly because, for no particular reason I can remember, we decided to break our years-long vegetarian diet with a steak dinner that night and then went into the studio and recorded it. I remember wandering around in a daze afterwards and we all felt something wonderful had happened – a night not like any other!'

Bonus Tracks

'A PHP's Advice – Alternate Version' (C.O.I.T.)

The second track on the album, shorn of all instruments except Allen's voice, Mike's bass and Steve's guitar, displays the intricate interplay between the three musicians – especially Hillage's remarkable dexterity, shifting from muted arpeggios to piercing lead and back again without breaking a sweat.

'Where Have All The Flowers Gone?' (C.O.I.T.)

This is not the Pete Seeger folk song, but a surprisingly straightforward bluesy number featuring Tim Blake on harmonica. It seems to have grown out of quite impressive improvised scat singing by Daevid Allen immediately following 'Master Builder' during live performances in 1973 – there's a rare recording on the *Gong In The 70s* album, released in 2006, in which Allen's scat is joined by Tim's excellent blues harp and Steve plays a Bo Diddley guitar rhythm before throwing in some 'Flying Teapot' riffs. After about two minutes Allen sings what sounds like improvised lyrics, each line starting with 'I don't want to know about love…' before the song suddenly lurches into four repetitive power chords as Allen sings the title, followed by a lead guitar break from Hillage.

The studio version follows the same structure, except it opens with some Pierre hand percussion before Tim's harmonica comes in and is in a completely different key. Oh, and it's unfinished, so there is no lead guitar over the four power chords, which come in after a tremendous drum roll from Pierre (who plays the living daylights out of his kit on this one). It ends with a few mysterious chords from Steve before Tim's harmonica fades into the distance.

It took until the 1977 release of the *Live Etc* album for this to see the light of day and was reworked by Allen as 'Hours Gone' on the 1979 New York Gong album *About Time*.

Shamal (1976)

Personnel:
Mike Howlett: bass guitar, vocals
Didier 'Bloom' Malherbe: saxophones, C&G flutes, bamboo flutes, gongs
Mirielle Bauer: marimba, glockenspiel, xylophone, assorted percussions & gong
Pierre Moerlen: drums, vibraphone, tubular bells
Patrice Lemoine: pianos, organ, mini-moog synthesiser
With the help of
Steve Hillage: acoustic & electric guitars on 'Bambooji' & 'Wingful Of Eyes'
Miquette Giraudy: vocals on 'Bambooji'
Sandy Colley: vocals on 'Shamal'
Jorge Pinchevsky: violin on 'Cat In Clark's Shoes', 'Bambooji', 'Shamal' & 'Chandra'
Recorded at Basing Street Studios, London, & Olympic Studios, London.
Producer: Nick Mason
Engineers: Phil Ault & Dave Hutchins (Basing Street), Ben King (Olympic)
Mixed at Sarm Studios, London
Original label: Virgin Records
Released: February 1976
Highest chart positions: Uncharted
Running time: 40:13
Current edition: UMC/Virgin 7714153 2019 2CD remaster with bonus tracks and selections from live concert at The Marquee, London, 1975.

Even before *You* was released, the 'crisis of splittingness' came back with a vengeance. A month after completing the sessions, Pierre Moerlen left yet again, to join Les Percussions de Strasbourg as a full-time member. He was replaced for a few weeks by Henry Cow's Chris Cutler before Laurie Allan rejoined. But Laurie only lasted a couple of months – at the end of October 1974, he was banned from setting foot in France after being caught with drugs at the border. He continued playing some gigs in Germany but was replaced for French live dates by former Yes and King Crimson drummer Bill Bruford, who had just a week to learn the full two-hour set. Bruford, in turn, was replaced in February 1975 by Brian Davison, ex-The Nice and Refugee, but he only lasted for a UK and French tour. Phew! Drummers, eh?

Changes were also afoot in the keyboard department, too. Tim Blake was asked to leave after bust-ups with other members of the band, including one occasion where a knife was thrown towards Daevid Allen's head. Mike Howlett told the author:

> Tim started ranting at Daevid and at one point jumped up on to the table brandishing a carving knife which he threw at Daevid from about five or six feet away. It missed Daevid but glanced off the arm of a female friend. No harm was done, but one of our roadies got up behind Tim, lifted him off and threw him out the door. That was the end of Tim.

Blake said later in the *Love From Planet Gong* box set sleeve notes: 'I have to admit it, when I should have been at my strongest, I totally cracked up and started behaving in a way that rapidly became unacceptable to my colleagues.' But the biggest upheaval came on 10 April when Daevid Allen left the band he had created five years previously. As usual, he had a somewhat whimsical explanation for his departure during a gig in Cheltenham, which he related in his 2009 book *Gong Dreaming 2*:

> I couldn't actually get on stage. It was as though there was an invisible curtain of force that was stopping me from going through the door. I threw myself at the open door and bounced back off – nothing. And this blew my mind so thoroughly that I just ran out of the theatre into the rain and started hitch-hiking on the road with all my clothes, my stage clothes, my costume and face painted with fluorescent colours. And then a woman looked at me so strangely that I started thinking I was a murderer and I was hiding in the bushes. Finally, I got picked up by somebody who had left the concert, was taken home, and then I had to realise that I had to leave Gong, so that's the way it all ended.

In hindsight, however, it's clear Daevid's dissatisfaction went way back to *Flying Teapot* and the difficulties he had with record companies and drummers, and keeping some kind of control of the monster he had created – Steve Hillage accepted that Allen was feeling frustrated at not being at the creative core of so much of the music on *You*, while Pierre said Allen believed the music was becoming too complex and virtuosic. He also had two young children to bring up, who had decamped to Deya with their mother Gilli. To cap it all, BYG had resurfaced and gone to court, forcing all Gong albums to be removed from the record shops. No wonder he'd had enough.

Somewhat perturbed, Virgin turned to Hillage to save the day. His first solo album, *Fish Rising*, had just been released and, as it featured several Gong members, was seen by many as another chapter in the Gong story. The record company advertised him as the new leader of the band, a role Hillage neither pursued nor wanted (a situation that the rest of the band weren't even aware of) and a truncated lineup finished a European tour, crowning it with a triumphant free gig to promote drug legalisation in front of 50,000 people in Rome's Piazza Navona.

In July Gong found a new keyboard player – Patrice Lemoine, born April 1953 in Marigny, France, from short-lived progressive rock band Arc. Lemoine had met Pierre Moerlen in 1970 and jammed with Gong after a 1974 concert in Strasbourg. A few weeks later Brian Davison left, citing irreconcilable musical differences, and Pierre was persuaded to return as joint leader of the band along with Didier Malherbe (who was still there). Mirielle Bauer became a proper member of the band in September.

In October rehearsals began for what would become *Shamal*, but hit another snag – Steve and Miquette felt the new lineup was heading into a different direction, and they didn't want to commit to another Gong tour. They decided to appear on the album as guests only and then concentrate on Hillage's solo career. So, after more shuffling than a group of magicians at a card-trick school, a five-piece Gong without Allen, Smyth, Blake and Hillage went into the studios at the beginning of December, with Pink Floyd drummer Nick Mason producing at the suggestion of Virgin Records. Mike said to the author:

> Nick came across as an intelligent and empathetic person and I liked him a lot. I still see him occasionally and we always have a laugh. Nick's input was very positive – for me especially, because I had somehow ended up as the singer and he was very encouraging and gave me a lot of confidence in the studio. I have told a lot of students I have taught over the years of how I learned from Nick the importance and huge value of the producer's communication with an artist over the headphones when the recording process is going on. It's hard to explain, but to be alone in a studio and being asked to perform your heart out is a very vulnerable situation. I have no doubt that what I learned from Nick gave me the confidence and understanding to go on and produce the later successes I did. Being a drummer, Nick also engaged well with Pierre, respecting his phenomenal talent and suggested a number of ways the drum parts could contribute more.

The result is a transition album that bridges two very different eras of the band. Gone are the 'silly' spirituality, the cosmic mythology and the space whisper. Gone also is Hillage's distinctive guitar sound, except sparingly on a few tracks, and only three of the six tunes have any vocals on them. But Howlett's warm, powerful bass playing is still holding things together – in fact, his playing is superb throughout – and Malherbe's Indian-influenced flute, plus his squealing hard bop on sax, counter-balance Pierre's more careful, constructed approach.

The new style extended to the gatefold cover, which sports a very well-manicured sand dune on the front, with not a single Pot Head Pixie in sight. Across the centre-spread is a glamorous shot by celebrity photographer Clive Arrowsmith of the band with gloriously-conditioned, windswept hair – Mike Howlett, in particular, looks as if he's just stepped out of a Silvikrin advert.

Viewed on its own merits, *Shamal* is a thoroughly accomplished and entertaining jazz-fusion album with the occasional quirky, Eastern twist, and I have to admit that repeated listens during the production of this book have led me to reassess it more favourably. The first four tracks, certainly, contain enough of the old playfulness to convince that, yes, it's still a Gong album – after all, the original Pot Head Pixie, Didier Malherbe, is still there. But the preponderance of tuned percussion – marimbas, glockenspiels, xylophones and the like – shows the direction the band was going, leaving the orbit of Planet Gong and entering a more predictable jazz-fusion universe. Mike said:

During this later period of my time in Gong, a tension developed between me and Pierre about whether there should be lyrics at all. I felt that it was important to have lyrics because otherwise, we would become too dry and serious, which was not what I understood was Daevid's intent, and nor was it mine. Shamal was effectively a compromise between these two camps.

'Wingful Of Eyes' (Mike Howlett)

You can usually recognise a Howlett composition – that fruity, elastic bass takes centre stage, operating almost like a lead instrument instead of just part of the rhythm section. That's so true of *Shamal*'s opening track, which kicks off with the bass for a few seconds before gentle drums and tuned percussion join in. Patrice plays a little electric piano arpeggio and then Didier enters with some mystical flute.

Mike plays the verse melody line high up on his instrument before taking lead vocals for the first time on a Gong song. It's a surprisingly spry, young voice – for some reason you expect all bass players to sing in the same deep register as their instruments – a little untrained and raw, perhaps, but endearing and listenable. The lyrics contain some of the cosmic hippy weirdness that many Gong songs have explored -'You are a kite upon the wind, blowing through eternity', he sings, 'your eyes are wise, you're wise, you're wise, your eyes, you rise…' – with the emphasis on sounds rather than explicit meaning.

Halfway through, a piece of frantic Pierre drumming brings us to a rocking little section during which Hillage gets to let rip with some lead electric guitar, heavy on the wah-wah, as Howlett and the band give us some very nice harmonies on repetitive lines alternating the words 'live' and 'love'. Then we are back to the gentler verse section, with my favourite lyrical couplet on the album: 'Why is the pussy in the well? Must be a cat that fell.' It ends on a minute-long instrumental outro, with some lovely acoustic flourishes from Hillage and tasty flute from Malherbe, merging almost imperceptibly into a long cymbal roll for the following track.

Mike says he tried with his compositions to continue some of the mythology, specifically the perspective of Zero the Hero. Where the trilogy chronicled Zero's journey from innocence and naivety to realisation and understanding, the lyrics on *Shamal* 'were aiming to speak from the perspective of someone who had been through such a cycle and to articulate some of the understandings attained'.

'Chandra' (Howlett, Patrice Lemoine)

A bit Brand X, a bit funky and a bit Zappa, 'Chandra' is a thoroughly unpredictable piece of work with more twists and turns than *Strictly Come Dancing*. Once again, co-writer Howlett dominates, his bass work channelling Percy Jones in the intro, as well as providing a funky groove in alternating chords of Em and Dm for Didier to blow over on saxophone. Mirielle is very much in evidence here with some spirited marimba playing, while Pierre's drumming matches Howlett in sheer funkiness. There are some subtle key changes, frequent stops and starts with bass and drums locked in tight unison, gorgeous sax improvisation from Didier and great little Canterbury-esque keyboard solos from Lemoine. Moerlen even squeezes in his tubular bells.

But that's not all. At the four and a half minute mark there's even a vocal section, written and sung by Howlett, with lyrics clearly chosen more for their sound than their meaning. There's quickfire repetition of 'You call, you grow, you know, you blow, you fall to the wall' and a memorable little couplet in 'Humpty-Dumpty had a forest of men, really ought to get it together again'. After another quickfire word salad, there's a slower section with more tubular bells that gently fades into a high-pitched keyboard flourish from Lemoine.

For me, this is one of the highlights of the album because of the musical dexterity and the variety of composition on display. And a chandra? It's a lunar deity in Hinduism, described as young and beautiful and carrying a club and a lotus.

'Bambooji' (Didier Malherbe)

Didier learned to play bamboo flute during a trip to India and Afghanistan during the early 1960s. But this tune is more Japanese than Indian, especially in the way it doubles up Hillage's guitar and a wordless female vocal from Miquette. It has a slow, steady step-like structure in a minor key, moving up and down scales while joined by tinkling xylophone notes and occasional muted percussion from Pierre. When Steve and Miquette join in, you have two tunes moving sinuously against each other before Didier plays faster 'up and down' phrases with martial drumming. After about two minutes the tune seems to come to a close before bursting back into life with Hillage's electric lead guitar, played with plenty of wah-wah against Didier's flute.

That section comes to a sudden stop with the banging of a gong, followed by another plaintive little flute tune, in a major key this time, accompanied by the rough strumming of a stringed folk instrument not credited on the album but sounding like a shamisen, a banjo-like lute with three strings. It may even be Jorge Pinchevsky strumming his violin – he is credited as playing on this track. This speeds up into a rather jolly little folk tune played on flute, shamisen and hand-drums. Finally, we end as we began, with Didier playing long, mournful notes against the sound of wind rushing through the reeds.

It's an absolutely gorgeous little tune that highlights not just Didier's mastery of all things wind-blown but the ability of this lineup to treat its material with the reverence it deserves – with 'Bambooji', less is frequently more.

'Cat In Clark's Shoes' (Malherbe, Howlett, Lemoine)

Like 'Chandra' earlier, 'Cat In Clark's Shoes' is one of those tracks that has had everything thrown at it, including the kitchen sink. Later Gong albums under Pierre would concentrate on more straight-forward compositions based on increasing layers of sound rather than grabbing you by the ears and dragging you across most of the continents of the world.

Mike Howlett's input into this track is evident right from the start, as his bass pops back and forth in a cunningly-difficult time signature that I couldn't even begin to guess at. Didier comes in with the sort of sax playing he would rarely attempt in Gong – hard, brash and sometimes squealing, channelling Coltrane more than his hero Charlie Parker. Lemoine's keyboards add a sort of big band backing and the marimba gamely attempts to keep up. There's even Jorge Pinchevsky's violin in there somewhere.

After about two and a half minutes of full-on, relentless improv in the single chord of Dm, a slightly eastern-sounding sax tune brings the track to a sudden halt. Then we have a succession of stop-start sequences in which sax and violin play little tunes that go up, while the bass heads down, with a touch of Didier's melodic whimsy that graced tracks such as 'A PHP's Advice'.

We're now at the four-minute mark and suddenly the track speeds up into something resembling a country hoedown, with Jorge improvising on violin before a series of staccato key changes leads us to some more whimsical sax and violin interplay, overlaid by what sounds like French cafe conversation! Finally, we pick up the pace again and fast sax and marimba interplay takes us home at the 7:44 mark, ending with a squeal from Didier.

I said earlier in the book that writing about music is like dancing about architecture – in other words, it's almost impossible to do! So it is difficult to convey the full effect of this big, impressive track – it sounds terribly disjointed on paper, as many Gong tunes do, but in practice, it is a wild ride that somehow fits snugly together. Here's Mike in his interview with the author:

> 'Cat In Clark's Shoes' was a reference to the well-known shoe brand, as well as being a playful reference to Puss in Boots; we were familiar with Clark's shoe factory in Street, next to Glastonbury, and Didier felt some mystical association because it happened to lie on the part of the Glastonbury Zodiac corresponding to Pisces, which rules the feet, of course! Also, Didier was able to express much more of his jazz roots on this album because we were able to stretch out and indulge our improvisational skills.

'Mandrake' (Pierre Moerlen)

Pierre wrote 'Mandrake' for a demo tape he sent to Virgin in the hope of getting a deal for a solo album following his post-*You* departure. When he rejoined Gong, this became one of just two tracks on the album bearing his name, a fairly low-key composition based on repetitive sequences of notes played on vibes, overlaid by Didier's flute and additional tuned percussion from Mirielle. Compared to 'Cat In Clark's Shoes' this is quite gentle and sombre until it gets to the two and a half minute mark, when things pick up a bit and Didier switches to saxophone, before returning to a quieter, more contemplative state that fades out with swishes of cymbals, rolling drums and breathy flute.

It typifies Pierre's later approach to Gong compositions – layers of repetitive tuned percussion, sometimes playing against each in different timings but creating a wall of sound that rings in the ears. It's clever and intricate but just a bit mechanical and lacking in humour. The title came from Didier and his interest in folk magic – a mandrake is a plant root that resembles a human figure so has been frequently used in superstitious rituals.

'Shamal' (Malherbe, Howlett, Lemoine, Moerlen, Mireille Bauer)
The album ends with some fairly straightforward jazz fusion, not unlike the sort of thing the Los Angeles band Spyro Gyra was doing at the time. There's a rich, funky bass line from Mike, a simple melody from Didier on sax, a bit of supportive organ from Patrice and a solid drumbeat from Pierre, most of it taking place in the single chord of A minor. After about three minutes there's a short vocal section during which Howlett sings 'Deep, deep within you' while Patrice's girlfriend and the band's cook, Sandy Colley, sings contrapuntal vocal lines over the top.

A middle section that mixes up time signatures, allowing Pinchevsky a moment to stretch out on violin and Pierre to show off a bit on drums, leads us back into the steady A minor section, with Didier blowing over the top, echoing some of the earlier vocal lines. Sax and some tuned percussion joust for the rest of the track's nine minutes, accompanied by ethereal vocals repeating 'There's a strange wind blowing through as all now'.

Like 'Mandrake, 'Shamal' is a fairly unadventurous piece of music, certainly compared to the first four tracks on the album, and has clearly come out of group jamming rather than being the inspiration of one or two members, although once again it is Howlett's bass that keeps it all together.

Bonus Tracks

'Bambooji [Out-Takes Edit]' (Didier Malherbe)
A mildly interesting early attempt at the tune, opening with a gong rather than the windy sound effects of the official track. There's a slightly different lead guitar section from Hillage and busier drumming from Pierre that ends with a slow drum and bass section.

'Chandra [Alternate Mix]' (Mike Howlett, Patrice Lemoine)
Good luck with noticing anything different to the official version of this track, apart from some slightly-more pronounced keyboards!

'Wingful Of Eyes [Out-Takes Edit]' (Mike Howlett)
Opening with some solo drumming from Pierre, this picks up from the middle 'learning to turn our fears into hopes' section of the original track before going backwards into the bass and drums intro. It ends with nice, drawn-out harmonies vocals that fade into the ether, offering an interesting alternative structure for the song but one that is inferior to the original version.

Gazeuse! (1976)

Personnel:
Pierre Moerlen: drums, vibraphone, marimba, timpani, glockenspiel
Didier Malherbe: tenor sax on 'Expresso', 'Anuria', flute on 'Shadows Of'
Allan Holdsworth: guitars, violin, pedal steel
Mireille Bauer: vibraphone, marimba, glockenspiel, toms
Benoit Moerlen: vibraphone
Francis Moze: fretless bass, gong, piano
Mino Cinelu: percussion
Recorded at Manor Studios, Oxfordshire, September 1976
Producer: Dennis MacKay
Original label: Virgin Records
Released: Late 1976 (released as Expresso in US)
Highest chart positions: Uncharted
Running time: 39:46
Current edition: 1990 Virgin CD

This is really where the story of Pierre Moerlen's Gong truly starts but, for contractual reasons, *Gazeuse!* – it means 'fizzy' or 'sparkling' in French – was released as a Gong album, like its successor *Expresso II*. So we will treat it as part of the official Gong canon, while accepting that, by this time, Pierre was firmly in the driving – as well as drumming – seat.

Like most Gong albums, *Gazeuse!* had its birthing pangs. A few more people came and went and the band suffered a major split down the middle, leaving Virgin Records to arbitrate until the lineup settled down into the one on the record sleeve – and even that barely survived the album's release.

Jorge Pinchevsky became a full member in January 1976 but was busted with a violin case full of drugs four months later and denied entry into the UK. The band briefly tried out former King Crimson member David Cross before deciding it didn't need a violinist after all. Sandy Colley, Patrice Lemoine's girlfriend, briefly became Gong's singer. But by May the band had split into two opposing camps over the issue of vocals – Mike told the author:

> When we started to think about the future direction of the band, in May 1976, the tensions grew. We even had a meeting with Peter Gabriel about joining Gong as the singer – this didn't go any further because he was intent on his own solo career – I think that was a Branson idea. Anyway, it came to a split, with Patrice and I wanting to continue with vocals, Pierre and Mireille wanting pure instrumental music, and Didier, as ever, vacillating between the two, but finally coming down on the instrumental side. And so I left the band. I think Didier stayed on because he was principally an instrumentalist, although he has written some fine poetry in French, and Pierre had great respect for his musicianship.

The band desperately needed another guitarist and bass player if it wanted to fulfil the record contract of two more studio albums. Virgin employee Nicholas Powell knew Allan Holdsworth and also knew he was on his uppers after a disastrous US tour with Tony Williams that resulted in the tour manager selling his instrument!

Holdsworth – born 1946 in Bradford, England – was described as the John Coltrane of guitar and took his playing to almost scientific levels, creating complex chord progressions that most musicians didn't even know existed. He made his recording debut with 'Igginbottom, then joined improvisational band Sunship with keyboardist Alan Gowen and future king Crimson percussionist Jamie Muir. That was followed by short stints in Ian Carr's Nucleus, a prog rock band called Tempest, Canterbury legends Soft Machine and Lifetime with jazz drummer Tony Williams.

When the call came from Powell about Gong, Holdsworth gratefully accepted. He said later in an interview by Anil Prasad in 1993, on the *Innerviews* website:

> I played with them and was intrigued with the lineup ... I thought it was a fascinating group. It was good fun. I didn't speak French and they were always arguing in French, so I never knew what the hell they were arguing about! But, I think the band had a lot of potential, it was just never reached. I recently listened to *Gazeuse*!, because it was re-released on CD. I thought I was terrible on it, but the band sounded good. It still sounded pretty fresh – especially the drums. Pierre [Moerlen] sounded great – it sounded like it could have been done yesterday. That says a lot about his drumming.

Flying Teapot bassist Francis Moze returned to provide the low notes, bringing in percussionist pal Mino Cinelu (because he thought Pierre played too much ahead of the beat), and Moerlen himself brought in brother Benoit. The fact the band now had FOUR percussionists strongly suggested that hitting things with sticks and mallets was going to be the way forward.

The album shows Gong marching steadily away from its psychedelic space-rock roots and heading firmly into jazz-rock territory, led by marimbas, xylophones and glockenspiels, with a bit of a Latin feel thanks to Cinelu's percussion. Holdsworth's fuzz-toned guitar is so precise it fits in perfectly with Pierre's tight-as-clockwork approach – even his improvisations sound carefully constructed and planned as if they were all written down on music sheets beforehand. Most of the tracks tend to establish a theme and a rhythm and then stick to them like glue – the only slightly unpredictable element is Didier's sax and flute playing, and even that is used sparingly over the three tracks on which he appears.

The album was released as *Expresso* in the States, named after its opening track, which explains why the follow-up was *Expresso II*.

'Expresso' (Pierre Moerlen)

Guitar and percussion kick things off with a descending opening riff that leads into Cinelu's congas, punctuated by Pierre's drums. The combination screams Santana, the Latin-influenced US rock band who by 1976 were experimenting with jazz. It settles into a steady beat, with Holdsworth and the percussionists playing riffs in tight unison before the guitarist gets a chance to stretch out with some improvisation. Holdsworth wasn't impressed with his own playing on this album, saying later to Anil Prasad: 'I can't think of exactly what it was, but there were moments that went by and I went, 'Oh, I wonder what happened to that?' You could hear something that I was thinking about, but then somehow, some way, I must have deviated and went slightly left or right of whatever that was.' Certainly, the lead guitar work here is more precise than inspired, and the improvisation doesn't really go anywhere.

After spending more than half its length switching about between two minor chords, it moves into F minor for an ascending series of chords – Fm, Gm, A flat and B flat – before returning to Cm for some concentrated percussion and then a return to the opening congas to repeat the main melody line before a sudden end.

Didier is on here too, but he plays little more than single notes following the main melody lines, fleshing out the sound rather than contributing anything outstanding to it.

'Night Illusion' (Allan Holdsworth)

Holdsworth fares better, in my view, on this self-penned composition that has some stylistic similarities to his later work on Bill Bruford's albums and his own 1985 release *Metal Fatigue*. It is built on some heavy guitar chords but, just when you think it's going to be a simple four-to-a-bar chug, it turns into a twisting, unpredictable guitar melody, with shifting, sliding keys that are almost impossible to follow. Some of his improvised work is absolutely stunning, with liquid notes piling in on top of each other. The percussionists play a simple supporting role here – this is Holdsworth's show and, in its comparatively brief length of three minutes 42 seconds, he creates a mesmerising piece of music.

'Percolations (Part I & II)' (Moerlen)

We've heard a track called 'Percolations' before, on *Angels Egg*, although that was a brief and seemingly random striking of various percussion instruments. This, on the other hand, is an intricately-composed piece of music played almost entirely by tuned percussion, involving repetitive, contrapuntal phrases that move through different keys, with what sounds like gentle violin support from Holdsworth. Occasionally, Moerlen picks the pace up with a steady drumbeat, but it doesn't last long, letting the tuned percussion return and take control.

At about the four-minute mark, everything slows down, there's a bang on a gong, then Part II kicks in with a faster marimba pattern and Moerlen provides swift, busy drumming utilising practically his entire kit to create rhythmic patterns and sounds. Seven minutes in, the drums take over for a three-minute solo section that peters out at the end of the track.

Anyone listening to this and thinking 'Mike Oldfield!' is not mistaken – there are, indeed, some similarities with that composer's work, and Pierre was long associated with him. He was part of the band that gave *Tubular Bells* its first live outing in 1973 and then appeared on Oldfield's 1975 album *Ommadawn*. In 1978 he would play on side four of *Incantations* along with brother Benoit and, during those sessions, would persuade Oldfield to play on the title track of a later Pierre Moerlen's Gong album, *Downwind*. Both brothers also toured with Oldfield, appearing on the 1979 live album *Exposed*.

'Shadows Of' (Holdsworth)

A drum roll introduces the second Holdsworth composition on the album, a reworking of an earlier track of his called 'Wish', which appeared on his 1976 album *Velvet Darkness*. The guitarist was not happy with the release – the tracks were recorded during rehearsals in New Jersey and put out without his knowledge or permission. The album has variously been described as a 'disaster' and a 'train-wreck' but, to be fair, features some great playing from Holdsworth and keyboardist Alan Pasqua.

'Shadows Of' is, however, a mighty improvement, taken at a slightly slower speed with long, soaring lines from Holdsworth and the tuned percussion this time simply supporting the melody and the chords. In the original, Pasqua took over on keyboards for a long solo – here it's Didier with a nice little flute section that occasionally soars like a bird over busy drumming from Pierre and Moze's bubbling fretless bass.

It's worth pointing out here that Moze has a style and sound that has drawn comparison to the great Jaco Pastorius, and his playing on this track fully supports that. It goes everywhere a bass can go without overshadowing Didier's flute or the Holdsworth guitar solo that follows it. After about five and a half minutes the track seems to come a natural end but no – following the briefest of pauses it picks up again, more subdued than before, with a beautiful flute solo followed by Holdsworth playing lightning-fast runs on acoustic guitar, before switching back to electric for a slow restatement of the main theme and, finally, a real finish.

'Shadows Of' is undoubtedly the highlight of *Gazeuse!*, a tour de force from Holdsworth that cements his reputation as one of the greatest ever jazz guitarists.

'Esnuria' (Moerlen)

A track with a similar Latin feel to parts of 'Expresso' – a busy samba rhythm with Cenuli's percussion to the fore. Holdsworth supplies some heavy chords and Didier joins in with slightly subdued sax – sometimes the guitar completely drowns him out. There's plenty of contrapuntal tuned percussion from Benoit and Mireille, plus funky bass from Moze, and the whole thing bounces along for five minutes before breaking down into a staccato section led by tuned percussion and Holdsworth's heavy guitar chords. Slowly, this builds back up to maximum funkiness and the tune powers home after eight minutes.

'Mireille' (Francis Moze)

Now this is embarrassing – a tune by Moze dedicated to Moerlen's partner. Actually, it's impossible to know if they were still an item at this stage, and Bauer was certainly living with Moze by the time she left Gong in 1978, so let us assume she had parted from the drummer by the time of *Gazeuse!*. This mostly gentle, contemplative piece sees Holdsworth playing subdued but jazzy guitar notes over Moze's keyboards – it all sounds fairly random and improvised. At the three-minute mark, Moze takes over on solo piano, picking out delicate notes and chords that fade gently into the night.

Expresso II (1978)

Personnel:
Pierre Moerlen: drums, vibraphone, marimba, timpani, glockenspiel, tubular bells
Hansford Rowe: bass, rhythm guitar on 'Golden Dilemma'
Mireille Bauer: vibraphone, marimba
Benoit Moerlen: vibraphone, marimba, percussion, tubular bells, glockenspiel, claves, xylophone
Additional personnel:
Allan Holdsworth: rhythm guitar on 'Heavy Tune', lead guitar on 'Sleepy', 'Soli' and 'Three Blind Mice'
Bon Lozaga: lead guitar on 'Golden Dilemma', rhythm guitar on 'Sleepy'
Francois Causse: congas
Mick Taylor: lead guitar on 'Heavy Tune'
Darryl Way: violin on 'Sleepy' and 'Boring'
Recorded at Pye & Matrix Studios, London, July-August 1977
Producer: Gong, John Wood
Original label: Virgin Records
Released: March 1978
Highest chart positions: Uncharted
Running time: 37:17
Current edition: 1990 Virgin CD

Gong est mort ... yet, vive Gong. In 1977 the band officially ceased to exist – only to rise Phoenix-like from the ashes. Sure, the Gong that made *Expresso II* was virtually unrecognisable from the classic 1973 lineup, and only used the name for contractual reasons. Indeed, gigs for the band at this time were booked under the name of Gong-Expresso. This was the last Gong album Virgin would release, not including the inevitable reissues and compilations – Pierre would move his outfit to Arista, while future Daevid Allen-led lineups would come out on a variety of accommodating labels.

But we're getting ahead of ourselves. There was enough going on in 1977 to keep us busy. In fact, the story starts at the end of 1976, when the *Gazeuse!* lineup called it a day, even before the album had been released. Didier Malherbe left to lead his own band, Bloom; Allan Holdsworth was recruited by drummer Bill Bruford to play on his debut album and to form UK with John Wetton and Eddie Jobson; and the ever-restless Francis Moze did a few gigs with Mother Gong and Steve Miller before disappearing into the musical mists.

Pierre Moerlen, meanwhile, headed to Finland to record with bassist Pekka Pohjola then went to New York, where he met bassist Hansford Rowe through mutual friends. Rowe – born in Virginia in 1954 – had little previous musical experience apart from playing in jazz clubs. He discussed meeting Pierre with Anil Prasad on the *Innerviews* website in 2017: 'We played together and hit it off. He played me the Gong album *Gazeuse!* which was the last one he had done, and the first one with Allan Holdsworth, and I thought it was really special stuff. Allan soaring above the tuned percussion players was great. I thought "If we're headed in that direction, I'm down with that."'

Gong's split was made official in April 1977, but plans were afoot to give the band another kiss of life. Former tour manager Jacques Pasquier organised a reunion festival at the Hippodrome de Pantin in Paris – 14 hours of music featuring solo performances from Lady June, Tim Blake and Steve Hillage plus appearances from Mike Howlett's new band Strontium 90 and Daevid Allen with Spanish folk group Euterpe. It ended with every possible Gong incarnation – Shamal-Gong, Gong-Expresso and, finally, the classic trilogy lineup, captured for posterity on the 1978 live album *Gong Est Mort ... Vive Gong*.

For Pierre Moerlen, whose story we are still telling at this point, it was a chance to show off his new Gong lineup. He told *Big Bang* magazine that he had been introduced to 'Hanny' – Hansford Rowe – at an opportune moment:

> Their drummer had just joined the US Navy, and I was offered to replace him, which I did for a few weeks. We played some nice soft rock stuff, and between the rehearsals, Hanny and I jammed. That's how it started. We decided to form a new lineup of Gong. But Virgin weren't interested. Eventually, a friend of mine in the New York office of Virgin gave us money to take the plane back to France. We started rehearsing in Strasbourg, with Mireille, Benoit, Francois Causse on percussion, and Jorge Pinchevsky on violin. After a few months of hard work, we played at the big Gong reformation concert at the Porte de Pantin in Paris. The Virgin people were there, and signed us after the concert, for one album.

The band toured France and Switzerland but soon lost Jorge and carried on as a quintet. Curved Air founder Darryl Way filled in for him on some of the live dates and ended up guesting on the album when recording sessions began in July but left before they were completed. He was replaced by guitarist Bon Lozaga, whose demo tape had found its way into the hands of Gong manager Graham Lawson. Lozaga – born in Germany in 1955 – later became a full member of Pierre Moerlen's Gong.

Allan Holdsworth also returned, playing guitar on four of the new album's six tracks, and Moerlen managed to persuade former Rolling Stones guitarist Mick Taylor to guest on the opening cut – they had played together on *Tubular Bells* back in 1973, and Pierre would go on to drum on Taylor's debut solo album. Meanwhile, percussionist Francois Causse – born 1959 in Tahiti – was plucked by Pierre from the ranks of the Strasbourg Philharmonic Orchestra.

The band went into the studios in July and the result is an album that continues pretty much where *Gazeuse!* left off – *Allmusic* considers it the strongest of the post-Allen Gong albums, and it certainly does have a clean, polished confidence about it. And where else would you hear two guitarists of the stature of Allan Holdsworth and Mick Taylor playing together (although probably at different times)? Bon Lozaga shows himself to be no mean guitarist himself, either, and 'Hanny' anchors things together with solid and occasionally funky bass.

Indeed, Rowe makes an immediate contribution with two tracks that fit very nicely into Pierre Moerlen's Gong world, while Mirielle offers two sole composing contributions, one the rather bravely-titled 'Boring'. Some listeners who have followed the Gong story from its inception may feel that a few of these tracks don't really seem to go anywhere, and tend to merge into one another. Certainly, this is worlds away from Daevid Allen's Gong and it's right that Pierre decided he should rename the band. Because of that, the remaining releases from this particular branch of the Gong tree will be dealt with in a separate section.

'Heavy Tune' (Pierre Moerlen)

This pretty much does what it says on the tin – it's a heavy tune, led by Moerlen's straightforward, four-to-the-bar drums, Rowe's solid bass and Holdsworth's power chords. Well, heavy for Gong – don't expect Rammstein. After a lengthy intro cycling through G, F and B flat, Taylor comes in with some jagged lead guitar before the tune heads to B flat for some repetitive phrases played on tuned percussion – there's Pierre on glockenspiel and vibraphone, Benoit on vibraphone and Mireille on marimba. The next section alternates between Gm and Am, with more lead guitar from Taylor, Howe getting pretty funked up on bass and, of course, the old tuned percussion banging away 19 to the dozen. Then we go back into the original heavy riff, which repeats and then staggers to a close.

It's nice to hear Mick Taylor stretch out like this – he is no Holdsworth, but I'll stick my neck out and suggest he's the best guitarist the Rolling Stones ever had. But despite its virtues, 'Heavy Tune' is one of the tracks here that doesn't seem to have any particular destination in mind – it comes and goes without making much of an impression.

'Golden Dilemma' (Hansford Rowe)

Hanny offers a faster, jazzier piece, led by rapid tuned percussion phrases and Lozaga playing chopping chords underneath. After about two minutes, it changes to a slower, funkier rhythm led by the guitarist, who then overdubs some angular, spikey lead guitar over the top. He's not bad on the fretboard and offers some interesting little phrases over a deceptively-tricky time signature. It ends with a short tuned percussion section.

'Sleepy' (Mireille Bauer)

A very repetitive piece, even by the standards of Pierre Moerlen's Gong, in which Mireille plays the same phrase on her vibraphone practically throughout, with Lozaga on rhythm guitar and Holdsworth wrenching out quite atonal lead lines. After about three and a half minutes everything stops except for the tuned percussion, Rowe offers a little funky bass improvisation and then we break into a faster section that allows Way to soar over the top on violin. Despite its title, 'Sleepy' is not sleepy at all – there's plenty going on here and the violin adds something a little different to the mix.

'Soli' (Rowe)

Another Rowe composition, in which he starts proceedings with a little funky bass riff in a similar rhythm to 'Golden Dilemma' and Holdsworth plays an unpredictable melody on lead guitar. Indeed, the entire track has some sudden stops and starts in it, there's a nice section in which Rowe takes the lead spot as the old tuned percussion bashes away alongside him, and then Benoit takes a vibraphone solo. That's followed by Holdsworth with a long solo that increases in intensity as the track drives on, to a point where he's providing a flurry of notes (and Benoit can barely keep up!). Then we're back to the opening melody to close.

As the standout track on *Expresso II* (and the longest at 7:37) 'Soli' still suffers from too much repetition – the PMG motto seems to be 'if it sounds good once, play it 101 times' – but is lifted to a higher plane by the presence of Holdsworth. In a 2017 interview with Anil Prasad, Rowe said of Soli:

> You'll hear Pierre and me do two fills based on disco octaves. They're there right in the middle of Allan's solo. Those things were a little wink to disco. We didn't do much pandering like that, but there are a couple of other tunes Pierre did where he's essentially trying to create a pop tune with disco-ish or funky-ish elements.

'Boring' (Bauer)

We're ready for something a little more laid back now, and we get it from this composition by Bauer. Not too laid back though – there's still plenty of marimba and vibraphone, plus Pierre on timpani and tubular bells, and Darryl Way gives us some choice violin improvisations over the top. In fact, his playing here is superb – dramatic and bold. About halfway through we stop for a few stabs of drums and bass (and the sound of someone urging them on in the background) and everything goes up a few gears, as Pierre's drums power us towards the finishing line under Darryl's violin. We get about 30 seconds of some Rowe bass lead towards the end before the band explode into a final flourish.

'Three Blind Mice' (Benoit Moerlen)

Benoit takes the lead here on at least five different percussion instruments but it is Holdsworth who is all over this opening of this track with his trademark fluid lead guitar, sometimes sounding just like Darryl's violin.

Again, repetition rules here and there are moments when percussion and drums are playing the same pattern time and time again and nothing much appears to be happening. Francois gets a bit of a bash at his congas, while Pierre, Benoit and Mireille throw practically every instrument they have into the mix. It ends suddenly after close to five minutes with the listener a little puzzled as to why someone unplugged Holdsworth for most of it.

Shapeshifter (1992)

Personnel:
Daevid Allen: acoustic, glissando and lewd guitarplay, vocals, midwivery
Didier Malherbe (aka Bloomdido Bad de Grass): bass, tenor, alto & soprano saxes, WX7, keyboards, wind synthesizer, dogs, piccolo & flutes
Shyamal Maitra (aka Banana Ananda): tablas, ghatam, djembe, darbuka, techno percs, programming, drums on 'I Gotta Donkey'
Keith Bailey (aka Keith Missile Bass): bass guitar, vocals on 'Shapeshifter' and 'Heaven's Gate'
Graham Clark (aka Albert (No Parkin) Parkin): violin & voices
Pip Pyle: drums, ten green bottles & scream
Additional personnel:
Charlelie Couture: vocals on 'La Bas La Bas'
Tom The Poet: instant radio poetry during US tour with Daevid on 'I Gotta Donkey'
Alain 'Loy' Ehrlich: keyboards on 'Give My Mother A Soul Call', kora on 'Spirit With Me'
Mark Robson: keyboards and sportin' vocals on 'White Doves'
Mike Howlett: bass on 'Goddess Invocation Om Riff' (possibly)
Peter Kimberley: vocals on above
Steffe Sharpstrings: guitar on above
Gilli Smyth: space whisper, vocals, whistle (human) on above
Twink: synthesiser on above
Recorded at Studio Davout, Paris, France between September 1991 & July 1992, except 'Can You: Can You' and 'Confiture De Rhubarbier' live at 'A L'Ouest De La Grosne', Bresse-sur-Grosne, France, 1 May 1992, and 'Goddess Invocation Om Riff' live in Glastonbury 1992 (but probably 1990)
Producers: Dino Watkyn, Nigel Gilroy
Original label: Celluloid
Released: October 1992 (1997 in US)
Highest chart positions: Uncharted
Running time: 65.33 (78:31 with bonus track)
Current edition: 1997 Viceroy Entertainment Group with bonus track but omitting 'La Bas La Bas' and 'I Gotta Donkey'

When they make the film of this book (which they surely will…) there will now be one of those connecting segments in which date sheets fall off a calendar. Or perhaps there will be a giant clock on the screen with the hands going round so fast they're in a whirl, and a tumble of images showing time passing, fashions changing, haircuts shortening and cars turning into small, featureless boxes on wheels.

Because we are fast-forwarding in time, folks, from 1978 to 1992 – a gap of 14 years before the surprise appearance of a new album by a band called Gong, and 17 years after the last Gong led by Daevid Allen. Not that everyone had been living quiet, retired lives during that period – a lot of things had happened to a lot of Gong people, and there were quite a few by this time. But I guess we should follow the fortunes of one D. Allen – aka Bert Camembert, Dingo Virgin and the Divided Alien – as he was the catalyst for this new Gong album and the return of the band to active duty.

When we last saw the tall Australian fella, he was being held back by a force field from joining his Gong colleagues onstage in Cheltenham. He retreated to Majorca, released some solo albums, formed New York Gong and worked with space-punk band Here & Now as Planet Gong. Then he went into semi-retirement in his home country for about eight years, and during that time put together a band with Byron Bay musician Russell Hibbs called The Invisible Opera Company Of Tibet, named after the force he believed guided Gong and, less prosaically, the English translation of the joint credits for the band on the *You* album. The IOCT, as we shall now call them, recorded one album during 1987, not released until four years later.

Stepping back on to UK shores in 1988, Allen used the same name for a new band that seemed to have an ever-changing lineup, including his then-partner Wandana Turiya and old pal Didier Malherbe, plus two musicians who would later form part of the new Gong, violinist Graham Clark and tabla player Shyamal Maitra. Calcutta-born Shyamal was a musical friend of Didier Malherbe and had played on some of his solo albums. He was introduced to Allen when Didier and Daevid met up in Nice after not seeing each other for 10 years.

Clark – born 1959 in Manchester – is a jazz violinist who, after leaving university, played in a quintet with noted saxophonist Andy Sheppard. As a teenage Gong fan, he had swapped a letter or two with Daevid Allen and met him after a Planet Gong show in 1977. By 1988 Clark had moved to London and went to one of Allen's first gigs as part of the UK IOCT on his return from Oz at The Tabernacle in Notting Hill (immortalised on a 2005 release, *Live in 1988: The Return*). Meeting Allen afterwards, the violinist realised Daevid was living not far from Clark's partner in Somerset and suggested hooking up. Allen offered him a gig, but it clashed with the funeral of his partner's father.

But they started rehearsing together two or three times a week, trying out songs from Allen's solo albums including *Good Morning*, *Now Is The Happiest Time Of Your Life* and *N'Existe Pas*. Clark said in an interview with the author: 'I was playing with him in various forms of the Invisible Co-Opera, as we called it at that time ... and then Daevid did some stuff in France with Didier and Shyamal and then they came over and I sat in on their tour and then I was in the band! I just happened to be around.'

Meanwhile, Allen had agreed a three-album deal with record company Demi-Monde, formed by Hawkwind bassist Dave Anderson, and took his band of minstrels, with Gilli Smyth's then-husband Harry Williamson, into Foel Studios in Wales in the summer of 1989. During this time the group was renamed Gongmaison, partly due to Allen's new-found interest in house music and partly because, in the old days, Gong used to live in the same house together.

But in late 1989 Williamson went back to Australia, and the band realised they needed a proper bass player – until then Harry had been playing the low notes on a synthesiser. They found one very close to hand – Here & Now's Keith Bailey, aka Keith da Missile Bass, who was now running the band's tour booking agency. Graham says: 'When we got Keith involved it changed things for the better, and it meant we could get into more of the earlier, rockier stuff. We started to write material as well because, well, that's what happens!'

In April there was a one-off Gong gig performed for a Central TV programme called Bedrock that did a sterling job resurrecting the careers of some 1970s bands including Hatfield And The North and Caravan. 'Central Gong', as we could call them, also pulled in guitarist Stephan Lewry and synth player Paul Noble, both from Here & Now, and saw the return of Gilli and *Camembert Electrique* drummer Pip Pyle to the fold. But this was a one-off – Allen, Malherbe, Clark, Bailey and Maitra continued touring as Gongmaison until they were made an offer they couldn't refuse by French promoter Thierry Leroy. Graham said to the author:

> Thierry, who was financing it, wanted to make a Gong album. We didn't feel we could call it Gong yet as there were only Daevid and Didier from the original band. We had Shyamal on percussion, but his approach didn't have enough weight to it. We got another man in called Nick Danger, who had played with Here & Now, but that didn't really work either. As Daevid had worked with Pip on the TV thing, he asked him to do the recordings. And then we had three old Gongsters so we could drop the 'maison'.

Gong were no longer mort. Vive Gong. Not only that, it turned out *Shapeshifter* was the fourth in the Radio Gnome, er, trilogy and had its own Zero the Hero story to accompany (and make sense of) the tracks. Zero was now Zerox Mandelbrat who, as the liner notes put it, 'is a king of urban sham-an-archist of endlessly changing shape, sex, race and age who appears out of a laser haze and offers initiation into an extra-terrestrial inner circle of 'self-initiates'. The initiate-to-be is given a free world-wide air-standby pass, valid for nine months. For this period he is only allowed to eat on planes; thus, he can only leave a plane for as long as he can do without food. And one last thing – he is not to use money in any way – hold it, touch it, borrow or promise it.'

The album, therefore, is made up of a series of musical postcards from Zerox's travels from England to Colorado, Ibiza, Mali, Ankara, the South Pacific, Berlin, Paris, Bombay, Byron Bay, and, er, Wigan. There was even a book to accompany the album, available separately, that explained the story in more detail, linking it to a journey Allen himself may – or may not – have taken. To add even more confusion into the mix, the album opens with a chilling threat to Allen's physical wellbeing that clearly did not emanate from the Planet Gong.

Shapeshifter is a mixture of solo Daevid Allen, Gongmaison and a touch of classic Gong. With no fewer than 22 tracks on the original CD – one of them clocking in at a mere six seconds – it bears more resemblance to the 'vaudeville' approach of *Angels Egg* than the sprawling cosmic rock of You. It contains more acoustic guitar than any Gong album since *Magick Brother* 22 years before – and it must be no coincidence than one of the bands spawned by this new lineup called itself The Magick Brothers.

Some of the tracks have their roots back in 1968, others came from Daevid's Australian years and were part of the IOCT and Gongmaison sets, still more were written once Keith Bailey had joined. It was a long recording session by Gong standards, stretching across 10 months from September 1991 to July 1992, punctuated by gigs across Europe and the US in various guises and changing lineups – talk about shapeshifting! Most of the sessions were at night to keep the costs down, which made things practically difficult for some members of the band. But there were no major rows and everyone worked hard to make the album as good as they could.

There may be nothing here that reaches the heights of the best tracks on the Radio Gnome Invisible trilogy, but there are certainly songs that stand out as prime Gong – the powerful 'Shapeshifter' and 'Can You: Can You', the gorgeous harmonies of 'Hymnalayas' and 'Give My Mother A Soul Call', the sheer acoustic beauty of 'Loli' and 'White Doves'. The album's drawback may be its length and the fact that 22 tracks are packed into its 65 minutes, with the result that, inevitably, some pass by without making too much of an impression. Here's Graham Clark's view, expressed to the author:

> It's hard for me to say it stands up with the trilogy solely because that is what I grew up with and that's partly what inspired me to play. But if you listen to it as an album without thinking of *You*, for example, it's a good album with some fine moments on it. Some of the grooves are great, Pip is wonderful, and I'm glad that I was involved in it.

'Gnomerique' (Daevid Allen)
A seven-second excerpt from Allen's tape loops introduces the album as 'Gong ... from the Planet Gong', just in case you were in any doubt. This leads directly into...

'Shapeshifter' (Allen, Didier Malherbe)
The 'You Can't Kill Me' of the album opens in a rather mysterious way, with an answerphone message in which an unidentified Glaswegian voice tells Daevid Allen 'You owe somebody some money and they want it back. I suggest if you want to keep your legs in the place they are now you pay the money'. It's easy to believe it's one of Allen's little jokes, but the sleeve notes and Graham Clark assert it was a genuine threat. Clark adds: 'I heard it on the answering machine. It was absolutely genuine. Daevid had no idea who it

was from or who he owed money to. We tried to work out who it might have been, but we had no idea who it was. Daevid thought the best thing to do would be to make it totally public.'

The recording merges into some ghostly electronic percussion that then bursts into the song proper through a rapidly descending guitar line. Previous entries in this book have stressed Allen's fondness for the ol' Devil's Interval – well, here it is, deployed again in the opening verses as the chords move from B to A to B and then to F. Allen's guitar is brittle, angular and repetitive before a fast run up and down the frets takes the song into F sharp – although still following the same pattern as the verses, in which he maintains that 'money is innocent'. This leads into a lovely, soaring violin melody from Clark in E – but written by Allen – which he repeats four times. Back in F sharp, we return to the ghostly percussive sounds – played by Malherbe through his WX7 wind midi controller – as Allen whispers various messages about the innocence of money.

There's a sudden shift into a slow section with guitar arpeggios played by Allen under a bit of gentle glissando. Then Bailey's bass takes us into a final section in A, in which Allen points out – quite accurately – that 'there is no politician who would be in that position if everybody used their voice', ending with the powerful exhortation 'it's OK for me to say no!'.

I call it the album's 'You Can't Kill Me' because of the power of the performance, the relentless, driving nature of the song and the defiant political nature of its message. It may not be quite as relentless as the *Camembert Electrique* opener, but it still works brilliantly as the first musical statement from the reformed Gong. And it turns the old hippy trope on its head – money is not the root of all evil, but just paper and metal. Was it possible, Allen asked, to detoxify money?

'Hymnalayas' (Allen, Keith Bailey)

A Tibetan gong vibrates through your speakers before Bailey starts up a rhythmic, funky bassline, and Allen begins to tell us the story of Zerox, a 'sensitive guy, he's got his pack on his back, plane ticket in his pocket, don't know when he'll be back'. The story and lyrics for *Shapeshifter* were written later, and the inspiration for Zerox's travels described in 'Hymnalayas' came through a Magick Brothers tour of the States in early 1992 when the band got standby air tickets that cost £300 for 30 days travel, so you could basically fly every day if you wanted to.

It has a travelling feel, this song, as it moves at a steady clip thanks to the pounding beat of Pip's bass drum. Then it heads into a chorus of sorts that was originally intended to sound like a 'Shepard tone' – named after scientist Roger Newland Shepard, it's an aural illusion in which notes go up and up but never seem to actually stop because you bring other notes in underneath as you go – but the band wasn't able to crack that. Allen's voice, tracked many times, sings 'bye, bye' but stops for each verse. Clark adds a frantic, exploding violin solo – later, that's topped by Didier on soprano sax.

At about the five-minute mark there's a false ending before the song shifts key and gear into a jazzy section, giving Clark a chance to shine, followed by more verses with a slightly different structure – there's a jagged rhythm to each of the last lines. That moves into a brief part with a slight ska rhythm and Didier blowing over the top, before we end with Allen singing 'what do we have to do to get through to you' as the guitar plays a repetitive downward riff – an adaptation of a tune called 'Boperatica' he had recorded with the Oz IOCT during a trip back to Australia in February 1990.

Surprisingly, 'Hymnalayas' doesn't tell of a journey to Tibet but rather to Denver via New York – in the *Shapeshifter* booklet Allen claims the airport is built on top of the Rocky Mountain Arsenal, the world's biggest stockpile of nuclear weaponry.

'Dog-O-Matic' (Dino Watkyn, Shyamal Maitra)

If any Gong track suggests house – or 'maison' – it is this, three minutes of pounding electronic beats put together by producer Dino Watkyn and Shyamal. It was originally in three-quarter time but was rejigged to a straightforward four-four in the mixing. There are some indistinct voices here, but it is impossible to tell what they are saying. At about halfway through it suddenly stops dead and we hear the word 'Gong' from the 'Gnomerique' tape loop. Then the relentless pounding starts up again, with Allen playing high-pitched, wailing guitar over the top and various sound effects coming in and out at random intervals.

If it all sounds a bit too Ibiza to you then, well done, because that was precisely the intention as Zerox (or Allen, take your pick) dances until 5am on an empty stomach and reaches a state of nirvana previously only attainable with the help of various psychotropic drugs. It fades out to another burst of tape loop before gently merging with…

'Spirit With Me' (Allen, Alain Erhlich)

Didier's pal Loy, a French multi-instrumentalist, composer and producer, plays a kora, a 21-stringed West African instrument, on a pretty but repetitive tune in which Allen sings 'calling down the spirit with me' over tumbling, twinkling notes.

Ehrlich was later to work extensively with Didier Malherbe on his solo albums and in the band Hadouk, as well as composing film soundtracks and inventing the gumbass, a cross between a guembri and an electric bass guitar.

The song is intended to suggest a spontaneous musical outburst in a Malian village, conjuring up the smells and sounds of a market, and it does have a certain simplicity to it – there's just Loy's kora and finger-picked acoustic guitar alternating between the chords of F and C, and Allen's voice singing suitably spiritual lines such as 'deep in meditation, tantric integration, intertwined in lotus, bonding into coitus'.

'Mr Albert Parkin' (Clark)

What sounds like 17 seconds of French gibberish is in fact a song Clark learned in primary school. He said to the author: 'Daevid just decided he was going to put it on the album. They got me to sing it and I'm not even sure I knew it was being recorded. Didier even corrected my French for me, which was very sensible. It's just a bit of silliness.'

'Raindrops Tablas' (Maitra)

A slightly longer – 21 seconds – burst of tabla-playing from Shyamal, along to a pulsating, almost watery beat suggesting heavy dollops of rain (Didier makes a reference to some precipitation bouncing off a zinc rooftop in the preceding track). There's also a travelling feel – in the booklet Zerox/Allen is riding a train to the airport.

'Give My Mother A Soul Call' (Yogananda)

A devotional chant composed by Paramahansa Yogananda that appears in the book *Cosmic Chants* published by the Self-Realization Fellowship. Gong's version is swamped in rich strings and soft 'oooohs', courtesy of uncredited composer and BBC producer Roger Bolton and his Fairlight digital synthesiser. The band went to his studio close to Peter Gabriel's Real World in Wiltshire – fact, the liner notes suggest Gabriel himself actually popped in for a listen. Allen excels himself in the vocal department here, his voice soaring over the strings while Clark plays high-pitched harmonic violin, almost like guitar feedback. A keyboard-generated bassline starts up, Shyamal provides some low-key percussion and Allen croons gentle, lyrical verses before his voice soars again for the title. It is exquisitely beautiful and reminds us just what a good singer Allen was. In *Shapeshifter The Book*, published by the Gong Appreciation Society 1992, he said that the music was inspired by 'my feeling of grieving ... for the thousands of years that free female beings have been enslaved by blind male conditioning and superstitious belief systems.'

'Heaven's Gate' (Allen, Bailey)

One of the interesting things about Shapeshifter the album is the juxtaposition of so many different styles, rhythms and musical atmospheres. For example, after the transcendental beauty of 'Soul Call' we go into the meaty thump of 'Heaven's Gate', built around a Bailey-composed repetitive bass riff with a bit of a Bo Diddley, 'Not Fade Away' shuffle to it (although Bailey disagrees. He told the author: 'I wrote it as a kind of tongue in cheek funky soul thing, deliberately commercial in feel to go with the lyrics.') Bailey himself takes lead vocals with what is more of a rap than a melody before the song suddenly breaks into an exquisite Allen guitar solo over gentle glissando and keyboards.

Allen takes verse two, in which he amusingly raps 'Don't do something ... just stand there', before a repeat of the guitar tune. Verse three is back to Bailey, with Didier breaking into occasional bursts of angry tenor sax. The song ends on a third and final rendition of the guitar solo. Lyrically, it's a song from Dr Zerox Missile Malestrum, a 'dodgy old charmer' attempting to sell us his wares – 'Whoopee,' he sings, 'it ain't free, it's a spending spree!'

'Snake Tablas' (Maitra)
Some more tablas from Shyamal, opening with a brief burst of Clark's French song from 'Mr Albert Parkin'. The title comes from Allen's story, in which a stage face is transformed into 'a writhing reptilian pagoda' with pythons, adders and cobras.

'Loli' (Allen, Clark)
One of Daevid's songs sounding very much like something from *Good Morning* or *Now Is The Happiest Time Of Your Life* – gentle, finger-picked guitar (with the odd strange note thrown in) in three-quarter time, a lyrical violin melody from Clark and gentle tablas from Shyamal. Pip's drums come in for the chorus of 'darling, all night long' and the repeat of 'I know it's all right', with gorgeous harmony support from Allen's double-tracked voice. In the second half bass and drums enter in earnest – Allen's still playing in three but the drums are in four, the bass is in six and Clark is playing over the top of them all. This goes back into the acoustic-led chorus before a gentle finish. It's a sublime little tune – not really Gong, but Allen at his sentimental, whimsical finest – and first appeared with different lyrics on a limited edition cassette tape of songs recorded in 1986 with the Oz version of the IOCT, known then as 'Lolli Song' (with two 'l's).

According to the storyline, it is inspired by a young woman writer in Bucharest who was almost Allen's lover. Returning to her home, he discovers her door locked and the buzzer broken. He says: 'Somehow it seemed appropriate that she would never know I had been there' – and there is certainly a sense of loss and what-might-have-been throughout the song.

'La Bas La Bas' (Charlelie Couture, Allen)
Otherwise known as 'Away, Away', Allen first recorded this with the Oz IOCT in 1987 – it appeared on the band's 1991 album. It's a folk calypso about the French nuclear tests in the Pacific, which started in 1960 and continued up to four years after *Shapeshifter* was released. Thanks to the tests, it was calculated that Tahiti was exposed to 500 times the permitted level of radiation, causing high levels of thyroid cancer and leukaemia. The full extent of France's toxic effect on the area and its inhabitants did not become fully clear until secret documents were declassified in 2013.

This deceptively upbeat, almost joyful, tune belies the seriousness of its content – with a 'bang, and a crash' an island of luminous coral was rendered unfit for human habitation. 'French person! Think about the future!' exhorts Allen, 'Think about you and me!' Bertrand Charles Elle Couture is a French musician and artist who, at the time of writing, has recorded more than 40 albums and film soundtracks. He provides a monologue in French over the song towards the end, describing the 'small island beyond the oceans' that has become a military playground 'poisoned for thousands of years'.

The song is dedicated to the Rainbow Warrior, the flagship of Greenpeace, which was sunk by the French government in 1985, killing a photographer.

'I Gotta Donkey' (Allen)
A brief but fun ditty that, strangely, opens with a radio discussion from Tom The Poet (real name Thom Kelly) in which he asserts that Dylan Thomas was his mother and he was a dolphin in a previous lifetime. The recording comes from the summer of 1991 when Kelly and Allen took over a late-night talk show on a Boston radio station. It goes into a few seconds of scratchy violin before Allen sings a jolly nursery rhyme-style song, where words such as 'hee-haw' turn into 'she sells seashells by the seashore' – inspired, apparently, by a walk along 'the seafront in Wigan' (a town in Greater Manchester which is nowhere near the sea). Clark plays pretty, childish violin tunes over the top and the whole thing comes to a sudden stop after just over two minutes, going almost immediately into ...

'Can You: Can You' (Malherbe)
From the ridiculous to the sublime. The apparent simplicity of 'I Gotta Donkey' contrasts with this nine-minute jazz workout, recorded live in France in May 1992 but originally part of the Gongmaison set. There is a stonking version on the 'Live At The Fridge' DVD, taped a year earlier and called at that time 'Kalipiege', in which Didier kicks things off by playing a bluesy, funky riff on his WX7 keyboard controller before bringing in Graham on violin and Keith on pounding bass, driven along by relentless drumming from Shyamal.

This version sounds like Didier's intro has been sliced off as it comes straight in with drums, bass and violin. After about five minutes, bass and drums keep the rhythm going – or, as Allen puts it in *Shapeshifter The Book*, 'the rhythm section settles to a brooding groove, the Missile Bass raises heavy eyebrows over a dangerous grin, the famous jellyfish eyes of Bloomdido Bad de Grasse bulge out euphorically, the shining brow of Graham dazzles blindingly'.

Clark improvises on violin, with Malherbe conjuring up noises and notes from his WX7, before Allen wrenches all manner of strange sounds from his guitar, many of which have little connection to the key the song is actually in. But, somehow, he gets away with it! The whole thing builds up into a cacophony of guitar and violin sounds before a sudden return to just bass and drums, the sound of audience appreciation, and Allen singing 'If I can do it you can too, we can do it if we try'. There's a few more lines of vocal and then we go back into the original violin tune and a sudden ending.

The longest track on the album, it's also the most exciting, channelling the 1971 *Camembert Electrique/Continental Circus* band – relentless, abrasive and musically brave. An even earlier version can be found on the 'lost' Didier

Malherbe and Yan Emeric album *Melodic Destiny*, released on cassette only in 1981 and 1992, under the name 'Driving'.

'Confiture De Rhubarbier' (Pip Pyle)
In another live recording from the same concert as the previous track, violin and keyboards merge in a mysterious soundscape as Pip randomly hits some of his drum kit. In the story, Zerox/Allen is floating over the River Seine in Paris, before he hears ...

'Parkin Triumphant' (Clark)
Six seconds more of Mr Clark's French lesson. C'est magnifique! Translated, part of it talks about 'a dancing gazelle in the Forest of Long Hair', which gives us the title for the next track.

'Longhaired Tablas' (Maitra)
Fourteen seconds more of Mr Maitra's energetic tabla abuse.

'Elephant La Tete (Malherbe, Maitra)
Keith says: 'And lastly Shyamal depict for me, if you will, a thousand royal elephants walking, well-fed, out of the front door of the Cafe Royal.' Shyamal then plays a slow, stately tabla rhythm to a mystical, Eastern tune from Didier on soprano sax, starting off slowly then doubling in speed as the tune progresses. There's a drone sound underneath it all that is probably played by Malherbe on keyboards. There is certainly a swaying sensation to the music that can indeed conjure up the images of a line of jumbos, holding each other's tails in their trunks, gently parading along. In the *Shapeshifter* book, Graham Clark is also given a credit for the tune.

According to the storyline, at this point, Zerox/Allen has woken up to a very hot curry on an Air India flight from Paris to New Delhi.

'Mother's Gone' (Allen)
This is the oldest composition on the album, first recorded in 1968 by the Banana Moon Band as part of a medley that included a Hare Krishna chant, 'Time Of The Green Banana', and 'Remember The Name'. The original version was loud and rocking, with Allen on electric guitar, Patrick Fontaine on bass and Marc Blanc bashing away on drums. The *Shapeshifter* version is a more gentle, contemplative affair with acoustic guitar, tablas and Didier's flute harmonising with Allen's gently descending vocal. It's basically a chorus, verse, and repeat of the chorus, lasting a mere one minute and 12 seconds, in the same key as the preceding track.

'Elephant La Cuisse' (Malherbe, Clark)
Didier's fast riff played on keyboards through his WX7 and Clark offering a big violin solo over it. It's a fast-moving piece in one key throughout with

bass playing a quick, bubbling riff, Didier providing stabs of almost big band sound on keyboards and Pip's drums powering everything along. Clark's solo is brilliant – it starts at 100mph and stays there throughout, soaring, dipping and diving like a frantic, wheeling seabird – and he keeps it going for three and a half minutes. It reminds me of an extended Frank Zappa jam when you think the musicians cannot possibly keep going at this level of intensity – yet they do. Towards the end, we get a repeat of the 'Elephant La Tete' theme but played faster and by what sounds almost like a big band.

La cuisse, by the way, translates as 'thigh' so this is a song about, er, an elephant leg. But really it accompanies a chapter in the story in which the hero is witnessing a mind-twisting Pooja ceremony.

'White Doves' (Viraj, Sunsinger)

Clark describes this as 'really a Magick Brothers track', but its roots lie in Allen's years in Australia. In the story Allen/Zerox has arrived in Byron Bay, where Daevid had spent most of the 1980s and is taken to the Bundagen International Community on the borders of the Bongil Bongil National Park. There he meets Solo Sunsinger, who is said to do incredible 'kirtans' – devotional chants with a big group – and Viraj, who is described as his soul brother. They sing a song for him called 'White Doves' that is reproduced here.

It was certainly one of the songs included in the set of the UK IOCT shortly after Allen returned to the UK in 1988, so it predates Graham Clark's involvement with the band. In the *Shapeshifter* version, Allen plays gentle, finger-picked acoustic guitar and Clark long, sweeping melodies on his violin. He believes this was actually recorded at Roger Bolton's studio in Box, Wiltshire – Bolton once again provides synth strings and extra bass. The layered harmonies and additional keyboards are provided by Mark Robson, who met Allen in Australia and was invited to be part of the Oz IOCT, later joining Kangaroo Moon and becoming one of the Magick Brothers. The liner notes suggest Robson actually performed on the following track, but that is probably a misprint.

The whole thing is gorgeous to listen to, providing a gentle end to the album – indeed, the last few seconds in which acoustic guitar and violin intertwine with each other is one of the most sublime moments on *Shapeshifter*.

During his visit to the community, Allen also talks about meeting Wandana – probably Wandana Turiya, sometimes referred to as Wandana Bruce, who became his partner and appeared in early lineups of the IOCT.

'Gnomoutro' (Allen)

A final few seconds from Allen's tape collages ends the album is suitably Gong-ish style.

Bonus Track

'Goddess Invocation Om Riff' (Allen, Gilli Smyth, Tim Blake, Didier Malherbe, Pierre Moerlen, Mike Howlett, Steve Hillage)

The 1997 reissue of *Shapeshifter* unaccountably removed 'La Bas La Bas' and 'I Gotta Donkey', replacing them with this live track allegedly recorded at 'Ynys Witren' during the Summer Solstice of 1992. It is, of course, 'Master Builder' from the *You* album but with a new intro featuring Gilli Smyth intoning lyrics adapted from a Mother Gong track, 'She Made The World'.

Ynys Witrin (note the slightly different spelling) was the ancient British name for Glastonbury. But here's the mystery – Gong didn't perform there in 1992. Instead, Daevid Allen, Graham Clark and Mark Robson appeared at the Glastonbury Festival as The Magick Brothers. And Gilli didn't rejoin Gong until 1994. According to the liner notes, other performers on this track include 'Steffe Sharpstrings' – alias Here & Now guitarist Stephan Lewry – and 'Twink', Here & Now's synth player Paul Noble. And bassist Mike Howlett is apparently there 'in spirit'. Once again, Lewry didn't join the band until 1994 – and by summer of that year, Didier had been replaced by Rob Calvert from Mother Gong.

If we cast our minds back to the potted history of the album above, we will recall a performance in Nottingham in 1990 for the Central TV programme involving all the musicians said to be on this track except Howlett. Before that, there was a rehearsal in Glastonbury, and I'm betting this recording comes from that.

As to the performance, it is as if the *You* lineup never went away – powerful, uplifting and note-perfect, with Didier, in particular, playing his heart out.

Zero To Infinity (2000)

Personnel:
Didier Malherbe aka Bloomdido Bad de Grass: doudouk (aka duduk), alto sax, bamboo flute
Theo Travis aka Theodophilus Acidopholus: tenor & soprano saxes, flute, keyboards, electronic samples
Chris Taylor aka Professor Paradox: drums & percussion
Mike Howlett aka Lorde Tonsil of Aplomb: bass guitar
Gilli Smyth aka Shakti Yoni: voicewhisper, horsewhisper & birdsong
Daevid Allen aka Sri Capuccino Longfellow: glissando & lead guitar, singing, piano
Additional personnel:
Mark Robson: guest vocal & keyboards on 'Wise Man In Your Heart'
Recorded at Moat Studios, London, between the full moons of Sept/Oct 1999
Producers: Mike Howlett and the Gong Eclective
Engineer: Tony Robinson
Original label: One Eyes Salmon Records/Snapper Music
Released: 2000 (re-released on Kscope in 2023)
Highest chart positions: Uncharted
Running time: 63:24
Current edition: 2023 Kscope reissue with lyric booklet

Gong were back, but it took another eight years before the next album appeared, this time heralding the return of bassist Mike Howlett to the fold. Once again, a lot of water had poured under the bridge and a lot of Gong people had come and gone. First out of the door was Graham Clark, who quit both Gong and The Magick Brothers. He said to the author:

> I left in early 1993. We were meant to be going back to the US as The Magick Brothers, but Daevid had problems with his back, and I was relieved. I thought, there's something wrong with that, you're supposed to feel disappointed. Then I thought, I'd rather not do Gong either. I tried to go back to being an academic, I was doing some research at Bristol University. A few months later my mother died and everything changed. I had to go back to look after my dad, and then he died. So I would have had to have withdrawn anyway.

Graham didn't close the door on working with Daevid Allen – in fact, he popped back on several occasions and was working with him on and off almost up to the latter's death.

The following year was a special anniversary – 25 years since Gong's first official gig at the Amougies Festival in 1969. To celebrate, a grand birthday party was organised across a Saturday and Sunday in October at the Forum in London. On the bill were the Invisible Opera Company of Tibet, Kangaroo Moon, Didier Malherbe's acoustic band Fluvius, Here & Now, Tim Blake, Shortwave, Lady June, Kevin Ayers and Mother Gong.

Two Gong lineups performed – the *Shapeshifter* band with Keith Bailey on bass and Graham on violin (although he suffered terrible sound problems) and, finally, Trilogy Gong minus Pierre Moerlen, who was touring with the stage show *Evita*, and Steve Hillage, who sent a message of congratulations. They were replaced by Pip Pyle and Here & Now guitarist Stephan Lewry. This performance was released a year later as *The Birthday Party*.

It wasn't until 1996 that this lineup reconvened again for what was, amazingly, Gong's first-ever North American tour. A year later, Pierre Moerlen rejoined on drums and the band toured again, taking in Japan as well as more US dates, but quit again – and for the last time – just two dates into a European tour. Poor Keith Bailey had to fill in for two dates before he was rescued by left-handed drummer Christopher David Taylor – born November 1964 – who had tasted mega-success with late-1980s pop group Roachford, as well as playing with The Cult and Edwyn Collins.

By 1999 Mark Hewins had replaced Lewry on guitar and Theo Travis was deputising for Malherbe. But Hewins didn't last long – he was gone by August that year – and Didier had stepped back to being a 'special guest' rather than a full-time Gong member. So when the band finally entered the studio to record the first Gong album for eight years, it was Theo – born 1964 in Birmingham – who took the lion's share of the windy responsibilities and would work with Gong on and off for the next decade, as well as with King Crimson, Soft Machine and The Tangent.

Zero To Infinity is, as the name suggests, yet another instalment in the story of our everyday hero. As Daevid Allen said in 2002, in a promotional interview with Lars Fahlin on the *Planet Gong* website:

> On the new album, Zero is out of his body. It's a bit like *Being John Malkovich;* he goes visiting people behind their eyes. Except that, unlike John Malkovich, he can't control anyone; he is just simply a watcher. But because he is a watcher, he can see the world from every point of view available, which gives him a certain breadth of wisdom. This is where the album takes us.

There was no accompanying book this time. Instead, the comprehensive sleeve notes tell the story and helpfully print all the lyrics, and we are introduced to some new Planet Gong characters including the triple goddess Magdelene, a mythical creature called a Gongolope and Lord Tonsil of Aplomb. Quite a bit of work had been put into the CD package, which was originally released in a transparent plastic sleeve with the title embossed on it, both in words and as the symbols *02∞*. There was also a double LP vinyl release in 2009 that included tracks from *Live 2 Infinitea*, recorded on the 2000 Spring tour.

The album cleaves closer to the trilogy format – gone are the little bits and bobs that were littered throughout *Shapeshifter*. Instead, we have 11 tracks, more than half of them busting the six-minute mark and one just 25 seconds shy of 12 minutes. With no violin or tablas, and the return of Gilli's space whisper, *Zero To Infinity* sounds more like old Gong. But there is a danger that things have got, well, a little bit predictable and, dare I say it, even tired. Some of the tracks sound like things we've already heard, while two of them are remakes of previously-released songs. Howlett, Travis, Malherbe and Taylor are on top form – the drumming is particularly snappy and powerful – but the band really needs someone like Steve Hillage or Steffe Sharpstrings to make the guitar sing rather than screech like rubber tyres on asphalt.

However, this is Gong, which means there are still moments here of bewitching power and musical wonderment.

'Foolafare' (Daevid Allen, Theo Travis)

Many Gong albums begin with a few seconds of something a little silly, like an opening fanfare, and *02∞* is no different. In fact, the fanfare element of track one is apparent not only in its name but in the fact that it's a short, stately duet between the two sax players that wouldn't be out of place at, say, the state opening of a parliament. Chris Taylor even offers up a suitably martial drum roll. The liner notes include unsung lyrics 'on this version' from Allen – is there another version in existence with a vocal? I've never heard one, but perhaps it had an earlier incarnation in his solo performances.

'Magdalene' (Didier Malherbe, Allen, Mike Howlett, Chris Taylor)

The first proper song on the album opens with a spooky little repetitive riff in B minor played in unison by Didier on duduk and Theo on tenor sax. Taylor comes in with a steady, danceable drumbeat and Howlett plays a bubbly, funky bass line underneath. It has a slight Latin feel to it – you could imagine doing something samba-ish to it on *Strictly Come Dancing*. The intro is punctuated with cries of 'Yo!' before Allen sings a long, drawn-out 'Magdaleeeeennnnne', rather like 'Seleeeennnne' on *Camembert Electrique*. 'Please teach me how to learn' says Allen, as our hero Zeroid sees the face of the triple goddess, represented by Magdalene, Diana and Witch Yoni, on a TV monitor in a Tesco supermarket. As you do.

The song is punctuated with frequent, perfectly-timed stops and starts, with an instrumental section in the middle in which Didier's mournful duduk hops about across various key changes, supported by Allen's glissando guitar. Returning to the final verse, it stops suddenly on the line 'show me how to yearn for you!'.

It's a smart, poppy little number written, according to the liner notes, back in 1997 – there are some who claim it was part of Allen's solo act, and he certainly did a few solo gigs in the years leading up to the recording of *Zero To Infinity*. However, the song is also credited to Didier, Mike and Chris, so clearly a lot of work went into shaping the composition during the early album rehearsal in August.

'The Invisible Temple' (Howlett, Gilli Smyth, Allen, Travis, Taylor, Malherbe)

The entire lineup is credited for this, the longest track on the album and one clearly inspired by the various temples Zero went through on *Angels Egg*. This particular temple also has an angel's egg at its centre from which steps a mythical creature called a Gongolope. The tune is just shy of twelve minutes and opens with Gilli's space whisper calling for Yoni over gentle glissando and drones, while Didier blows a suitably mystical, Eastern refrain through his bamboo flute. Through Smyth's poetry, heavily-laden with echo, we learn that the Witch Yoni flies out of the sky 'dissolving dream destroyers who stamp like mice in jackboots on imaginative schemes'.

Bass and drums come in at the 2:45 mark, Mike playing a funky riff similar to the one he employed on 'The Isle Of Everywhere', Chris keeping a steady, mid-paced beat going and Didier taking the first solo on alto sax. We get a bit more space whisper of 'Beyond the veil ... Zero to Infinity!' before Theo takes the second solo on tenor sax over shifting chord changes. There's another break for more space whisper and then Daevid takes a guitar solo, notable more for the nasty squeaking, screeching sounds he gets out of it rather than the interesting melodies he produces. Theo duels with him on sax as the backing slowly fades out of earshot, leaving sax and drone to bring things to a close.

Not before time, I'm afraid. It is rare for a Gong tune to outstay its welcome but 'The Invisible Temple' doesn't have enough in it to hold our interest for nearly 12 minutes – it lacks the drive and drama of the *Angels Egg* temples, or the instrumental excitement of 'The Isle Of Everywhere' and lays bare the band's shortcomings in the guitar department. Call me a mouse in jackboots, but it really needs a Hillage, or someone similar, to make this track sing.

'Zeroid' (Allen, Howlett, Smyth)

A track that tries to channel the spirit and energy of New York – the band played there in May 1999 – by opening with a circular, discordant guitar riff, a loud, insistent beat from Chris and Theo wailing on tenor sax. The verses are growled rather than sung over one nasty chord, an F something or other, stabbing away like someone being clubbed on the subway, with frequent pauses for absolute silence. In between, we get aggressive sax from Theo, a hint of theremin and some glissando guitar over steadily climbing key changes.

Halfway through we stop for an indistinct bit of dialogue and then the band crash in again as Daevid produces a slightly more orthodox guitar solo that screams, shouts and rips your ears off, ending with a screech that disappears into silence. The music comes back with a gentler section in which Gilli intones a short piece of poetry before a sax solo from Theo brings us back to the opening guitar riff, fading out on him blowing away.

'Wise Man In Your Heart' (Allen, Howlett, Pierre Moerlen)
The oldest track on the album dates back to 1969 when Allen penned some lyrics to the tune of what sounds a little like an old English folk song – put it into three-quarter time and you will see what I mean. But he did little with it – perhaps he offered it up as a possible track for *Angels Egg* or *You,* but it clearly wasn't used. It wasn't until early 1976, after Allen had left Gong, that Mike Howlett visited him in Deya and came up with the bass riff that flows throughout the entire song over a percussion loop from 'Love Is How Y Make It' on *Angels Egg*. The final result was released on Allen's second solo album, *Good Morning*.

Fast-forward 24 years and Allen decided to bring the song out, dust it off and start all over again. So Howlett repeats his bass riff but a bit faster, Chris Taylor supplies a basic four-to-the-bar beat, Theo Travis provides quite haunting soprano sax and there's gentle supporting keyboard drones and some warm backing vocals from Mark Robson. Allen fills out the sound on glissando guitar and his voice is a little more at the front of the mix than on the original. The result is, I think, an improvement on the original, not only in the individual musicians' performances but in the fact that, at eight minutes, it's about two-thirds the length of the original, which does go on a bit. But it begs the question of whether Allen really had enough material for an album at this stage, especially as this is not the only previously-released song to get an airing.

'The Mad Monk' (Allen, Travis, Howlett, Taylor)
From the sombre wistfulness of 'Wise Man…' we jump straight into a slice of pothead pixie madness, with jumping drums and bass from Chris and Mike, hilariously knuckle-fingered piano chords from Allen and Theo following along on tenor sax, with the occasional addition of spooky-sounding keyboards.

The story, at this point, has Zeroid meeting the Mad Monk, who tells him that the only way to happiness is through happiness itself and reveals to him the mysteries of 'Lafta yoga'. He also teaches him how to make a proper cup of tea. The song bounces along happily with its repeated chorus of 'Lafta yoga show me the way!' for a brief but satisfying three and a half minutes, ending abruptly on a slightly-dodgy piano chord from Allen.

Perhaps the song was inspired by the story of a real mad Buddhist monk, Ji Gong, who lived in the latter half of the 12th century and, while kind-hearted and generous, shunned the usual monastic codes, enjoyed eating and drinking and frequently travelled about in tattered robes. He is usually depicted in scruffy attire, carrying a bottle of wine in one hand and a fan in the other.

By the way, 'Lafta Yoga' was a phrase coined by Steve Hillage, who used it to title one of the sections in his song 'Aftaglid' from debut solo album *Fish Rising*.

'Yoni On Mars' (Travis, Smyth)
Theo uses a theremin to get a spooky, outer space sound at the opening and then plays a mysterious Dr Who-like melody as Gilli speaks lines about the

Witch Yoni heading off to walk her dog on Mars. Busy percussion and a pulsating, bouncing bass keep a bit of a funky rhythm going throughout, topped by Theo's tenor sax. He also plays interesting, shifting keyboard chords, mostly in a minor key, along with Allen on glissando guitar.

It's a little contrived in its attempts to depict the outer space travels of the witch, but it is never less than interesting and its six minutes pass surprisingly quickly.

'Damaged Man' (Travis, Allen, Howlett, Taylor)

The liner notes say: 'The Gongolope, in the guise of Professor Paradox, reminds Zeroid of the tragic endless cycle of war and its consequences for all beings.' As we know, Prof Paradox is a nom de plume for Chris Taylor, so perhaps he was the creative force behind this track. The lyrics are Allen's and suggest that 'behind the mask of the dictator I know there is a damaged man, a frightened little boy', which is very understanding of him. Perhaps we can think of some former world leaders who fit the description. Strange keyboard sounds, twisted glissando and a repetitive piano loop rather like the soundtrack of a psychological horror movie, allows Allen to pretty much improvise his own melody over the top as he tells us about this sad tyrant machine-gunning all the women and children.

Howlett's meaty bass comes in, providing low, menacing notes as Theo's flute mixes with Allen's haunting vocals. It probably all goes on a bit too long – at the three and a half minute mark the whole thing breaks down in a melange of sounds from sax, guitar, bass and drums all fighting each other – as a telephone starts ringing to take us directly into the next track.

'Bodilingus' (Travis, Allen, Howlett, Taylor)

The phone is picked up. 'Hello?' says Zeroid. 'Hello,' replies his body. 'Is that my virtual you? This is your body speaking.' Then we crash into a steady, funky beat in G minor rather like something the Talking Heads may have come up with, as Allen speaks over bass, drums and occasional electronics about his body talking to him. His tongue, his bowels, his feet, his bum and, finally, his spermatozoa are apparently demanding his attention, giving him no peace at all. Punctuating these verses are lyrical little choruses in E minor – 'speak with your body, feel with your mind, dance with your heart and soul'.

It ends with Allen repeating 'I call it body language' before a cheeky little nod to Kevin Ayers' 'Stranger In Blue Suede Shoes' in the final line 'Thank you very much!'. The sleeve notes say this track came from an idea by Theo, although it bears some resemblance to the cut-and-paste work Allen did on Divided Alien Playbax 80, relying more on the beat and clever wordplay than actual melodies. It does, however, create one of the standout tracks on the album, simply because it is so different to everything else that has gone on here, and has its tongue firmly in its cheek.

'Tali's Song' (Allen)
Another old song refurbished, this comes from about 1980 and was originally released on Allen's 1982 mini-album *The Death Of Rock*. That version was entitled 'Tali's Birthday Song' and consisted of just Allen's voice and Elizabeth Middleton on piano. Here we have Chris on drums, Mike on bass, Theo on flute and Allen on guitar and vocals, trying hard not to swamp what is really a dark and wistful nursery rhyme. They don't entirely succeed and, in the process, lose what charm the original had. It doesn't really fit the story – the lyrics clearly make this a song about Allen's children with Gilli Smyth, Taliesin and Orlando, and Gilli's daughter Tamsin, and touches on the time he has spent away from them. There is real poignancy in the opening verse as Tali sits in a garden 'by the wishing well, wishing he could find a way to break the magick spell that keeps his father far away across the windy seas'. It's that band called Gong, Tali.

It's a clever little song in three-quarter time with lots of interesting, shifting chords but the original is by far the better version. On an album that is over an hour long, Allen could have left this one alone and moved straight on to the final track.

'Infinitea' (Allen, Howlett, Travis, Taylor, Smyth)
It's like infinity only with lots of tea involved. In the story, Zeroid 'finds all the characters in this episode gathered together in the heart of the forest where they follow the example of the animals and form a huge circle which becomes an invisible temple'. It's an instrumental led by Chris Taylor's quite funky drum rhythm, Theo's ska-ish keyboard stabs and Mike's dancing bass lines. Allen adds sweeping glissando and Theo plays long, slow tenor sax lines while Gilli adds some space whisper. Theo lets loose with a bit more tenor sax improv round about the six-minute mark, then it all slowly fades away – probably into infinitea. It's a fairly uptempo piece but with an added brooding atmosphere as if something is about to happen – you can imagine this being used as an introduction for another song. Live, it would go straight into 'The Mad Monk'.

Acid Motherhood (2004)

Personnel:
Kawabata Makoto: guitar & bouzouki
Cotton Casino: synthesiser & voices
Daevid Allen: guitar & vocals
Josh Pollock: guitar
Orlando Allen: drums
Dharmawan Bradbridge: bass
Additional personnel:
Gilli Smyth: guest vocalist on 'Supercotton'
Greg Sheehan: percussionist on 'Monstah!', hang on 'Olde Fooles Game'
Recorded at Tiger Eye Studios, Australia, February & September 2003.
Producer & engineer: Zubin Henner
Executive producer: Orlando Allen for Rob Ayling of Voiceprint Records
Original label: Voiceprint
Released: March 2004
Highest chart positions: Uncharted
Running time: 47:52
Current edition: Original issue

The trouble with *Zero To Infinity* is that it sounded like Gong on remote control. That's not just my opinion – some of the band members felt exactly the same. Daevid Allen was 'restless for change' and was particularly concerned after seeing a double poster advertising both Gong and Tchaikovsky's *Swan Lake* at Blackburn City Hall. He said on the *Planet Gong* website in 2004: 'Perhaps we had become a surrealist pantomime. I had originally thought that Gong had such excellent musicians … well, what could go wrong? Alas! Seeing the *[High Above The] Subterranea* DVD confirmed my suspicion and [Mike] Howlett voiced it succinctly. We had become a comfy armchair of a band.' Some of Allen's most exciting and challenging music was being recorded not by a Gong lineup but by his many offshoots, including The University of Errors and Brainville, and in his collaborations.

Towards the end of the tour, Allen received a letter from a fan he identified as Christi-eye Queen of the PHP. They met, became lovers, and she introduced him to her favourite band – Acid Mothers Temple, a Japanese psychedelic group formed in 1995 and led by guitarist Kawabata Makoto. How to describe the music this band has made over the last 25 years? 'Extreme' and 'head-melting' are just some of the adjectives bandied about, and the many albums they have released range from transcendent drones to frenzied freak-outs. Much of the music seems to be improvised from start to finish, and suggests an almost telepathic connection between the various members, but especially between Makoto and synth-player and singer Cotton Casino.

Like Gong, the AMT appear to have had a constant churn of band members – nearly 30 at the last count – and like Gong, they have appeared under a variety of different names as well as spawning a number of like-minded offshoots. In fact, it is a surprise the two bands had not been packaged together before. Allen contacted Makoto and Casino and they agreed to do three gigs together in the USA, billing themselves as Guru & Zero. The first gig took the normally unflappable Allen by surprise. He said in 2004:

> Makoto & Cotton arrived sleepwalking and barely acknowledged my presence before a minimal sound check after which they slept at strange angles all over the dressing room until a few seconds before showtime. They awoke and were onstage in a flash and before I was quite set up, they suddenly began in total syncro with a ferocious wall of feedback. But I rose to the occasion in my own way without much thought. It was fun to play, but would I have stayed to listen?

By the second gig Allen had succeeded in breaking through Makoto and Casino's reserve and forging more of a personal and musical relationship, with the result that this performance was a far more successful meeting of minds and sounds – selections from two of the gigs were eventually released as part of Allen's series of limited edition Bananamoon Obscura CDs. From that moment on Allen decided there should be a merging of AMT and Gong, initially dubbed <you'N'gong>, comprising seven musicians: his 28-year-old son Orlando, a drummer and record producer who, from the age of 15, had played with various dub, reggae and jazz bands; Indonesian bassist Dharmawan Bradbridge, 27; guitarist Joshua Pollock, 39, a faculty member of Allen's University of Errors band: Makoto, 38, and 33-year-old Cotton; Gilli Smyth; and, of course, the then 65-year-old Allen.

One might have thought Allen would be reluctant to bring his own son into the fold, but he said, in an interview with Emily Bick, on *The Quietus* website in 2014:

> It was Orlando who has been hesitant to join Gong, in spite of being a professional drummer of high reputation here in Australia since his mid-teens. I guess he wanted to make it as himself and not ride on the parental coat tails. One night we were talking about roots music and I pointed out that Gong was his own family musical roots. Maybe then he began to consider it as a possibility. I find it enormously exhilarating gigging with Orlando. We have a telepathic link and of course a huge respect for each other which is a huge advantage.

According to Allen in 2004, the recording process was 'full of pain and conflict. Orlando took on an extraordinary workload to rebuild his studio while also rehearsing. The promised finance was withdrawn long after we had begun to spend it. I became an unpredictable volcano and the style and culture and generational conflicts loomed large and took a huge emotional toll on us all'. Writing on the Planet Gong website, he was at pains to point out that there is no bass on half the tracks and no saxophone on any of them. Oh, and there are three lead guitarists.

One of them, Josh Pollock, recalls some of the conflicts were not just between the Gong team and the Acid Mothers – they were also within Allen's own family. The weather didn't help, either. He said to the author: 'I can tell you with no fear of hyperbole, it was f***ing nuts, easily the most insane, strife-ridden creative project I've ever been involved in. And that's not even including the droughts and floods.'

Recording sessions were planned at Orlando's Tiger Eye Studios in Australia in February 2003, sandwiched between the gigs with Kawabata and Cotton and the only live performance by the lineup under the name <you'N'gong>. Indeed, this was supposed to be a <you'N'gong> album – it became Gong much later, probably more for financial than artistic reasons. But things didn't start well. The studio in the house where Gilli Smyth and Orlando were living wasn't finished yet and the technical glitches were causing Allen to become more and more agitated. Josh says:

> The culmination was a knock-down, drag-out screaming match between Daevid and Orlando/Gilli straight out of a Cassavetes film. Daevid was kicked out of the studio and not allowed back until long after I left. Though it ended up not being the case, I was absolutely certain at the time that I had witnessed the disintegration of that family and that they would never speak again.

As if in sympathy, the weather also took a turn for the worse, ending one of Australia's longest droughts in a century with a deluge that created an almost impenetrable lake between the studio and Daevid's bungalow where the rest of the band members were staying. With the entire recording session threatening to become a wash-out, Josh waded to the studio to find no-one particularly interested in doing anything. He said:

> So it was just me and the engineer Zubin. And so I was like, 'Well, where are the drumsticks?' A lot of the base of that album was recorded by the two of us that day. We did what we could before we had to leave, and then, thank God, Daevid was eventually allowed back in the house to put stuff on top. I think Daevid liked to frame the lack of bass as an offbeat creative choice on his part, but the truth of the matter was that Dharmawan Bradbridge was just so bummed out by what had happened that he got the hell out of there and never came back. If I had known that that would be the case, I would've just added the bass myself.

Allen eventually returned in September to put some finishing touches to the album before it was handed over to Orlando to be mixed. But the story doesn't end there. Allen received copies of the mixed recordings during a

Above: The classic trilogy lineup in 1974, with Steve Hillage, Gilli Smyth, Mike Howlett, Tim Blake, Didier Malherbe, Daevid Allen and Pierre Moerlen.

Below: Nearly 50 years later, the current lineup of Ian East, Dave Sturt, Fabio Golfetti, Kavus Torabi and the mysterious Cheb Nettles.

Left: Gong's debut album, the rough but charming *Magick Brother*, released in 1970. (*Snapper*)

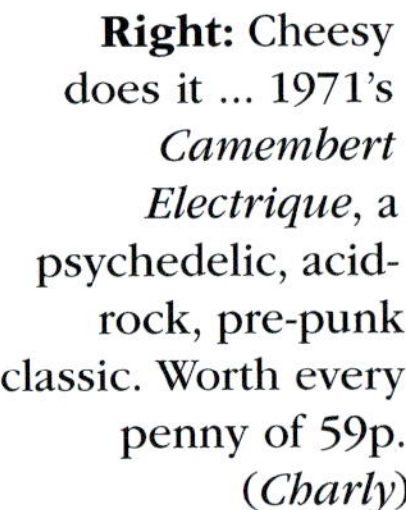

Right: Cheesy does it ... 1971's *Camembert Electrique*, a psychedelic, acid-rock, pre-punk classic. Worth every penny of 59p. (*Charly*)

Right: Comin' up behind yer is the soundtrack album *Continental Circus*, recorded before *Camembert* but released in 1972. (*Mantra*)

Left: The teapot has landed! The Radio Gnome Invisible trilogy kicks off with 1973's *Flying Teapot. (UMC/ Virgin)*

Left: Number two in the trilogy, with Mike on bass, Pierre on drums and Steve playing all over it like a guitar dervish. If *Angels Egg* (1973) is not your favourite Gong album, then you need to increase your tea consumption. *(UMC/Virgin)*

Right: Gong is one and one is ... the space-rock sound reaches its zenith on *You* (1974). *(UMC/Virgin)*

Right: The band split apart, but 1976's *Shamal* still contains some of the old magic. *(UMC/Virgin)*

Left: Pierre takes over on *Gazeuse!* (1976), helped by jazz guitar legend Allan Holdsworth. (*Virgin*)

Left: Gilli Smyth practising her space whisper during a 1971 performance – an essential part of the early Gong sound.

Right: Gong on French TV in 1971 with Gilli, Daevid and Christian Tritsch.

Left: Didier Malherbe, the heart and soul of Gong, interviewed on French TV.

Right: Steve Hillage reveals that he never glid before in TV footage from 1973.

Left: Daevid Allen and Mike Howlett, also from 1973, glid along together.

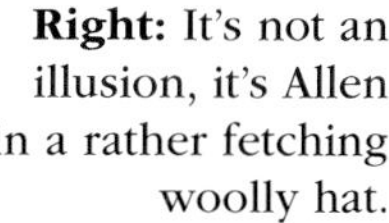

Right: It's not an illusion, it's Allen in a rather fetching woolly hat.

Left: Pierre resurrects his brand of Gongness with *Expresso II* (1978). (*Virgin*)

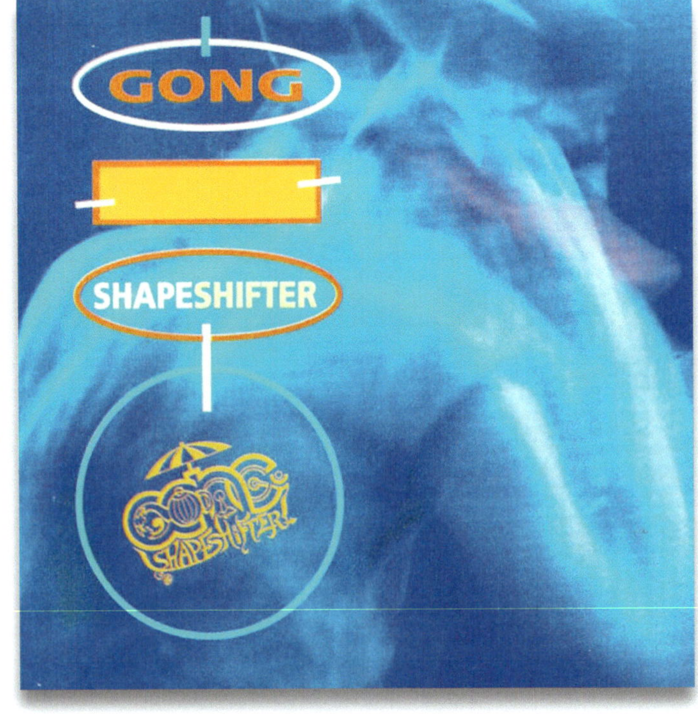

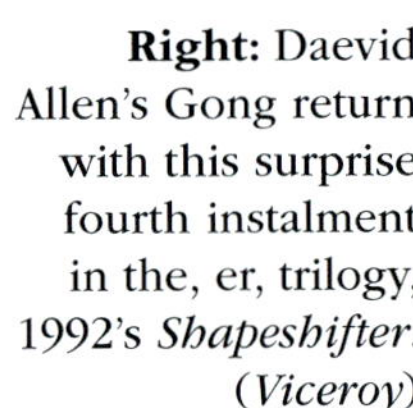

Right: Daevid Allen's Gong return with this surprise fourth instalment in the, er, trilogy, 1992's *Shapeshifter*. (*Viceroy*)

Above: The CD release *Zero To Infinity* (2000) came in a transparent sleeve. (*One Eyed Salmon/Snapper)*

Left: A thoroughly disturbing picture of Daevid Allen graced the sleeve of the troubled *Acid Motherhood* album in 2004. (*Voiceprint*)

Left: *2032* is the year we make contact again with the Planet Gong – while 2009 was the year most of the classic lineup returned for a new album. (*G-Wave*)

Right: Daevid Allen's last Gong album, *I See You* (2014), featured a new, revitalised lineup, plus his son Orlando on drums. (*Madfish/Snapper*)

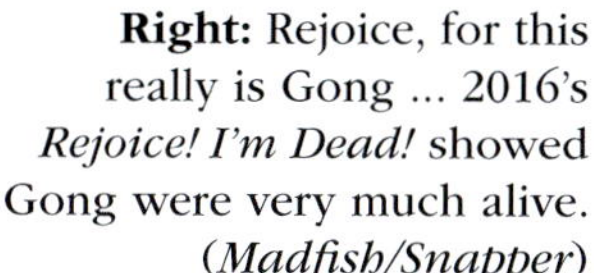

Right: Rejoice, for this really is Gong ... 2016's *Rejoice! I'm Dead!* showed Gong were very much alive. (*Madfish/Snapper*)

Left: No Allen, no pixies, no teapots ... just the most incredible psychedelic music, as 2019's *The Universe Also Collapses* breathes new life into Gong. (*Madfish/Snapper*)

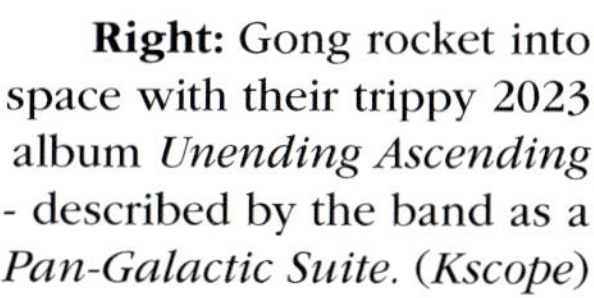

Right: Gong rocket into space with their trippy 2023 album *Unending Ascending* - described by the band as a *Pan-Galactic Suite*. (*Kscope*)

Left: New Gong leader Kavus Torabi with Ian East, on stage in 2019. (*Chris Walkden*)

Right: The new lineup get pretty damn cosmic on stage in Sheffield in 2019. (*Chris Walkden*)

Below: Gong become Steve Hillage's backing band as he revisits his classic 1970s tracks in Amsterdam, 2019.

Right: A pensive Pierre Moerlen before a PMG gig in 1979.

Below: Hillage and Allen interviewed on the BBC about the Canterbury sound.

Right: Kavus and Dave Sturt find interviewer Steve Davis surprisingly interesting in 2016.

Left: Mike Oldfield plays on the title track of *Downwind* (1979), the first album released by Pierre Moerlen's Gong. (*BMG*)

Right: The fifth studio album by Pierre Moerlen's Gong, *Leave It Open* (1981), was their last release on a major label. (*Esoteric*)

Left: If you want 30 minutes of two people drumming, then PMG's *Second Wind* (1988) is for you. (*Gonzo*)

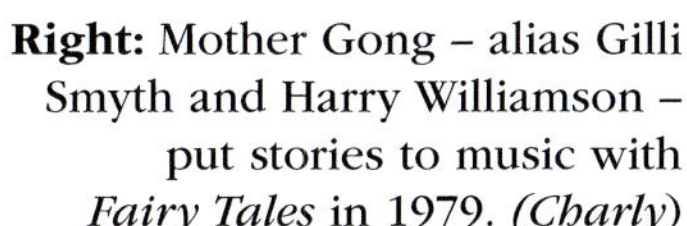

Right: Mother Gong – alias Gilli Smyth and Harry Williamson – put stories to music with *Fairy Tales* in 1979. *(Charly)*

Left: Only 3,000 copies of Mother Gong's *Robot Woman* were pressed in 1981, so the 2019 box set delighted fans. (*Import-L*)

Right: There are at least two versions of *Wild Child*, first released as a cassette in 1991, then a CD in 1994, but it's one of Mother Gong's best albums. (*Voiceprint*)

Left: Gong meet space-punks Here & Now to create ... Planet Gong! They delivered some *Live Floating Anarchy* in 1978. (*Charly*)

Right: Gong play 'house' music ... well, almost. That's the thinking behind *Gongmaison* (1989), which features Graham Clark on violin and Keith Bailey on bass. (*Voiceprint*)

Left: Daevid Allen goes back into his distant past to recreate early Soft Machine demos with The University Of Errors on *Jet Propelled Photographs* (2004). (*Cuneiform*)

University Of Errors tour and listened to them on a portable CD player in the band's van. After a few minutes, he took the headphones off and, looking perplexed, asked if Josh could listen and see what he thought. Josh said:

> Eagerly, I did so, only to find, as Daevid had, nothing recognisable in the recordings. Literally nothing. Everything seemed to have been replaced with keyboards and drum patterns – not even the musical/melodic contours remained. Had I not been told beforehand, I wouldn't have had any reason to think that there was any connection to the Acid Motherhood sessions at all. I told Daevid, and he was like 'Well, you're the one who's going to have to tell him [Orlando]! He won't listen to me!' Which, as diplomatically I could, I did, in a very carefully-worded email, which he probably didn't particularly enjoy getting, but to his credit, he never gave me a hard time about it. We had to hire someone else to start from scratch. I love and respect Orlando a great deal, and understand that he is coming from a very different corner of the musical universe than I.

The final mix of *Acid Motherhood* certainly does what Allen intended, which was to turf Gong out of their comfy armchair and set them tap-dancing on molten lava. It's loud, aggressive and relentless, moving through most of the tracks at breakneck speed and barely letting up through its 48 minutes. Guitars are raw and powerful and what bass exists is occasionally so low it makes notes that only mountains can hear. Allen's vocals are frantic and excited – he's almost shouting the lyrics rather than singing them – while Orlando more than holds his own on drums. There are a few quieter, acoustic moments but they sound as if they have been parachuted in from an entirely different album.

Despite being credited as songwriter on only five of the eleven tracks (and being kicked out of the studio!), Allen dominates proceedings throughout. Gilli's space whisper also keeps things planted well and truly in Gong territory. Josh comes out of this well, getting more than half the songwriting credits and filling the tracks with his deliciously nasty guitar sound.

However, it's interesting that none of these tracks were ever played live after 2006, the year of the last Acid Mothers Gong performances. The random, improvised nature of AMT performances coupled with the fraught recording sessions meant the *Acid Motherhood* album had caught a moment in time rather than laying down the definitive versions of these compositions.

The album is graced with one of the most disturbing covers of all time, showing a naked pregnant woman with Daevid Allen's head superimposed on top. If that isn't bad enough, the figure is duplicated and then pasted in the other way round, with their hands positioned so they are cupping each other's buttocks. Really.

Josh, for one, wasn't impressed. He says: 'I remember seeing it for the first time and thinking, Well, great, we've just cut our potential listening audience by 90%.' The centre-spread, meanwhile, has some, er, explicit pictures of a young pregnant woman overlaid with some equally candid descriptions of the sexual organs, or 'yoni', of the shankini, a 'conch woman' in Hindu mythology. Oh, and the back shows Kawabata sitting naked on the toilet.

You would expect *Acid Motherhood* to be Gong's 'Marmite album' but, interestingly, it was reviewed very positively when it was released, hailed by Allmusic as 'heavier, wilder and noisier' than anything they've ever done before but still 'whimsical, light-hearted and entertaining ... Did it succeed? Holy shmoly, it did!'.

Josh says: 'I'm so glad people found things to like about it! It's hard for me not to hear how it pales in comparison to what we might've accomplished if the studio had actually been functioning properly and the leader of the group hadn't been banned from the studio for the vast majority of the session. But, you know, woulda, coulda, shoulda…'

'Ocean Of Molasses' (Orlando Allen, Kawabata Makoto, Josh Pollock, Dharmawan Bradbridge)

Credited to four musicians because it was taken from a jam session – the title came from Josh Pollock's frustration at not being able to get anything done at that point. He said: 'It's like trying to move through an ocean of molasses!' There's the crashing of doom-laden discordant electric guitars, lingering on like the strings of a dying piano, Dharma's slow, ominous bass notes and a funeral march on the drums. A final slab of distorted sound leads us into…

'Supercotton' (Orlando Allen, Kawabata Makoto, Josh Pollock, Daevid Allen)

Look on 'Supercotton' as a sort of statement of intent from this Gong lineup, containing all the elements that have been fused together to make the album: Allen's playful lyrics, a pounding bass riff (played not on bass but by Josh tuning his guitar E-string way down), Orlando's jazzy drums, guitars that crackle and sting, synth loops and lots of background bubbles and swoops. Josh built up the basic track from Orlando's drums recorded during a jam session, and Allen added to it later when he was allowed back in the studio.

The song is almost like a manga animation turned into sound, with a spoken word intro from Allen, in a slightly dodgy Japanese accent, setting the scene: 'This is the story of beautiful Mango Cotton and how her marma-lady voice got stolen by one DJ (dodgy) Queenie Nylon Day-glo Doof only to be won back by Cotton's very own altered-ego Supercotton after the acid mother of all battles!' Then Dharma's bass and Orlando's drums crash in and off we go on a wild eight-minute ride with cries of 'Mango!' as if it's a 1960s superhero TV series. Batman!

Allen raps rather than sings, with short, snappy rhymes – 'Much too old/ Much too young/and she's got/The cutest bum'. The music stops every now and then for seemingly unrelated little guitar sounds and then charges on again, with occasional clangs like the clashing of samurai swords. There's an absolutely barmy section of guitar pyrotechnics and synth sounds with Orlando hitting what sounds like metal sheeting, then funky guitar chords taking us into a glissando section that could easily have come from earlier Gong recordings if everyone was completely out of their skulls.

The track ends with some sort of complete instrumental breakdown, topped off with screaming lead guitar from – well, someone; with three lead guitarists, it's difficult to know who is playing what, although Pollock's deceptively random guitar style is much in evidence. It could well be that all three are playing different things, in different keys, at the same time.

It is 8:36 of complete madness, an absolutely wild ride that makes some of Gong's earlier work seem like a snooze in a comfy armchair in comparison. The Pot Head Who?

'Olde Fooles Game' (Greg Sheehan, Daevid Allen)

A moment's respite from the madness as Allen croons a fairly gentle two-minute ballad about trying to make sense of the world. 'We are all young fooles in an olde fooles game,' he sings, 'livin on a planet that will never be the same.' Words that are as true now as they have ever been. I say gentle, but this still has plenty of things going on in it, despite Allen claiming there are only three instruments involved: a child's tambourine, a tiny Swiss UFO and a headless electric guitar scraped with a metal rod. But I think Australian multi-instrumentalist and composer Greg Sheehan is playing a hang here, a convex tuned steel drum, and there are undoubtedly more percussion instruments involved than Allen is letting on. It was one of the last tracks to be recorded long after everyone else had left the sessions.

'Zeroina' (Allen, Mike Howlett)

The stark difference between Acid Motherhood and its predecessor is brought home by this remake of 'Zeroid'. It seemed like the toughest thing on *Zero To Infinity,* but here it has been sped up and fed through various effects pedals to make it sound like thrash metal. It starts at 100mph and stays there, with all sorts of nasty guitar sounds laid over it and Orlando bashing along, trying to keep up. There are no vocals because, really, you can't sing over something like this, just hang on tight as it storms through its almost three minutes length with those repetitive guitar riffs Allen is so fond of, with what sounds like a jet engine in the background. It's crazy and exhilarating and wonderful and was first unveiled during this lineup's only live outing as <you'n'gong>.

'Brainwash Me' (Josh Pollock, Allen)

Amid the chaos comes this deceptively catchy little number, a cheerful stomp based on a simple electric guitar riff created by Josh Pollock and performed mostly around one chord, with Allen shouting out lines about the brainwashing effect of Hollywood and the 'shiny silver screen'. There's a chorus of sorts that's more of a chant with a bit of an Eastern melody to it, in which Allen sings the satirical lines 'I never asked for choice, You gimmee choice, Don't want a choice, It's simply too complicated'. There's synthy whistles and whooshes underneath, plus a middle eight over shifting, shimmering guitar chords as Allen croons 'I love you for your dream body, I'll give you everything, Everything but full control, Sex and drugs and rock'n'roll.'

The subject matter is perhaps a little clichéd, but there's no denying the barmy power of this track and the enthusiastic performances from all concerned. The drums are by Josh – it was one of the tracks he built up with Zubin after the big Allen family fall-out. He said he repeatedly pleaded with Orlando to replace the drum track, but the latter never did.

'Monstah!' (Pollock)
Literally two and a half minutes of the same distorted C major chord played with Monstah-rous aggression by Pollock, with all manner of industrial sounds and guitar squeals over the top of it, in what feels like alternating bar lengths of three and four beats. Drums and bass pound along in unison and the whole thing ends with a bit of feedback. Bonkers but brilliant. Again, this is a Josh track and his drums were left on. In his view this is 'a bit of a botch and not what I intended at all', but it fits perfectly in an album that one could describe as an inspired botch.

'Bible Study' (Das Ubuibi)
A cut-up recording of former US president George W Bush talking about 'the need for weapons of mass destruction' over a tape loop of murmuring sounds and someone running a plectrum up and down the top strings of a guitar. It ends with Bush allegedly saying 'My job is to smoke the bible – and that is exactly what I'm gonna do'. The track is credited to 'Das Ubuibi', the mysterious creator of the Big City Orchestra, a loose collection of 'anti-art' performers formed in 1979 in Los Angeles who worked with Allen on and off for about 20 years.

'Bazuki Logix' (Kawabata Makoto)
Kawabata plays his bouzouki – and maybe even more than one; the sound is full and dense – plucking mid-paced, ringing arpeggios in alternate chords of E minor and C major. Allen comes in after about two minutes with shimmering glissando notes that soar and swoop over the top before the track fades out after four minutes. It's not the most complicated piece of music but shows off Allen's dexterity with a guitar and a metal gynaecological instrument.

'Waving' (Pollock, Allen)
Gentle finger-picked acoustic guitar accompanies Daevid's soul-searching croon in a wistful song that sounds more like one of his 1970s solo albums

than the work of Acid Mothers Gong. 'You ask me how I taught myself to turn the force around, look fear and anger in the eyes and turn it into sound,' he sings as the chords move back and forth between two major sevenths of D flat and E flat. The guitar is accompanied by some whistles and warbles on synth and sparing use of glissando that build up during a 90-second long instrumental outro at the end. It's a Pollock composition once again put together after the bust-up, with Allen adding his vocals a few months later.

'Makototen' (Makoto, Pollock, Orlando Allen)
From a contemplative ballad to an intense fourteen-minute jam built around Pollock and Makoto's thrashing guitars. This probably has more of an AMT influence than any other track on the album, starting slow and menacing with an Eastern-influenced guitar figure before bursting into life with a fractured rhythm similar to that used by Genesis in 'Watcher Of The Skies'. Synth sounds, swirls and screeches accompany frantic, rising guitar chords and there's a solo there of sorts that adds to the general cacophony. It has the same intense, relentless, overpowering nature of some of King Crimson's doom-laden instrumentals, although it pretty much outstays its welcome after about ten minutes, leaving you looking at your watch for the remaining three and a half. It sounds as if it could be the basis for something but, compared to 'Supercotton' earlier, feels unfinished and half-formed. Nevertheless, it shows what a big, nasty noise this lineup could make.

'Schwitless In Molasses' (Allen, Pollock, Makoto)
A restatement of the opening track 'Oceans In Molasses', with the addition of surreal German artist Kurt Schwitters reciting his Dadaist poem 'Ursonate'. Obviously, Schwitters wasn't an AMT or Gong fan as he died in 1948, but a recording of his voice has been used here to accompany those heavy, sludgy, doomy electric guitar chords and random drumming that opened the album. 'Ursonate' is his most famous work, an early example of 'sound poetry' that took him ten years to develop, finally completing it in 1932. 'Molasses' actually opens with an unidentified voice in an American accent explaining: 'So I just want to let you know that I've opened up a new health spa…' This sometimes turns up on digital downloads as a separate track entitled 'Schwitter's Health Spa', although it clearly isn't him.

Talk about molasses, this certainly feels like one is wading through something sticky – the drums plod slowly, the bass sounds thick and liquidy and the guitars are like dropping a bucket of treacle on the innards of a grand piano. Things pick up a little bit under Schwitter's wordless mouth music, with some apparently aimless twiddling, then we revert back to that lurching, zombie sound. At the end, as the last chord dies away, you can hear an unidentified voice go 'Phew!'.

Phew! Indeed.

2032 (2009)

Personnel:
Daevid Allen: voice, guitar
Steve Hillage: guitar
Gilli Smyth: voice, space whisper
Miquette Giraudy: synthesizers
Mike Howlett: bass
Chris Taylor: drums
Theo Travis: sax and flute
Additional personnel:
Didier Malherbe: Duduk on 'How To Stay Alive' & 'Pinkle Ponkle', soprano sax on 'The Year 2032', flute on 'The Gris Gris Girl'
Yuji Katsui: electric violin on 'Escape Control Delete' & 'Portal'
Elliet Mackrell: violin on 'Dance With The Pixies'
Stefanie Petrik: backings vocals on 'City Of Self Fascination', 'Digital Girl', 'How To Stay Alive', 'Escape Control Delete', 'Dance With The Pixies' & 'Guitar Zero'
Rhythm tracks recorded by Ian Grimble at v2khz Studios, London, February 2009. Gilli Smyth's voices recorded by Nick Spacetree of Flamedog Productions. Yuji Katsui's electric violin recorded by Tatsuki Masuko at Float, Tokyo.
Produced and mixed by Steve Hillage at A-Wave Studio, London, Spring 2009
Additional production by Daevid Allen at the Bananamoon Observatory, NSW, Australia.
Original label: G-Wave
Released: September 2009
Highest chart positions: Uncharted
Running time: 75:25
Current edition: Original issue

In November 2006 Gong staged their third and largest 'Unconvention', a gathering of most of the family at the Melkweg in Amsterdam. It saw performances by practically every band and artist associated with Daevid Allen and his creation, including Acid Mothers Gong, The University Of Errors, Didier Malherbe's Hadouk, Mother Gong, the Steve Hillage Band – for the first time since 1979 – and the classic trilogy lineup with Hillage on guitar and Tim Blake back on synthesisers. It was a tribute to the influence Allen had on progressive rock and jazz, and an illustration of how far and wide his teapot had travelled in the last 40 years.

But it was also tinged with sadness, because two important members of the family were missing: Pip Pyle, who died in August that year in Paris aged 56, and Pierre Moerlen, who died in his sleep in the mountains near Strasbourg the year before at just 53. Chris Taylor filled in on drums, but Pip and Pierre were there in spirit and in the hearts of all of us who made it to the Dutch capital for that unforgettable weekend.

Allen was now 68, white-haired and wrinkled with age and experience, but his enthusiasm for music remained undimmed. The next few years saw him touring with Brainville, Here & Now, Josh Pollock, The University Of Errors, Big City Orchestra – it seemed he couldn't say no to a gig, be it in Europe, the US or even Brazil.

Then in June 2008, there came another opportunity for Trilogy Gong to get back together again – that year's Meltdown Festival at the Queen Elizabeth Hall in London was curated by Massive Attack, who wanted Gong on the bill. Daevid Allen, Gilli Smyth, Mike Howlett (wearing a monk's cowl) and Steve Hillage played together in the UK for the first time since 1975, with Theo Travis on sax and flute, Chris Taylor on drums and Miquette Giraudy on synths.

A review in The Independent said: 'It's a lineup that fans have dreamt of for years, and tonight they delivered two unremitting hours of mind-crushing delight.' It was becoming inevitable that this band would go into the studio to record the final instalment – honestly, definitely – in the Planet Gong story. This lineup had unfinished business.

A tour was planned, and the band wanted new material to play. But getting all the participants together in a studio at the same time was an almost insurmountable challenge. After all, Steve and Miquette were busy with their own band, System 7, while Mike was an in-demand record producer with a string of hits under his belt, and a university lecturer in music technology. In the event, a lot of the album was done 'in cyberspace' which, according to Hillage, helped to give it a contemporary feel.

It began with writing sessions in Australia, where both Daevid and Gilli were living, during November 2008. Then Hillage and Giraudy came back to London and put together the basic music tracks with Howlett and Taylor – Mike made some contributions to some of the tracks that are reflected in the credits. Hillage said on the *Planet Gong* website:

> We were communicating a lot with Daevid and Gilli over the internet and sending him rough tracks that way ... We finished building the tracks, and then Miquette and I went to Australia in April 2009 after some System 7 shows in Tokyo. Daevid had recorded a lot of his vocals by then and we worked together to finish off the record. Then we went back to London in May 2009 to mix the record. Daevid came over to participate in that too. The album's direction was very much Daevid's idea. We all wanted to capture the feeling of 'this is where Gong is here and now'.

Allen's idea was to bring the story of Zero the Hero and his interactions with the denizens of the little green planet to a close by suggesting 2032 would be the year when 'the existence of Planet Gong will be officially recognised by astronomers on Earth and will signal the first public arrival of these space visitors'. Of course, they had visited our world before, back in the late 1960s, and were returning to check up on how we are doing. I can't help but suspect the report card will say 'could do better'.

The Pot Head Pixies always brought with them a message of love, not just for each other but also for the slightly-squashed sphere we live on, and the album is preoccupied with matters of an ecological nature, like a cosmic Al Gore. Many of the songs have a 'green' aspect, influenced no doubt by growing fears over global warming, most obviously in the internet single 'How To Stay Alive', which added the line 'without killing the planet'.

Other influences on the album include its hi-tech method of production, resulting in tracks such as 'Digital Girl' and 'Escape Control Delete', and the 2008 'credit crunch' that inspired Allen to rip into the 'Wacky Baccy Banker'. Tracks like 'Robo-Warriors' and 'The Year 2032' hark back to earlier compositions – the former clearly inspired by Mother Gong's Robot Woman trilogy – while one composition has its roots in a song only available on a DVD of a 1971 French TV performance!

At more than 75 minutes, *2032* was Gong's longest studio album so far, released on CD and as a limited edition double vinyl, which made it easier to read and decipher Allen's intricate drawings within the titular numbers on the cover. Inevitably, its sheer length means the album can meander in parts and there are a few songs that come and go without making much of an impression – I defy any Gong fan to hum 'The Gris Gris Girl' to me. But, as with all Gong releases, there are some tracks that capture the spirit and mythology of the band so perfectly they would now be regarded as classics if they had been released 35 years ago.

Here's *Allmusic*'s summing up: 'Self-conscious silliness rarely works well, and *2032* does indulge in rather a lot. At the same time, though, it's still Gong and, when it's good, it's still great. And that makes it all worthwhile.' My sentiments entirely.

'City Of Self Fascination' (Daevid Allen)

The opening track sets up the story – the Octave Doctors, representatives of the planet Gong, return to Earth to see how we've done since the late 1960s, and wonder why human beings seem to 'wanna kill kill kill, wanna win win win as they spin spin spin'. And they haven't even met Donald Trump yet. An Earth citizen tries to explain: 'I live in my bubble and I watch TV and my boys go to war to keep the poor away from me'. And, in the third verse, Zero the Hero – now an Octave Doctor inhabiting a human body – gives his impressions: 'You block out the sun, fight the light, chop out the beautiful sky to take another bite, teachin' all of the kids to live by the knife.' Clearly, things haven't gone down too well.

Musically, the track has a sinister but swaggering feel to it – it's built around Chris's funky drums in solid 4/4 time and a rising and falling guitar and bass riff mostly in A and D. Allen recites, in a rasping whisper: 'We come from an alien nation to the city of self-fascination'. The song drops into B flat for the verses, but they each have a slightly different chord progression to them – the first alternates between B flat and A, the second between B flat and F, the third ... well, you get the picture. There are times when Allen is virtually rapping the lyrics, especially during the Zero verse.

At slightly over six minutes it meanders a bit, especially for an opening number. But the guitar riffing is great – in fact, I'm surprised Hillage doesn't get a writing credit on this – while Allen's voice is full of personality and Taylor makes those drums swing.

'Digital Girl' (Allen, Steve Hillage)
This was one of the earliest tracks to be written for the album and was performed live by the band at the Meltdown Festival in 2008. You can tell Hillage's influence – his guitar is all over it, providing the little riff that opens it up, a meatier riff for the main body of the song and a brilliant solo about two-thirds through. There's an appealing, slightly Latin staccato rhythm to it all, over which Allen virtually speaks the lyrics until we get to a nice, catchy chorus in 'Now she's here, then she's gone, now she's back where she belongs', with his vocals supported by Stefanie Petrik. Even Gilli gets a short spoken word section in the middle. The only musician to be poorly served here is Theo, who gets little to do except follow Steve's guitar chords.

In the story, Earth is now populated by a 'new variety of highly-evolved, smart young women' who are 'super-fast thinkers, have no desire to procreate and effortlessly understand the digital world'.

'How To Stay Alive' (Allen, Hillage, Mike Howlett, Chris Taylor)
For many of us, this was the first track we heard from *2032* as it was released on the internet shortly before the album went on sale, accompanied by a somewhat primitive but amusing video animation created by Mood Magic in Tokyo. After a little fanfare of chords and female voices singing 'Take me to your leaders..' it settles into a mid-paced dance rhythm, with Allen rapping the lyrics over the top about 'a sweet green planet, nothing on it, nothing to it, nothing in it'. Hillage provides chopping D flat minor and B minor guitar chords and riffs, with glissando support and Howlett's pumping, dancing bass.

There's no chorus here, really, apart from some repetition on lines such as 'one great family of conscious humanity', and a few mentions of the title. Didier makes a welcome return to the fold to provide a duduk solo – his instrument of choice by this time – and Gilli's space whisper soars over the top. At more than eight minutes it's a little too long for its content – the edited internet version is superior – but there's a hypnotic quality to it, more of a soundscape with beats than anyone's traditional idea of a song. It ends with some synth and glissando swirling sounding uncannily like the end of 'Sea Nature' from Hillage's 1978 solo album *Green*.

Strangely, I don't recall this being played live. Instead, it was used as intro music as the band took to the stage.

'Escape Control Delete' (Allen, Hillage, Miquette Giraudy, Howlett)
As we all know, holding down Escape, Control and Delete at the same time on your computer empties the internet of kitten pictures or something like that. Anyway, this handy little trick is the hi-tech title of track four on the album, another big joint effort but this time also crediting Giraudy, who provides an intro of kettle-drum-like synth notes before drums, bass and rhythm guitar kick in. Then Hillage plays the verse melody line in E major on guitar before crashing into B major for what will be a chorus.

Allen's vocals come in at the 1:45 mark – he's communicating a message from the Octave Doctors, in which they instruct the listener to 'look up in the sky, there's somebody calling'. In the chorus, Allen says 'it is time to escape the control of the rich', pointing out that 'if your luck runs out then it's terminal beep beep beep beep'. So don't say you weren't told.

Stefanie Petrik is on backing vocals here for the chorus, and Yuji Katsui of Japanese instrumental band Rovo supplies some tasteful, almost not-there violin. It ends with Hillage's heavily-delayed guitar phrases and warm synth strings.

'Yoni Poem' (Gilli Smyth, Giraudy)
The two Digital Girls in the band work together on this, a description of different types of witches and what they get up to in the forest. Gilli provides haunting poetry while Miquette provides all manner of strange sounds beneath. According to the story, 'Yoni is the eternal spirit of nature, the voice of animals, the smell of plants materialised into witches who move between that world and the world of humans'. This merges into…

'Dance With The Pixies' (Allen)
A gentle jig-like rhythm fades into view, with bass, sax and muted guitar in unison playing a vaguely traditional folk melody while Gilli speaks the verse over the top. Daevid and Stefanie take over for the chorus, which changes each time lyrically but always ends with a repeat of the title. After the three-minute mark, it moves into a faster jig played on violin by Kangaroo Moon and former IOCT member Elliet Mackrell, punctuated by repeats of the chorus, before coming to a sudden end (as folk tunes generally do) after about four and a half minutes.

When critics accuse Gong of 'silliness' it may be tracks like this that they will use as evidence – it's an uncomfortable merging of space rock with Irish traditional music that tries a little too hard to be whimsical and fun but ends up sounding forced and out of place. Even Allen and Stefanie's vocals don't seem to be, well, very together in the chorus, suggesting not a great deal of time was devoted to its production.

'Wacky Baccy Banker' (Allen, Hillage)

What rhymes with banker? Tanker. Sri Lanka. Ah yes… Allen goes for the obvious rhyme here as he becomes the voice of the Switch Doctor, recounting his experiences as a merchant banker. Written after the banks had blown up the economy with their greed and stupidity, Allen pulls no punches as he depicts a coked-up money man with 'speed on a drip-feed' who turns into a spliff-puffing protester with 'no house and no job and no car'. But it's a story of redemption as the banker discovered his real home, free of the greed, is with Radio Gnome. In reality, of course, stupidity and greed never die; they just find homes in new, empty heads.

A slow sequence of power chords, with glissando and synth warbles over the top, leads into a sudden bugle call for a cavalry charge, then crashes into what is almost a punk rock song with power chords from Hillage. Allen sings in his most naughty, Cockney boy voice as Hillage hits chopping chords beneath him. There's a chorus of sorts using the chord sequence of D flat, A major, B major and back to D flat again, and a nasty, spiky guitar solo from Hillage.

The song feels like it should end round about the five and a half minute mark, but it goes on, as glissando flows in and synths whistle and swoop along with Gilli's space whisper and Theo takes a sax solo that brings the track to its eventual end after nearly eight and a half minutes. Along with 'How To Stay Alive' it's another track on the album that would have benefited from a bit of editing.

'The Year 2032' (Allen)

What's this intro? It's 'Radio Gnome Invisible' from *Flying Teapot* – but slightly different. The original, if you recall, was that steady, rolling rhythm in A minor, with the bass alternating between A and E. 'The Year 2032' has that same style, same rhythm but a semi-tone down, with the bass playing A flat and E. So, I hear you ask? Yes, I thought you'd say that. Nothing really except that it's connecting the song waaaay back to 1973 in a very clever, almost-the-same-but-not-quite kinda way. The point is that this song suggests the story is coming full circle – Zero started his adventures 36 years ago and here we are still trying to channel peace and enlightening energy and a generally good vibe.

Over this gentle cosmic plod our hero Zero points out that, despite all this peace and love being directed at our planet, we still have 'bomb blasts in the bus station, bodies on the road, innocent detainees'. But there is hope – 'in 2032 we'll all come back for you'. Theo gets more to do on this song – he improvises over a lot of it – but Hillage takes the last minute or so with some understated lead guitar.

'Robo-Warriors (Smyth, Giraudy)

According to the liner notes, Robo-Warriors are peace machines that can resolve the conflict of opposites by 'absorbing and transforming conflict into a single unified field'. Gilli explains their manifesto over robotic drums and synth whistles; her voice manipulated to sound suitably robotic and artificial. If this sounds a little familiar to Mother Gong fans then, of course, it is inspired by that band's *Robot Woman* trilogy and tracks such as 'Machine Song'. In 'Robo-Warriors' Gilli reminds us all that 'leaders rise, leaders fall, Humpty-Dumptys all'. Humpty-Dumpty? How did she predict the rise of Boris Johnson?

'Guitar Zero' (Allen, Taylor)
To a steady beat from Chris, Allen plays a simple riff on guitar in 4/4 time (with a 2/4 thrown in to keep things interesting). Then Gilli sings lyrics that date back to at least 1971 when the band appeared on French TV to perform a number of tracks including 'Never Fight Another War', a song that doesn't appear to have ever been commercially recorded and released except on a very hard-to-get DVD. Lyrically, it's not that complicated, just a repeated chant of 'Never fight another war', with Stefanie on vocals. Sax improv and space whisper keep things a bit interesting, and Hillage provides some guitar riffs later on that sound very much like his work on 'The Golden Vibe' from his *Fish Rising* album. Everything ends on a bit of sax madness from Theo.

'The Gris Gris Girl' (Allen, Hillage)
It's that old Bo Diddley shuffle again as Allen sings us the story of the 'girl in green', taken originally from a poem, in which the Switch Doctor splits into male and female, the latter travelling across the planet trying to reconnect with her other half. In fact, this is a composition with different sections and rhythms to it – it opens with guitar arpeggios and Didier on flute before the 'Not Fade Away' shuffle starts. Allen sings over shifting, unpredictable chords, with frequent stops for staccato guitar and vocal lines. It loses its shuffle at about the four and a half minute mark as Taylor gets his head down and gives the drums a bit more of a straight-forward pummelling, and Hillage adds his trademark lead guitar. After that, Allen sings over some gentle guitar plucking from Hillage before things pick up again under the lyrics 'The soul call! The soul call! Remember the soul call…'

It's a song that takes repeated listens to get your head round and is even more difficult to describe, but I'll tell you what it reminds me of: 'Sally Simpson' by The Who, a story song with the same insistent movement to it but not nearly as complicated. The title references a 'gris-gris', a voodoo amulet from West Africa that is said to protect the wearer from evil.

'Wave And A Particle' (Smyth, Giraudy)
The third and last composition on the album by Gilli and Miquette reminds us that everything is a wave or a particle and nothing is truly solid (and waves are particles too. Or is it the other way round?) Anyway, it's unusual to have a song about quantum physics but here it is – not really a song, of course, but a poetry recital with sound effects. It's a short, two-minute performance from Gilli that ends, amusingly, with the line 'nothing stays still, even my tongue'.

'Pinkle Ponkle' (Allen, Hillage, Smyth)
Didier's back with his duduk for what is mostly an instrumental, with Allen singing some Eastern-y chant lines inviting us to 'surrender to the cosmic lover', Gilli space whispering and Taylor giving us a busy drum rhythm, heavy on the toms. Every now and then Allen hums something that sounds like 'Deya Goddess' from his 1977 solo album *Now Is The Happiest Time Of Your Life*. There are synth sounds from Miquette and subtle flute from Theo, while Howlett on bass plays a riff not too dissimilar to 'Master Builder'. Towards the end Hillage enters with lead guitar buried deep in the mix – it's like all the elements of past Gongs are coming together in a rich aural soup.

'Portal' (Hillage)
Shades of 'Fohat' here as Hillage plays a series of power chords over bubbly synth before Taylor sets up a galloping rhythm on drums – think 'Robin Hood, Robin Hood, riding through the glen' – while lead guitar wails impressively. Gong have definitely saved the best until last as this rip-roaring instrumental powers along like a runaway train. There's rich power chords bouncing back and forth before heading down, down, down the neck of the guitar, then crunching riffs over synth swoops. Theo gives us some bristly, raw sax before repeated guitar riffs echo back and forth, as the synth gives us something akin to 'A Sprinkling Of Clouds' before things slow down and dissolve into a swirling wash of sound. Gilli announces 'the portal is open'.

So here we are – it's been a long journey, meeting many marvellous characters along the way but finally we are in the final phase of preparation for 2032. The portal is open and all we need to do is have the tea and biscuits ready for when our visitors arrive.

I See You (2014)

Personnel:
Flamedog Allen (aka Orlando Allen): beat/crash/kick/vocal
Unicorn Strut (aka Dave Sturt): bass & invisible operas
Spiral K. Octoflash (aka Kavus Torabi): crunchbox & scythe guitar
Fabuloso Golfcart (aka Fabio Golfetti): winged guitars/glissando
Eastwinds i.e. Windows (aka Ian East): saxo/flutes/lungs
Dada Ali (aka Daevid Allen): bi-focal vocals 'n' gliss
Additional personnel:
Shakti Yoni (aka Gilli Smyth): sprinkled space whisper
Engineered, mixed and produced by Orlando Monday Allen at Flamedog Records Studios and at the Bananamoon Observatory Studios in NSW, Australia
Additional production by Dave Sturt and Daevid Allen
Rhythm section for 'I See You', 'Occupy', 'The Eternal Wheel Spins', 'You See Me', 'Pixielation' & 'Thank You' recorded by Alex Angeloni at Mosh Studios, Sao Paulo, Brazil
All saxes and woodwind recorded remotely by Ian East in his own studio
Gliss guitar on 'Shakti Yoni & Dingo Virgin' recorded by Tony Robinson at Moat Studios, London
Original label: Madfish (Snapper Records)
Released: November 2014
Highest chart positions: Uncharted
Running time: 62:07
Current edition: Original issue

I See You wasn't intended to be Daevid Allen's last Gong album, of course. It was yet another twist and turn in the story of a band that refuses to die and regenerates itself more frequently than *Doctor Who*. The fact that Allen sadly departed this planet shortly after it was released has given the album a bit more poignancy, a greater emotional wallop. Tracks that, initially, were just good songs turned into epitaphs – particularly the final two, 'Thank You' and 'Shakti Yoni & Dingo Virgin'. Grown Gongsters have been known to burst into tears upon hearing the latter.

Or perhaps not so unintentional. In 'Thank You' Allen appears to be saying farewell to everyone who has shared his flying teapot with him, so perhaps he had an inkling this was going to be his last Gong recording, although he fully intended to join his new, young band on stage.

But first, let us go back to 2009 as the *2032* lineup toured the new album. Mike Howlett and Theo Travis couldn't make all the gigs – Mike's academic career in Australia was calling him away from the bass while Theo was being wooed by someone called Steven Wilson. Travis brought in two musicians who would eventually become full-time members – bassist Dave Sturt and saxophonist Ian East.

Sturt – born 1960 in Middlesbrough – had worked with Theo as part of experimental instrumental group Cipher since 1996 and was a member of ambient prog band Jade Warrior. His credits also include session work with Pink Floyd's David Gilmour, film composer Michael Kamen and Be Bop Deluxe singer and guitarist Bill Nelson. Londoner East was a graduate of the Royal Academy of Music as well as musical director and composer for a wide range of bands and artists.

In 2011 Steve Hillage had a disagreement with Daevid Allen over the future direction of the band – he preferred to tour the classic trilogy songs, but Allen had itchy fingers and wanted to record new material – so he and Miquette Giraudy returned to System 7 duties. The following year Allen decided to get Gong going again – he wanted Orlando to play drums (even though his son had tried to distance himself from the band for years, having been brought up with it for most of his life) and a new guitarist was required. At one point Adrian Belew of King Crimson was considered and was seriously interested until his manager talked him out of it. Instead, Allen went to Brazil for another Gong Global Family gig and returned with Fabio Golfetti.

Fabio – born April 1960 in Sao Paulo – learned to play guitar as a teenager and was co-founder of the influential Brazilian psychedelic band Violeta de Outono. A big Gong fan who corresponded with Allen, in 1988 he also founded an offshoot, The Invisible Opera Company Of Tibet (Tropical Version Brazil), inspired by his hero's music and philosophies. In 1992 he invited Allen to an ecological festival in Brazil and the pair performed together. Fourteen years later Golfetti was invited to join Allen's Glissando Orchestra at the Gong Unconventional in Amsterdam, which was followed by a short tour of Brazil as Gong Global Family. Fast forward to 2012 and now he was part of the new lineup. Dave Sturt told the author: 'He was fantastic, perfect, a marriage made in heaven. He was very excited and really keen to work with Daevid, see how he worked and how he put compositions together.'

This band toured in 2012 and the following year, but there was one more piece of the jigsaw to be slotted into place. The catalyst was an interview on snooker legend Steve Davis's progressive rock radio show on Phoenix FM, a community station serving not Phoenix, Arizona, but the slightly less exotic locations of Brentwood and Billericay in Essex.

A word about Mr Davis. Most readers will know him as a snooker wizard who dominated the game during the 1980s, winning six world championships. Viewed as a nice but bland bloke from south-east London – earning the ironic nickname of 'Interesting' – he raised a few eyebrows by revealing he was a progressive rock fan and particularly fond of French Zeuhl outfit Magma. In 1996 he started his own radio show playing prog music and interviewing some of the genre's practitioners.

It was at a Magma concert in France that he bumped into Kavus Torabi, founder of Knifeworld and member of Cardiacs and Guapo, and the two hit it off so much that Kavus – born December 1971 in Tehran, Iran – became a regular contributor to the show. He takes up the story in an interview with *All About Jazz*:

> A few years back, I got a call from Steve saying that we were going to have Daevid Allen on the show [in fact, it was down to Dave Sturt who was trying to drum up publicity for a tour]. Both Steve and I were a bit in awe. I've been a huge Gong fan since I was a kid. We went down to their rehearsal and before doing the radio show, we went out for dinner. Daevid and I clicked right away. We did the radio show and Daevid was just vibing out. Daevid and I swapped numbers and he'd get in touch whenever he was over. Then there was a gig at Cafe Oto, where Marshall Allen and Daevid Allen were playing together. That night, after he'd played, he asked me to join Gong. I mean, when Daevid Allen asks you to play guitar in Gong, you don't say no ... He hadn't even heard me play.

Dave Sturt said to the author:

> Kavus came along for a rehearsal on April 22, 2013, which was the day I first met him, and we had a jam and threw some ideas around, and Kavus played some of his ideas as well. It went very well – I'd never come across anyone quite like him. And he played guitar unlike anyone I'd ever known.

Shortly after, Gong went to Brazil for two gigs – without Kavus because he wasn't quite a member of the band yet – and checked in to Mosh Studios in Sao Paulo, run by a friend of Fabio. The musicians felt a little unprepared but started jamming, running through some of the ideas that had been rehearsed earlier and, slowly, some basic rhythm tracks took shape, including 'I See You', 'You See Me' 'Occupy', 'The Eternal Wheel Spins', 'Pixielation' and 'Thank You'. There were also three takes of Sturt's song 'Zion My T-Shirt', with Orlando playing along to the composer's demo, and a track called 'Change The World' – yes, the alternative name for 'Rational Anthem' from the first Gong album. The band played this live during the 2012 tour and recorded it at Mosh for possible inclusion on *I See You*. Orlando took the approved recordings, edited them into shape and then they were sent to the individual members in various parts of the world for additional embellishments, including Allen's vocals.

Additional tracks were later composed and demoed by individual band members before being disseminated through the internet and added to remotely. Dave Sturt acted as the lynchpin, sending and receiving the individual members' recordings, eventually handing them over to be mixed by Orlando at his studio in Australia. Unusually, some of the drums were recorded quite late in the process. Orlando put together 'A Brew Of Special Tea' from Daevid's tape loops, while Dave Sturt supplied an out-take from

Cipher's 2002 album *One Who Whispers*, which became the song 'Shakti Yoni & Dingo Virgin'. A few other tracks dated back to 2012 and were performed live by the Gong lineup that year.

The result is a band reborn – the youthful energy and attack provided by the new lineup seem to have rejuvenated Allen. The songs are strong and mostly concise, the performances full of brash confidence, the musical styles a mix of ska, funk and almost heavy metal. Sturt's powerful bass punches out of the speakers, Torabi's guitar is almost as quirky and offbeat as Allen's and Orlando's drumming rises to the occasion. If there is any criticism I would make it's that Daevid's voice is sometimes a little too quiet and occasionally gets swamped by the rest of the band.

But this is a new, revitalised Gong – where *Zero To Infinity* and *2032* attempted to recycle past glories, *I See You* carves a new, jagged musical furrow for the 21st century. OK, there are some nods to the past. Everyone gets a silly name, just like on practically every Gong album, and the cover and inside booklet are replete with Allen's doodles and designs – once again, much easier to read on the LP release than the CD. As for the title, Allen explained to Joe Asmodo of *Eclipsed* magazine in 2014:

> *I See You* could be understood as a kind of esoteric statement (as the cover artwork suggests) but also as an allusion to all these insane things round NSA and Edward Snowden ... This is 'seeing you' as an act of intrusion and it is difficult to trust an invisible presence. In this respect, I am suggesting that we are smart enough to see that we are being seen.

The band was looking forward to touring the album with Daevid Allen after its release in late 2014 on CD and three-sided vinyl LP. Reviews had been almost overwhelmingly positive, with website *The Progressive Aspect* calling it 'their best album in years'. But Dingo Virgin was suffering some health problems – he fell down and broke his shoulder while in Australia in 2014, and then was diagnosed with lymphoma after discovering a lump on his neck. But he had lived with skin cancer for about twelve years and fully expected to see off this latest bodily invasion.

Both Kavus and Dave recall the production of *I See You* as a frustrating time. Kavus said to the author: 'With Orlando and Daevid in Australia, Fabio in Brazil and me, Dave and Ian being over here [in England] it was a very piecemeal method of recording. I think it was extremely important for Daevid and Orlando to work with each other – I feel this album was Daevid's gift to Orlando and Orlando's gift to Daevid. Artistically, it's a record of compromises, but I'm really glad we made it.'

Dave adds: 'It was a stressful time and so hard to keep the communication going. What Daevid was going through and what Orlando was going through, bloody hell, his father was dying and his mother failing and he felt really under pressure as well in that it was a lot to take on. It wasn't an easy album from that point of view too. But I'm surprised to listen to it again and find how much life there is in it, how much energy and power.'

'I See You' (Music: Orlando Allen and Dave Sturt, Lyrics: Daevid Allen)
The track that opened the album and gave it its title began life as a groove developed by Dave Sturt on bass and Orlando Allen on drums during rehearsals for the 2012 tour, when it went by the title of 'One By One', and was later further developed at Mosh Studios in Brazil. Daevid Allen always called his bass players the 'mothers' of the band and, from Christian Tritsch onwards, they have all played a major part in Gong's studio and live performances. The first few seconds of 'I See You' tell you who is in charge here as Sturt's bass, Allen's vocals and Orlando's drums jump out of the speakers.

According to the liner notes, the melody was inspired by 'upward swoops of pre-war orchestral portamenti experiments' and name-checks those old proggies Ligeti, Varese, Penderecki and Stockhausen. The phrase describes sliding from one note to another, rather like a violin – it was used as a vocal effect back in the 17th century, but it wasn't until avant-garde composers such as Hungarian Gyorgy Ligeti came along that it became the primary motif. In 'I See You' it refers to the way the song moves up and down in semi-tones, with each chord slipping into the next.

It opens with cymbals setting up a constant rhythm while bass drum, bass guitar and Allen's vocals jump in and out in unison. Again, the very informative liner notes explain how Daevid tried various ideas before realising that syncing his vocals with the drums 'hit the jackpot'. It's why, at the start, his lines are so short: 'I see ya! I miss ya! Hey listen! Who? Let's go there!' Dave adds: 'It took him a long time but when he finally sent through the recording of him singing with all the harmonies it was quite astounding. You can hear where he's also got melodic lines from the bass, and some really nice moments where he is totally freestyling.'

It sets up a tension in the song that isn't released until Allen sings 'in your dreams' and the track suddenly ups and gallops along, heading off on its 'portamenti' journey from A flat to A to B flat to B ... you get the picture. There's a brief pause in the gallop for Ian East to ape the rise and fall melody with his sax – intentionally or not reminding the listener of the way Didier's sax did something very similar in 'The Pot Head Pixies' from *Flying Teapot*. We quickly go back to the galloping rhythm before the track is broken up with Allen's repetition of 'Saturday night blues' and plays out with just a soundscape from glissando guitar.

The original recording went into a fast ska rhythm under East's sax improvisation, with the whole thing lasting a good 10 minutes. This was chopped off and positioned later in the running order as 'You See Me' – although I always put it back where it belongs as it creates a great six-minute opening number! And, amazingly, this all came out of just one take.

'Occupy' (Allen)

The Occupy movement sprang up in 2011 in response to the austerity and economic hardship imposed on ordinary people by countries attempting to deal with the financial crisis caused by greedy and irresponsible banks. Starting on Wall Street in New York, it spread to nearly 1,000 cities across 82 countries, consisting mostly of huge groups of protesters gathering and building camps in streets and squares. It began as a non-violent protest but, as often happens, was marred by violence from both the police and some anarchic elements in the crowds. By the time *I See You* was released most of the protests had died down, occasionally flaring up again for various reasons until 2016.

Allen said he came up with 95% of the song while walking by the Pacific Ocean, and believed it had some stylistic links to Japanese 'speed-rock' bands he discovered while touring Japan with you, me & us, a 2013 trio formed with Henry Cow drummer Chris Cutler and Japanese pianist Yumi Hama. It's certainly pretty speedy, powered along by simple, raw guitar riffs with sax wailing over the top and Allen's cries of 'Occupy!', but punctuated by dreamy, slow saxophone themes over sweet guitar chords and gentle slide from Fabio.

'Occupy' was played by the 2012 touring band but then put on ice as most of the repertoire at that time came from the classic trilogy. But later the *I See You* lineup used it as the basis of a jam at Mosh Studios in Brazil – where it went under the name of '757' due to the time signature changes – and various members began to contribute more to it. So it's credited to Allen, but Ian wrote the sax theme and Dave the chord sequence that supports it.

'When God Shakes Hands With The Devil' (Music: Kavus Torabi, Lyrics: Allen)

Kavus got into Gong when he was seventeen and Daevid Allen and Steve Hillage – 'two of the great riff masters', he says – were massive influences. But that meant, later in his musical career, he would occasionally compose riffs that sounded, well, a little too Gongish, so he'd put them to one side. He came up with this riff while waiting for Allen to turn up for the first rehearsal. When Allen heard it, he started dancing around and scatting over the top of it, before asking: 'Got any more like that?' Kavus replied: 'Yeah, f***ing hundreds! Twenty-five years' worth!' Finally, all those riffs he had that sounded too Gongish had a home.

Well, here's one of them, a fiendishly tricky little guitar figure in G minor that feels slightly Eastern, jazzy and spidery all at the same time. It's backed by a slow, funky groove from Orlando and Dave – the latter contributing a fretless bass part that is both meaty and liquidy, if that is possible. Liquid meat? Sounds disgusting, but this isn't – it's sinuous and warm. The guitar riff is doubled up by Ian's high-pitched flute with gentle gliss underneath – a second riff introduces the guttural spoken-word chorus.

There's a slightly more melodic and quite lengthy middle section, but even that has harmonies that sound just a little off – deliberately so, to give the song a menacing air. There's a third section that operates as a kind of coda, with Ian playing a repetitive atonal flute phrase over Dave and Orlando's groove and Allen repeating 'C'mon, c'mon' before everything dissolves into decaying echo.

Allen wrote the lyrics, which take a well-deserved pot-shot at the unholy links between religion and business designed to beat, batter and abuse the people. 'The fat cat smiles, the contract signed, he can be proud/The Church agrees his private army will be used to stop the crowd'. As I write this, current US president Donald Trump has just used the US army to attack and teargas protesters so he can be photographed holding a bible upside down. Allen saw it all coming. The title may also be a reference to a Neil Young quote about rock and roll being the devil's music – he said: 'I think that's where god and the devil shake hands – right there.'

The song displays Kavus's ability to come up with strange, quirky guitar phrases and chord sequences that shouldn't really work together – but somehow, they do.

'The Eternal Wheel Spins' (Music: Fabio Golfetti, Lyrics: O. Allen)
Originally written by Fabio for his other band, Violeta de Outono, this was another Mosh Studios recording completed in just one take from an original demo. The liner notes say 'Orlando and Dave took his original idea into drums & bass hyperdrive', and Dave certainly remembers plenty of musical development going on in rehearsal. He recalled to the author: 'In the end section Fabio did some random gliss stuff while I developed the bass line, which sometimes can control the harmony. That became the area where Kavus put on that amazing guitar solo.' Unusually, Orlando wrote the lyrics and sang it, with Daevid restricting himself to counterpoint gliss.

It opens with Gilli announcing the title before drums and bass kick off a pounding, running beat under glissando guitar. Orlando vocals are double-tracked, harmonising with himself – he has a gentle, almost feminine voice. Kavus's guitar solo is angular and spiky, threatening to head off into an entirely different key but somehow restraining itself, while Fabio's is more orthodox and a bit more like the classic Hillage sound. At about the five-minute mark there's some short guitar interplay reminiscent of the work King Crimson was doing in the 1980s, followed by a brilliant, finger-tangling final solo from Kavus that seems to me to be channelling a bit of Robert Fripp's classic KC sound. It ends with a final surge of sound that disappears into the ether.

'Syllabub' (Music: Sturt, Lyrics: Allen)
The first jamming session with Kavus involved just Allen, Sturt and Ian East. Orlando came over for the second and they played through some ideas, including 'Syllabub', an idea from Sturt that grew out of the 2012 rehearsal of what became 'I See You'. We had better let Dave tell the story: 'I took the "One By One" groove that became "I See You", cut it together and created

some ideas, playing around with different grooves. When we rehearsed together again as Gong "I See You" went down a different route and I used those ideas to develop "Syllabub".'

It opens with a collage of sound, some of which is a time-stretched rehearsal recording, including crashing gongs, Gilli intoning 'I Seeee Youuu' and cries of 'Banana!', before a sequence of eight heavy metal chords crash in, reminiscent of the opening of 'Fohat Digs Holes In Space'. This leads into a lurching, 'up and down' nursery rhyme melody in 6/4 involving Allen's vocals, Sturt's bass and Orlando's drums. The staccato lyrics echo the approach on the title track – 'Take y time, stick around, loosen up,' Allen sings, 'I wanna talk about, whatcha got, whatcha think.' There's a middle-eight of three-quarter time cheesiness, like the music on a fairground carousel ride, before we head back into the 6/4 verse. By this time, guitars and flute are playing little contrapuntal bits and bobs, punctuating the lyrics.

A quicker 6/8 section takes us back into the middle-eight before Ian lets loose on sax over laid-back atmospheric guitars from Kavus and Fabio. The liner notes suggest this is 'an interesting mix of familiar Gong elements with a friendly nod to Zappa' – I don't quite see the nod myself, but it is an entertaining and unpredictable four and a half minutes. Incidentally, Dave remembers taking charge of this one and telling the rest of the band what to play 'and that's not usually me!'.

'This Revolution' (Music: Sturt, Lyrics: Allen)

A poem written by Daevid specifically for the 2012 European tour that, according to the liner notes, 'addresses the frustrations with current politics and reassures that in the absence of a specific direction the force of intelligent innovation will soon give flower'. It apparently provoked strong reactions, presumably because its rose-tinted vision could be seen as being a little naive. 'This revolution will not be on TV thanks to Gil Scott-Heron,' Allen insists. 'This revolution is from the source of our thinking, our stories, dreams, our poetry…' If only he was right. As I pen these words, countries across the world have been convulsed by Black Lives Matter protests, and these are most definitely being televised. It appears revolution has no choice but to take to the streets.

The poem was originally accompanied by high-octave bass sounds composed by Sturt, but he later took out some of his parts to emphasize Ian's lyrical sax melodies, Fabio's gliss and Kavus's Ebow guitar. Daevid ends with the touching words: 'Shine on love ... shine on.'

'You See Me' (Gong)

The tail-end of 'I See You', chopped off and standing alone. Introduced by some space whisper and excerpts from Daevid's tape loops over glissando guitar and busy, expectant drums, it goes into the ska rhythm mentioned above, cycling round the chords of F#, G, F# and B flat. Ian on sax improvises over the top before a collision of riffs from all the instruments creates an anarchic ending that almost, but not quite, dissolves into chaos. As the liner notes state, it was indeed a feat of mixing by Orlando that no-one's contribution here gets swamped.

'Zion My T-Shirt' (Music: Sturt, Lyrics: Allen)

The band were living in a hotel apartment in Brazil during the Mosh sessions, where Dave instigated a 'listening session' of demos to identify possible tracks for the album. This was one of the demos he played, dating back to the late 1980s when he was a mature student in Middlesex, recording a Tibetan children's choir in the university studio. He played around with the recording and reversed some sections, creating the melody from it and finding nice accompanying arpeggios on his bass. In fact, it was originally TWO songs that Dave thought could become tracks for the band he was in at the time, Jade Warrior, and recorded it once while working on the album *Now*.

Orlando wanted to have a go at it, recording his drums along with the demo, but it seems none of the three takes he did actually ended up on the album, so he probably re-recorded it when he returned to Australia. It opens with a muted gong sound and the choir singing a simple rising and falling melody, accompanied by what sounds like a harp or similar instrument – later used as the band's 'walking on' music for live gigs. There's atmospheric noises behind the children's voices, which seem to phase in and out of hearing. Unless you are one of the 1.2million people in the world who speak Tibetan – and there are many different dialects – it is difficult to identify which lines are being sung backwards, if any.

A sweep of the harp heralds the song proper, a ballad in D minor anchored by Sturt's melodic bass notes and Orlando's fairly gentle drumming, with Fabio playing sweet slide glissando notes over the top. Allen sings lyrics that, say the liner notes, are 'a group reply to a postcard from a friend in the UK'. He points out that while he's happy to 'zion your t-shirt or your old LP' he shouldn't expect the singer to remember his face after 40 years. But, he later admits, 'I recognise that crazy stare ... I'd recognise that anywhere'. There's a faster middle-eight section in C minor before the song moves back to its original key and tempo under Allen's narrated lyrics.

The contention that this was originally two songs is supported by a sudden move at the four-minute mark into a faster, busier instrumental section based on a rising guitar riff, with Ian playing double-tracked flute. Towards the end, Fabio's gliss slows things down and Allen 'la's' over an exquisitely-played bass solo from Dave, before we fade out on glissando and Gilli space whisper.

'Pixielation' (Music: Ian East, Lyrics: Allen)

'Pixielation' began life as a flute salad improvisation in 2010, which Ian then used to jam with the band in soundchecks on that tour and also in 2012. He said: 'We were playing so much material from *Camembert* and the Trilogy back then it inevitably absorbed some of that older Gong band influence, as well as Didier's approach given that I was learning and adapting many of his parts at that time.' Originally it was called 'Tory Rebellion', which tells you where it was coming from, but Daevid didn't want to deal with a narrow political subject so preferred to broaden the message to a larger global environmentalist one and thought it would be a suitable vehicle for a last hurrah from the Pot Head Pixies, becoming Pixie Rebellion before settling on its final name.

Ian said to the author: 'Personally, I'm very happy that the PHPs made an appearance on what turned out to be Daevid and Gilli's final Gong album. The slow/abstract gliss and flute sections plus the coda were originally arranged so that Gilli would have a space to perform some poetry and space whispers. Alas, due to her health problems, she didn't add any parts, so those sections became instrumental interludes.'

For me, this is very definitely Ian channelling Didier Malherbe – it has the same child-like, nursery rhyme quality as 'A PHP's Advice' from *You*, as his flute cycles up and up, punctuated by nice little funky notes on Dave's bass and, er, some clapping. The lyrics are an address to the people of this planet by one of Allen's Pot Head Pixies – really the only bit of the original Gong mythology that turns up on this album – and, as usual, they are a little bit critical of the way we run our lives. 'We watch some of you and wonder if you're really as silly as you look!' sings Allen (sadly, the answer is almost certainly yes).

The song is punctuated with sudden fast sections as Allen sings 'Think! Think of it!', followed by peaceful moments of glissando, before the verses come back in again. At the 3:50 mark, it turns into a cheeky little instrumental with Ian referencing the theme from *The Woody Woodpecker Show* over discordant guitar riffs, before ending in what sounds like the pixies taking off in their flying teapot.

It's a track that divided the band somewhat – Kavus felt it was too much like the more whimsical material from classic trilogy Gong and should have been left off the album. As it happens, you won't find it on the vinyl version – it wasn't finished in time for the deadline.

'A Brew Of Special Tea' (O. Allen)

This is Orlando's tribute to his father, a collage of sounds including excerpts from early Gong interviews, tape loops from *Camembert Electrique* and extracts from an early Daevid Allen poem 'Capt Shaw & Mr Gilbert', ending on a few seconds of 'Givin' My Luv To You' from *Angels Egg*.

'Thank You' (Daevid Allen)

'Thank You' sounds like goodbye. Yet it was one of the first tracks to be attempted by the new lineup in Brazil, before Allen was diagnosed with his new cancer and, presumably, before he realised this would be his last Gong album. In it, Daevid thanks everyone ever involved in Gong and, possibly, his own personal life – the children, the dreaming, the believing, the healing, the feeling. And, in a no doubt accidental nod to Abba, he says 'thank you for the music'. Talking to the author, Dave says: 'At his age, any album could have been his last so maybe that was in the back of his mind.'

Allen had recorded it as a 'scratchy' demo and was very clear about how he wanted the song to go, although it was tried out in a few different tempos. Dave remembers spending an evening in the Sao Paulo hotel, transcribing it. There are echoes of the spirit of 'You Can't Kill Me' in the earlier verses – 'it doesn't matter if you hate me, it doesn't matter if you left me, it doesn't matter if you kill me'. But where the former was a blast of defiance, 'Thank You' is an upbeat, celebratory stomp.

Musically, it is one of the simplest songs Gong have ever done, a slow blues alternating between the chords of F and C for half of its 10-minute length, with Allen repeating the same melody for 16 lines of vocal. Orlando plays steady, powerful drums while swampy blues guitar runs throughout.

At the 3:50 mark, it quietens down, passing through a mysterious soundscape of atonal guitar notes and gentle gliss, before gradually building up again into the 'Thank You' section as Allen expresses his gratitude for, well, everything and everyone, really. Guitars, drums, bass, sax and Gilli's space whisper (lifted from various previous albums) collide until the track ends with a guitar chord sliding down – like the ending to Jethro Tull's 'Aqualung'!

'Shakti Yoni & Dingo Virgin' (Daevid Allen, Gilli Smyth)

The band felt the album needed to end on something ambient and reflective, but by this time Daevid was too ill to play. So Dave Sturt trawled through some glissando improvisations made in 2001 when Allen spent a day recording with Cipher for their 2002 album *One Who Whispers*. He said to the author: 'I found a couple of pieces that were really nice so I edited them together, did a bit of a treatment on them and sent it to Orlando and he got Gilli to sing over it. And Gilli was struggling by then, too. I'm glad we managed to get that to work so well.'

How to describe a nine-and-a-half minute glissando and space whisper ambient track that pays tribute to the immeasurable influence of Shakti and Dingo on all who love, listen to and have played with Gong? I cannot truly do it justice except to suggest that the sounds seem to be coming from beyond the veil, creating notes that appear to vibrate the very walls of your home. It's mystical, ethereal, sometimes dark and foreboding – a bit of a downbeat ending, perhaps, but one that underscores the sheer anarchic joy Allen and the band have put into the previous tracks.

It fades out to the sound of birdsong. Or was that the birds in my own garden singing along in unison? I'm not entirely sure ...

Rejoice! I'm Dead! (2016)

Personnel:
Ian East: soprano/tenor sax, flute, Swanee whistles, bells, shakers
Fabio Golfetti: guitar, gliss guitar, vocals
Cheb Nettles: drums, vocals
Dave Sturt: bass, hi bass EBow, vocals
Kavus Torabi: vocals, guitar
Additional personnel:
Graham Clark: violin on 'The Thing That Should Be' and 'Someone You'll Never Be'
Steve Hillage: guitar on 'Rejoice!'
Didier Malherbe: duduk on 'Model Village' and 'Through Restless Seas I Come'
Daevid Allen: vocals on 'Floating Anarchy Manifesto', 'Kapital [Original Demo]', 'Glastonbury Town'
Recorded at Brixton Hill Studios, London.
Engineered by Gong and Nick Howlantz
Mixed by Mark Cawthra and Dave Sturt
Produced by Gong
Original label: Madfish (Snapper Music)
Released: September 2016
Highest chart positions: Uncharted
Running time: 59:42 (Deluxe 2CD version 141:03)
Current edition: Original issue

Daevid Allen reckoned he would die in his 84th year. Sadly, he was seven years out. In February 2015 he told fans in a moving message that he had been given six months to live. He said in a statement on the *Planet Gong* website:

> It is now confirmed that the invading cancer has returned to successfully establish dominant residency in my neck. The original surgery took much of it out, but the cancer has recreated itself with renewed vigour, while also spreading to my lung ... I am not interested in endless operations. In fact, it has come as a relief to know that the end is in sight. I am a great believer in 'The Will of the Way Things Are' and I also believe that the time has come to stop resisting and denying and to surrender to the way it is.

He died a month later. He left behind him a huge body of work that was a testament to his musicianship, work ethic, restlessness and seemingly endless flood of ideas. From 1963 to 2014 he had produced astonishing, groundbreaking and genre-bending music, poetry and art, and was at the heart of a quiet but insistent movement that spread across the globe. He wasn't perfect by any means – he could be hard-hearted and selfish when he wanted and sometimes needed to be – but he was undoubtedly inspirational, musically, politically and spiritually. His romantic partnership with Gilli Smyth was long over, but they seemed to be somehow still joined psychically together – a year later Gilli died of pulmonary pneumonia at 83.

Daevid had battled skin cancer for some years and had to go back to Australia every three months for treatment, but it became very clear towards the end of the making of *I See You* that he was extremely ill. A massive tour had been planned to promote the album, but there was no way Allen was going to be able to do it, leaving the rest of the band to fulfil dates without the man many fans considered WAS Gong.

It was particularly heartbreaking for Kavus, who had just joined the band he loved to work with a man he had admired since his teens only to see everything fall apart (the second time it had happened to him; first was when he joined Cardiacs not long before Tim Smith suffered a heart attack). He told the author: 'I didn't think Daevid would die from this – he just seemed to have so much life. In 2014 we played in Brazil and Daevid must have had his cancer at this point, and he was still doing three or four costume changes a night, packing up all his own equipment and then doing the bars until two or three in the morning. He had the most extraordinary energy. So, of course, we thought he'd beat this.'

Initially, the band was sceptical about carrying on without him. Kavus, in particular, didn't want to front Gong – he wanted to be the guitarist, not the singer. Most of the gigs were cancelled, leaving ten or eleven that still needed to be fulfilled – and Allen insisted the band play them. Kavus told the author: 'I distinctly remember leaving my flat before the first gig in France and honestly feeling like a condemned man – I thought how did I end up in this f***ing position, where I have to go out and play to a disappointed crowd who expected to see Daevid Allen?'

Before the tour, the band needed to find a new drummer – Orlando had his own career to think about, and it would make life a lot easier if the Gong drummer was based in Britain rather than Australia, so Kavus recommended Cheb Nettles. Cheb, born in ... well, we don't know. The trouble is, Cheb Nettles is notoriously shy and retiring, and he is rarely pictured. All we can say with any certainty is that he was born to play Gong and his inventive energy behind the drum kit helped give the new lineup the added impetus it needed.

A strange thing happened on the tour. The sound of the band was amazing. Former Gong members including Steve Hillage and Mike Howlett were joining them on stage and giving their seal of approval, while Daevid Allen was over the moon with the performances on recordings sent to him in Australia. Eventually, he delivered them a message that officially passed on the Gong baton to this exciting new lineup in an email to the band:

> Can I just simply say that it is super clear to me that Kavus, you are the perfect fit with Dave, Ian and Fabio and that Cheb, you are the perfect fit

> with Kavus! I feel you are all equally on the brink of a whole new era of Gong, musically, lyrically and spiritually and that pretty much all you have each done until now has been a preparation for this time ... At last I am free to let go of it, so now it is up to you guys to carry it on into new unknown heights and depths far beyond anything I could ever imagine myself.

By the end of the tour it was clear there could be a future for this version of Gong, but if it was to carry on it had to make a new recording, one that had to be amazing, otherwise, it was just a covers band. Kavus said: 'Until we made *Rejoice!* I was still ambivalent about this being Gong.'

Tentative preparations began with the band looking at some of Allen's poetry and seeing if any of it could be set to music. It was, however, an uncomfortable process trying to shoehorn existing lyrics, many of which didn't really scan or rhyme, into some of the tunes the various members had floating around in their heads. They were also insistent that the new album couldn't go anywhere near the Pot Head Pixies or the Octave Doctors – it was felt that would come across as too bogus. So this approach appeared to be a non-starter until they hit upon three words from one of the poems – 'Rejoice! I'm dead!' – and realised that was the title of the new album, right there.

Allen always had a positive attitude towards death – he saw it as a goal to be reached rather than something to be feared. When he heard of a friend who had passed away, he would respond by saying 'Yes! He made it!'. It may sound callous, but perhaps it is a more positive approach towards the inevitable than most of us have, and it helped him to embrace his own end with open arms. The line 'Rejoice! I'm dead!' hit a chord with the band, particularly with Kavus who has been obsessed with death since he was seven.

The poetry was abandoned, and instead, the band decided this would be the 'death album' but a positive one. It would be an album about transitions, about changes – and the more they worked on it, the more it made sense for this band at this particular time. Kavus said: 'It was us saying goodbye to Daevid with that record.'

A lot of the ideas originated from Kavus, Dave, Ian and Cheb while Fabio was in Brazil, although they all share the credits for the music, while one of the tracks began life as a Daevid Allen demo, offered up as an alternative to 'Occupy' on the *I See You* album. But there was one song that convinced them they could successfully write Gong music – Kavus told the author: 'I knew we could make an amazing record – I knew we were great writers and players. The moment when I thought, oh yeah, we've got this was when we wrote 'The Unspeakable Stands Revealed'. When it expanded and we were playing it, it was really exciting. And then the other stuff followed.'

The result is an album that bursts with vitality and ideas. It feels a little more together, a little more organised than *I See You* yet retains that album's impudent energy and adventurism. The musicianship is superb, the arrangements are exciting and climactic and there's enough humour and spirituality running throughout to stop you missing those mischievous little pixies. And the love and respect for Daevid Allen goes all the way through like a stick of Blackpool rock – his voice is there, mostly figuratively but sometimes literally.

The record company clearly had enough faith in the album to release it on double-LP and as a limited edition, LP-sized hardback book containing two additional CDs, one with out-takes from this and the previous release and the third with a 5.1 surround sound mixed by Bruce Soord. It garnered almost universally positive reviews, summed up by seven words from a reviewer on Amazon: 'If you like Gong, you'll love this.'

'The Thing That Should Be' (Music by Ian East, Fabio Golfetti, Cheb Nettles, Dave Sturt, Kavus Torabi. Lyrics by Kavus Torabi)

The key to this version of Gong is vocal harmonies. In the past, the bulk of the singing duties had fallen on Daevid Allen, with occasional support from the few others in various lineups who could hold a tune – plus, of course, Gilli's space whisper. But the new Gong had four singers who together could create some heavenly harmonies, and they exploit that to the full in this powerful opening track. It begins with two heavy metal major chords – G and A if you want to try it at home – before the unaccompanied vocal harmonies burst out of the speakers with the opening line, introducing the title of the album: 'The time has come again, rejoice, you're dead.'

The lyrics were inspired by a mystical experience Kavus had after sampling a psychoactive plant called salvia divinorum, also known as Sage of the Diviners. As stated before, he was just seven when the inevitability of death hit him and he made it almost his life's work to find out what it was about, what dying really meant. Flash forward 24 years and deep understanding came about thanks to puffing on the opioid-drenched leaves of the plant, which is still legal in most countries. He said to the author:

> Within two seconds of taking this stuff, I lost all logic, time, everything. I found myself somewhere in which every atom of my being felt completely familiar. It was like going somewhere and within two seconds saying ah, this place. I came back, not an atheist. I came back, not afraid of dying for the first time since I was seven.

As he says in the lyrics, 'language, time and reason all dissolve, now that everyone is everything'. Yes, it does sound like hippy-dippy cosmic nonsense but, having spoken to Kavus, I know he is deeply sincere about the experience and the effect it had on him. The song is about embracing death, but it's not morbid or downbeat in any way – it's triumphant and positive.

Musically, this began life as a sketch from Fabio called 'Thank You George' because the slide guitar melody sounded a little like George Harrison. It comes in after every verse, starting on A flat, sliding up and then down to D and then E while the band thunders along in A. In fact, the song pretty much remains on that chord for nearly two-thirds of its length before heading down into F sharp for a blast of soprano sax from Ian, followed by several repeats of the lyric 'You know that nothing means a thing'. Heading back into A for some more instrumental work it then moves through a final sequence of chords that I have to say sound reminiscent of early Pink Floyd before coming to rest after, in Gong terms, a scant three minutes and 37 seconds.

It was a track that came together very quickly – the band had the melody done and dusted in a day – and it provides a confident, uplifting opening to the album. The band felt it was the right thing to start on because it didn't necessarily sound like quintessential Gong – it told the listener something different was happening now.

'Rejoice!' (Music by East, Golfetti, Nettles, Sturt, Kavus Torabi. Lyrics by Daevid Allen, Torabi)

'Rejoice!' was put together quite early on in the Gong songwriting process and helped to establish the sound of the album. Like the previous track, it exploits the band's harmony vocal abilities in a soaring chorus that manages to combine both joy and pathos – there's some bitter-sweet major sevenths tucked away in there to tug on the heartstrings. Kavus said to the author: 'It felt a bit naughty doing that in a Gong song. But I remember going to the pub after working on it all day and realising what a great chorus we had.'

It opens on a bit of guitar and sax interplay, a climbing tune that has Kavus on the offbeat, Ian on the on, before settling down with a steady beat in 5/4 over two repetitive chords, A flat and B flat, although there are some odd notes floating about in there too. Kavus sings the first two verses; there's a repeat of the climbing tune, then a third verse before the powerful chorus of 'Rejoice, I'm dead! At last, I'm free!' This is followed by a tricky little riff before heading back into the fourth verse and another rendition of the chorus, punctuated by a short, syncopated guitar riff like something from King Crimson in the 1980s.

At the two and half minute point, we reach a gentler glissando section, with Cheb's tom toms keeping things going as Fabio's gliss builds up. Ian takes a sax break that's heavily echoed before Kavus provides a menacing, atonal guitar solo. Then the guitar sound changes as we welcome back an old friend, Submarine Captain Spillage, to the fold. Steve was a strong supporter of the new lineup, joining the new Gong for gigs, and had been a friend of Dave's for seven years. His playing takes the song almost into 'Master Builder' territory as he soars over repetitive guitar and bass riffs, with Cheb's drums kicking up a thunderous storm.

By the seven and a half minute point, we have an almighty collision of sound and rhythm, with guitar and sax duelling for attention as bass and drums drive everything onwards before we erupt back into the chorus again in something approaching a musical orgasm. The remaining few minutes find the band alternating between repeating the 'Rejoice!' line and a version of the opening stepping riff, while Hillage adds little bursts of lead guitar here, there and everywhere, before a slow fade.

If 'The Thing…' was a short, sharp introduction to a new Gong, 'Rejoice!' showcases the band's ability to create long-form tracks full of fire and passion but also with moments of glissando beauty. At more than ten minutes long, 'Rejoice!' shows the listener that this band means business.

'Kapital' (Music by Allen, East, Golfetti, Nettles, Sturt, Torabi. Lyrics by Allen)

'Kapital' was one of Daevid's tunes, offered up as a possible track for the *I See You* album but ultimately rejected in favour of 'Occupy' with which, of course, it shares a particular political viewpoint. The original demo is included on disc two of the deluxe boxset and consists simply of Daevid singing and playing the guitar riff. The band wanted to do something with it but couldn't see how to turn it into a full-length song.

Meanwhile, Fabio had, completely separately, come up with a driving instrumental full of repetitive little riffs that he called 'Electricity' (and is also included on the bonus disc). It was Cheb who realised that the two could be knitted together into a single entity and it worked completely. It was even in the same key of E, give or take a bit of dodgy guitar tuning from Daevid. Kavus says: 'It had gone from being a one and a half minute Daevid sketch into a tune. I don't like to imagine a time when we don't play that one live. It's a really good live track. It kind of replaced 'Occupy' – I felt 'Kapital' was a better tune.'

It fades in with driving guitar chords and pounding drums as Fabio and Kavus sing the lyrics, their vocals electronically treated to sound menacing and threatening: 'We occupy your dreamworld ... Kapitalista, pleased to meet ya.' It is punctuated with bursts of E seventh chords (with an added G I think!) going bam! bam! like a double-punch. Then it crashes into Fabio's 'Electricity' riffs, briefly revisits the main lyrics, then ends on repetitive blasts of chords after just three minutes and 20 seconds. It's a short but powerful piece of music that's as angry and disturbing as anything Allen had done in his long musical career.

'Model Village' (Music by East, Golfetti, Nettles, Sturt, Torabi. Lyrics by Sturt)

Dave and Fabio were the main drivers behind this gentler offering, but one with a disturbingly dark heart – Fabio sings the verses and Dave the middle eight. It's a bit Kinksy, a bit Dukes of Stratosphear, a bit XTC but with a mysterious, *Handmaid's Tale* twist in it. It was inspired by the miniature model villages the band would pass as it toured the UK – there were even fantasies about doing a gig that could be streamed to a model village somewhere. Gong Live at Legoland, perhaps.

It opens with Dave playing major seventh arpeggios on a keyboard, along with an excerpt from an out-take from the *I See You* sessions, a spoken word piece from Daevid Allen called 'Floating Anarchy Manifesto' that was presented as an alternative to 'This Revolution'. His denunciation of corrupt, dishonest capitalism sets the scene for a description of, as the title suggests, a model village – a perfect blue sky, manicured lawns, church bells ringing and a police officer with nothing to do because there's no crime.

Guitars, bass and drums take over now in a rolling three-quarter time (mostly) as Dave and Fabio tell the story of this rural utopia. It sounds idyllic and just what we imagine many little English villages to be. But there's something strange going on, hinted at in the added tritone in the guitar phrases – what we have all come to know as that ever-present motif in Gong songs, the Devil's Interval. As the song progresses, we learn that things are not quite what they seem – there are 'rules here to guide you, and constantly remind you you'd be useless without us. We know what's best. We are born to rule you.' So we're looking at an enforced idyll, full of people who are 'virtuous and mindless, obedient and silent'.

But there's yet another layer here, because there is revolution in the air – the friendly shopkeeper is passing on secret information to radicals waiting for their cue to rise up. There will be a revolution here soon, some floating anarchy perhaps – come back in a few months and the model may be in pieces. But the people will be free.

The song sees a welcome return to a Gong recording by Didier Malherbe, playing his favourite instrument these days, the duduk, mostly in gorgeous harmony with Ian East during the middle eight but coming into his own as the tune slowly winds up and ends. It is a marvellous piece of songwriting, part 'Penny Lane', part *Village Of The Damned*, a six-minute short story that probably Ray Davies and Andy Partridge would have sold their souls to have written – and the first time Sturt had penned lyrics to a song.

'Beatrix' (Music by East, Golfetti, Nettles, Sturt, Torabi. Lyrics by Allen)
Dave Sturt had composed the tune and asked multi-instrumentalist pal Christopher Piers Ellis to play piano on it before presenting it to the band. Dave played it to Allen, who spontaneously came up with some French lyrics about his then-girlfriend Beatrix, with Ian East's sax put on later. It's in a three-quarter time 'French cafe' style, with a low acoustic bass, Ian playing long, mournful notes on tenor sax and Dave's pianist pal Chris Ellis tinkling l'ivories. Think of a more ethereal, downbeat version of 'Prostitute Poem' from *Angels Egg* but with Daevid instead of Gilli. In fact, the similarities become even more pronounced when, at just before the two-minute mark, bass and sax play a pretty major key tune as Daevid's voice fades into the background.

'Visions' (Music by East, Golfetti, Nettles, Sturt, Torabi)
Fabio dominates this slow, gentle four and a half minute instrumental with his glissando guitar, Ian adds some low-key soprano sax, Dave plays his hi bass

EBow – a hand-held electronic bow that helps to create long, slow notes – and Kavus adds some electronically-treated wordless vocal harmonies. Kavus says: 'This one has really grown when we do it live. The tune is so quiet that if there is any noise from the audience, any talking from the bar, it really puts you off.' Glissando instrumentals are difficult to describe – they are washes of sound that transport you to another world, but they can also outstay their welcome. Thankfully, 'Visions' is just about the right length and provides a moment's respite before we reach the centrepiece of the album.

'The Unspeakable Stands Revealed' (Music by East, Golfetti, Nettles, Sturt, Torabi. Lyrics by Torabi)

Track seven on the album is a multi-sectioned beast clocking in at nearly twelve minutes, and it's the composition that, as mentioned above, pointed the way forward for both the band and the album. Kavus told the author: 'Beforehand we did have 'Kapital' and we did have 'The Thing That Should Be' but when we got this one it stood up on its own feet and was a piece completely written by us and it was so epic as well. This is what the new Gong is going to be like and it gave us a bar to aim for.'

It's mostly a combination of Kavus and the mysterious Cheb – the former came up with the verses, Cheb part of the melody for the chorus and the big epic cycle at the end. But Gong is not one of those bands in which someone comes up with a completed song and tells everyone else how to play it – an approach that did for The Beatles in the end – but one in which ideas are elaborated upon, coloured in and, sometimes, twisted into new exciting shapes.

So it was with 'The Unspeakable…', which opens almost tentatively with Fabio's gliss and Kavus playing cosmic, twinkly little notes over the top. Then comes Dave with a funky, bouncy riff on his fretless bass, the drums pick up the pace, Ian blows some sax over the top and soon we're driving along joyfully in a lengthy instrumental section with a vibe that's not a million miles away from 'The Isle Of Everywhere'. The opening 5/4, 5/4, 5/4, 4/4 bass line was the first part to be written – Kavus, Ian and Dave then jammed over it at Kavus' studio. He came up with the wonky guitar riff and Ian and Fabio later developed the harmonic sequence.

At about the three-minute mark some spikey guitar riffs take control as layers of harmony vocal sounds build up underneath before chopping guitar chords bring in the first verse, with Kavus singing: 'Well, here's the question, all information is at stake.' The verses are punctuated with a rising and falling riff played by Kavus and doubled up on soprano sax by Ian, repeated under the chorus of 'reflections that reveal the mystery further, serve only to reflect the thing itself. It's only the unspeakable within that resembles the more the mystery itself'.

We're now at the seven-minute mark and the song has entered a more reflective section, with Ian blowing long, flowing notes over guitar arpeggios, alternating between D major and B major, interrupted by some heavy metal guitar chords and chunky riffs. Finally, we reach the 'big epic cycle' as the chunky riff moves back and forth between B flat and G major, Cheb sings the chorus over the ending (in a key too high for Kavus!), Ian is going all-out on sax and Fabio's gliss sounds like a string symphony before the whole thing seems to disappear into hyperspace.

Wow, what a track. A simply stunning piece of music that ebbs and flows like the tide but finally reaches an astonishing sonic climax that could level the Himalayas. As Kavus said when the band first put it together: 'Bloody hell, there it is!'

And what, you may ask, is the Unspeakable? It is the other, the beyond – this is the Death album, after all. But it's also a message of hope, that everything we could want to know can be found by looking inwards. Kavus says: 'All the great mysteries that we are searching for, that have faced Mankind forever, we can access by looking within. The answers are in us somewhere.' Within you, without you, as someone else once said.

'Through Restless Seas I Come' (Music by East, Golfetti, Nettles, Sturt, Torabi. Lyrics by Torabi)

A sadder reflection on the death of the Divided Alien, about his voyage into the 'other', and a song that got Kavus choked up with emotion as he wrote the chorus. It was also a difficult composition for the band to get right. Kavus told the author: 'When we first played it, it really sounded great, but for a long time we could never get it back to how it sounded. We all knew what a nice song it was – maybe it was the pace or maybe the way we approached it.'

The nautical theme is a typical Kavus device – 'I always do nautical songs, I don't know why. I really like writing about the sea as an analogy. I love watery and nautical language.' Perhaps it's because he used to live in Plymouth. It certainly does strike a sombre note, with a gentle gliss soundscape in A flat minor over which Kavus sings a fairly simple but endearing melody that flows up and down like the sinuous heaving of a mighty ocean. 'All heroic voyages,' he sings, 'and this will be my last.' There's a touch of Steve Reich in its opening minimalism, although there is still a lot going on in the rest of the song, with some Fabio slide guitar, Kavus finger-picking and Dave playing solid, mournful bass notes. The vocals are quite high and, to me, there's a touch of Daevid in them at times (he had a higher voice than Kavus, who finds some of the classic Gong songs a challenge to sing).

In case all this sadness makes you want to take a boat into the middle of the Atlantic and throw yourself overboard, the song suddenly picks up its heels at around the four-minute mark and dances into a minor key jig-like rhythm in, I think, 7/8. To the sound of some crashing guitar chords, Kavus sings the chorus that got him so choked up: 'Mystic, fool, radiant jewel, teacher, wise man, sage. Golden flame, none more sane.' Yes, they are all descriptions of Allen, but why none more sane? Kavus said to the author:

> There was this idea that Daevid Allen was some kind of crazy guy, out of his gourd, wigged out, a damn crazy hippie, but Daevid certainly wasn't. He seemed extremely balanced, sane and sorted. I didn't find him crazy; he was really good fun to be with. People called him an eccentric but he wasn't really.

Finally, we end with the band's final farewell to 'a beacon blazed ... Journey's end, welcome friend, now your crossing's done', followed by guitar arpeggios and Didier Malherbe's duduk fading into the distance. The captain has been swallowed up by the sea – but the ship sails on.

'Insert Yr Own Prophecy' (Music by East, Golfetti, Nettles, Sturt, Torabi. Lyrics by Torabi)

The album finishes pretty much as it started, with guitar power chords and the massed harmonies of the Gong vocal section. Of course, it's still about Death with its references to 'the cradle up to the grave' in the opening chorus, but it's still a welcome blast of sheer joy after the reflective nature of the preceding track. Frantic guitar and sax riffs, held together by Cheb's pin-sharp drumming, punctuate verses about losing friends along the way, and how we need to hold each other close and say 'I love you' before the dance is over. It's all done at an astonishing breakneck speed – originally it was even faster, but the band thought it sounded a bit too 'Cardiacs' and set about slowing it down and Gongifying it a bit.

At around the three-minute mark, the song goes into a lengthy psychedelic 'lull' based on Steve Hillage-ish guitar arpeggios, vocal 'aaahhh's and intermittent sax interjections from Ian. It builds up slowly, helped by Dave stroking his bass with his EBow to create long, low sounds, Fabio's glissando washes and Kavus's increasingly energetic strumming, before crashing into a final end section in three-quarter time that cycles the chords of D, E and B flat – almost the ol' Devil's Interval that Daevid Allen loved so well. The sax and Cheb's voice repeat the guitar riff from the front of the song, but considerably slowed down, before the band end together at the nine-and-a-half minute mark.

This was largely one of Cheb's tunes – the band came up with the psychedelic lull in the middle, and Cheb brought in the end section – and has become a live favourite for both band and audience. Kavus said: 'We always end gigs with this one. The build-up in D is a key moment live – if we are over-running this is where we can shave a bit out. If we are headlining and time isn't important, this can go on for several minutes. We keep it going round and round and building up this psychedelic section. It's like foreplay – you know the big orgasm is coming.'

Bonus Tracks

'Floating Anarchy Manifesto' (Allen)

Gong had just delivered the new album when the record company revealed it was planning a deluxe version, and needed material for a second CD. After a desperate search through hard drives, they came up with this spoken-word piece by Daevid, originally written and recorded in 2014 as an alternative to 'This Revolution' on *I See You*. In the end, it was shelved, to be resurrected as the intro for 'Model Village'. This is the full-length four and a half minute version in which Mr Allen takes capitalism apart with witty, incisive lines and rhymes. 'No more paranoid politicians playing snake oil salesman for the golden throne, no more armament mafioso ordering murder down the phone,' he says. Right on! It's probably a bit too long for its own good, but I love the ending. His voice softens and there's almost a catch of emotion in it as he says: 'Shine on love. Shine on ...'

'Someone You'll Never Be' (Music by East, Golfetti, Nettles, Sturt, Torabi. Lyrics by Torabi)

Composed mostly by Kavus and Cheb, this was recorded during the *Rejoice! I'm Dead!* Sessions, but ultimately rejected – Kavus thought it sounded too much like one of his tunes and not Gong. The end section will be familiar – it's the same as the one that finishes 'Insert Yr Own Prophecy'. Kavus explained: 'I like things being thematic so we used it again but when the album was mixed I was very keen it shouldn't be on the album. It was a bit too navel-gazing. It wasn't Gong enough. I dug my heels in a bit on that, really felt it was out of place.'

I see what he means. It sounds more like a Dukes of Stratosphear track, with Kavus singing and strumming the chords of A flat and E, on electric guitar over psychedelic keyboard and vocal backing before going into a more subdued version of the 'Prophecy' ending. It's interesting and entertaining, but it doesn't sound very Gong.

'Kapital' (Allen)

The original demo offered up for the *I See You* album but rejected in favour of 'Occupy'. As stated above, it uncannily seemed to fit with…

'Electricity' (Golfetti)

The original demo of the instrumental that became part of 'Kapital' on the album.

'Glastonbury Town' (Allen)

This recording and the next, come from Kavus Torabi's very first jamming session with Daevid Allen, Ian East and Dave Sturt on April 22, 2013, in a London rehearsal studio. This is clearly a work in progress as Allen sings half-thought out lyrics to a gentle descending guitar figure reminiscent of 'Pretty Miss Titty'. It opens with Allen solo as the rest of the band gradually join in, with Kavus playing EBow guitar. It is of historical rather than musical interest, although it does have some very nice melodic lines in it from both Kavus and Dave on bass, ending on some chat from the band.

'Celestial Brigadier' (Allen, Sturt, Torabi)
A spontaneously improvised piece of music, with Allen on gliss and Kavus on guitar and EBow. It's nearly fourteen minutes long but doesn't really go anywhere, not that it was intended to I guess. But, again, it has its moments of melodic beauty and it is clear even from these first tentative steps that there was a meeting of musical minds going on.

'The Paragraph Time Chose To Forget' (East, Sturt, Torabi)
In 2015 Ian, Dave and Kavus formed The Inspiral Trio to play at a tribute gig for Daevid at the inSpiral Lounge in Camden Lock, London. They went on to play totally improvised gigs around the UK, some of which have been captured for posterity and placed on the internet. This is their only commercially-available recording, from a 2016 concert at The Lighthouse in Deal, Kent. It's a gentle, atmospheric number played mostly in G with a bit of a major seventh feel – Kavus plays long, Frippian notes on guitar, Dave reaches both low and high for lovely, fluid bass notes and Ian adds soprano sax. And at 4:25 it's just the right length for this sort of thing!

The Universe Also Collapses (2019)

Personnel:
Ian East: flute, bass clarinet, soprano, tenor and baritone sax
Fabio Golfetti: electric guitar, gliss guitar and singing
Cheb Nettles: drums, piano, theremin and singing
Dave Sturt: bass guitar, synthesiser and singing
Kavus Torabi: singing, electric guitar, acoustic guitar and harmonium
Recorded and mixed by Frank Byng at Snorkel Studios, London
Produced by Gong
Original label: Kscope (Snapper Music)
Released: 2019
Highest chart positions: Uncharted
Running time: 42:04
Current edition: Original issue

Gong had shown there was life after Daevid Allen, but *Rejoice! I'm Dead!* had Dingo Virgin all over it – most of the tracks were about him and his death, and some of the recordings were even developed out of his demos. The reaction from critics and fans was overwhelmingly positive, but the band had to prove it could stand on its own two feet, that it could be new and original while still staying true to Allen's spirit and legacy – and it was prepared for this to be the last album if it didn't work.

The result was this psychedelic tour de force, described in various reviews as 'a truly miraculous rebirth' (echoesanddust.com), 'a genuinely psychedelic record for the 21st century' (*Prog* magazine), 'simply a new Gong, and these are the musicians who are destined to play that music' (The Progressive Aspect) and a five-star rating on Amazon if you remove the complaints about the vinyl pressing!

At the heart of the album is the 20:37 track 'Forever Reoccurring' – the first time a Gong song has taken up the entire side of what used to be an LP. *You* came close in recording terms – as stated before, the entire sequence of 'The Isle Of Everywhere' through to 'You Never Blow Yr Trip Forever' was done in one live take, solos included. But here the band had to craft something that was a single musical entity but still provided enough variety to keep the listener enthralled throughout.

The decision was made very early on while touring *Rejoice! I'm Dead!* that the follow-up would be a 'psychedelic' album. Kavus said: 'All the best music is psychedelic, whether you're talking about Stravinsky or My Bloody Valentine, but in my mind I thought we're not making a fusion album, we're not making a jazz-rock album, we're not making a punk record – we're making a psychedelic album. So we had mapped out the territory in which we wanted the album to exist before we started writing it.'

Dave Sturt told the author: 'This time it was about stamping our own identity on what we were doing without reference necessarily to anything that came before. It was going to be specifically psychedelic, focused on one kind of approach. That was the basic concept of where we were coming from.'

There were no lyrics, to begin with. It was all worked out instrumentally, in a similar fashion to how *Rejoice!* was done – endless hours in the rehearsal studio contributing ideas and riffs to see where they were going and where they fitted. Most of the riff work came from Kavus and the mysterious Cheb who, apart from being a great drummer, is also a very good guitarist.

Gong didn't start off with the idea of creating an epic track that would occupy the whole of what we used to call 'side one'. But as musical themes flooded in from every member of the band, it became clear that many of them seemed to fit together. Dave said to the author: 'We came up with one idea and then another and then another, and they seemed to slot together. The whiteboard became one of the most important tools in the production of the album – every day we would have to photograph it and then write it back up the next day because it was so complicated.'

The mix of talents worked to the band's advantage – Kavus and Cheb were the instantaneous composers, while Dave, Fabio Golfetti and Ian East preferred to listen back, think about it and then return to rehearsals with new ideas. Dave added: 'Often it felt like I was hanging by my fingertips because it kept changing all the time and all the parts are really quite hard to play and really intense.'

It is, indeed, an incredibly complicated album once you delve into it and start deconstructing the various parts that make up the whole. And it's certainly a challenging listen – maybe not for prog heads who were brought up on 'Close To The Edge' and 'Echoes', but for those who love Gong for its whimsical, nursery-rhyme elements *The Universe Also Collapses* requires some concentrated listening. Lyrically, the album is also quite dense – Kavus tends to write impressionist lyrics that create a mood and communicate feelings and ideas rather than story songs or dialogues with Pot Head Pixies.

There's also a 'controversial' final track that split some sections of the fanbase because, to their ears, it sounded too much like a Knifeworld or solo Kavus number and not enough like Gong. In fact, the final line of that song, 'There Is Only Now', was intended to be the album title until a Google search revealed it was a fairly well-used phrase by artists including the Souls Of Mischief.

But, as the quotes above suggest, the album was very well received and, more importantly, the tracks worked live. I recall sitting in the audience of a theatre in Aylesbury when the band, supporting Steve Hillage, decided to open with 'Forever Reoccurring', and feeling the frisson of expectation and excitement that went through the theatre. People couldn't believe they were actually going to do it, and there was a sense that this band we have followed for decades was still making challenging, surprising music…

Kavus said: 'I felt like we were making the record we had to make. We had to really go hard on 'this is our version of Gong' and see if people liked it. When we finished the mix, I knew we had made an album we could be really, really proud of. The album sounds like what us five sound like playing together.'

'Forever Reoccurring' (Gong)
Gong realised fairly early on in the rehearsal process that they were writing one long piece that would take up the whole of 'side one' – and almost entirely in the chord of E. Kavus said: 'It changes key for about 30 seconds then goes back into E, so we knew it was going to be this propulsive thing that just keeps moving forward, it doesn't take any side-steps in the way that 'Rejoice!' does. We wanted this thing to just keep moving forwards and upwards.'

It can be fairly easily divided into various sections, although the joins are organic – it's not an obvious collection of individual songs like the Genesis opus 'Supper's Ready'. During rehearsals and recording, various sections were given names like 'Fishy' or 'Scofey's Gravy' – named because Kavus thought his guitar sounded a bit like John Scofield – but these titles do not appear on the album.

And there's also a cunning mathematical basis to it all – all the timings can be divided into 30 beats, so there are sections in a count of five or six, or ten or even fifteen. Kavus says Ian was very big on checking the maths every time they would write a new bit. But he added to the author: 'I have this phrase since going back to my first proper band – never let them see the graph paper! The minute you are showing people the workings out, that people can hear what you are doing, it's spoiled. If you start hearing the counting, if it feels like we're trying to shoehorn things in, then we've done it wrong. It should be seamless and invisible.'

'Forever Reoccurring' fades gently in, developing a pulsing rhythm played by Kavus on guitar going through a tremolo pedal – it represents the formation of something, probably the universe itself, so it doesn't have too much detail at the beginning, just a feeling of the primordial elements starting to come together. Early ideas in rehearsal to embellish this section were discarded – it has to be almost formless as it builds and builds for about two and a half minutes before the vocals came in.

Fabio's playing glissando, Dave some 'impressionistic' Ebow bass, the drums doing washes and Ian is pulsing along with Kavus. Theremin and keyboards were also overdubbed. The opening line – 'There is only now you know' – mirrors the last line of the entire album, which we'll come to later. The lyrics suggest everything is happening all at once – history, the present, the future, all wrapped up together in a glistening, pulsating ball of nowness. There's a bit of a chorus of sorts, more of a chant really on the lines 'and behind the meaning is another meaning and between the meaning more'. This melody is repeated a few lines further on with 'it's going faster, always going faster, really going faster now' before drums and bass kick everything up a gear.

When the drums come in it's like a release from the tension of the previous four and a half minutes and you start getting more form – the drums are playing in 6/8 against the rhythm of the pulse (with the occasional added

3/4!), creating a pleasing and interesting juxtaposition of rhythms. Dave, meanwhile, is thinking in 4/4 but he said: 'It's not really 4/4, it's a dotted rhythm over the 15. It's best not to think about it after a while and just learn the part, play it and feel it'.

Lyrically, Kavus is singing about opposites – devil and angel, birth and death, the 'fiery explosion of light' from the Big Bang and the initial rapid expansion of the universe but, of course, 'the universe also collapses'. They are all, says Kavus, contained in the same single moment – your death is there as part of you when you are born. While we are experiencing everything in a linear fashion, at the same point as the Big Bang is happening, the universe is also collapsing.

At the 7:23 point comes a riff, featuring that ol' Devil's Interval, played on sax in 15/8 but thought up by Fabio, initially on guitar, to complement a faster, more intricate, jazzy riff created by Kavus that appears slightly later in this section – in fact, the track originally started with Kavus's phrase, written in rehearsals, before everything grew, both backwards and forwards. There's also a solo from Kavus that he dubbed 'The Frenchman' and a vocal section over Fabio's riff but this time played gently on guitar.

So far, we've had about twelve minutes of music all played in one key – Dave's bass occasionally slips into a C, but for the most part, this is E-zy does it. Then at the 12:00 mark, we move briefly into F sharp before descending back into E, doing this a few tantalising times. There's a lovely, rising soprano sax phrase that starts on E flat (which gives the E a major seventh feel, chord fans). There's also an interesting clash of metres here, with some instruments in five, others in six but the entire thing, thanks to Ian's calculator, adding up to 30, which is fast replacing 42 as the number of, well, everything really. Listen also to Cheb's incredible drumming here, inventive, packed with variety but never straying from the rhythm.

Then we go into what I have dubbed the 'chugging' section – a chopping rhythm (still in E) that reprises Ian's sax melody from a bit earlier. The band members all went round a microphone and recorded their feet stomping along with the drums for this. There's a dramatic melody written by Dave but played by Ian and Fabio as a 'canon', in which they each start the tune at different points, so they overlap each other. Fabio then enters with a very Steve Hillage-y guitar solo and we get an actual chord sequence going beneath him, ending up now in A major ...

By 15:43 we know we are seriously entering some sort of build-up to a finale – the riffs have got even faster and the rhythm has doubled up before we enter what is fast becoming a trademark of the new Gong – the psychedelic lull. The lyrics become a bit more personal and reflective – you have come out of your trip and back into yourself, while the Ego dissolves and you are back to you.

Kavus explained to the author: 'It's inspired by wanting to do something that had the same feel as the section between 'Tropical Fish' and 'Selene'. We wanted the same feeling that feels like it's floating before the next bit, just a bit of a breather.'

But we still have The Big Finish to come – another fast riffing section that powers us through to the end of the track, with keyboard swirls over a sequence of chords that are almost like The Universe Also Collapses Variations, written by Cheb. With a final chord, the song disappears into the ether at a phenomenal 20 minutes and 37 seconds.

Kavus said: 'Special mention to Frank Byng, who recorded this track and mixed it. I think he did a lovely job and it's certainly my favourite-sounding recording that we've made.' Dave added to the author: 'It's such a joy to play and it has really come into its own live. When we played it in Aylesbury supporting Steve Hillage we weren't sure it would work as the first number. But every time we did it there was an astonishing response.'

Ian adds, also in discussion with the author:

> When writing 'Forever Reoccurring' the structural threads that underlie the piece magically and instinctively occurred when we were composing/ jamming together, formed possibly due to some kind of collective consciousness that seems to occur between us when together. I tended to check the maths after the event, at the beginning of the process anyway, pretty gobsmacked to discover what was occurring. We sometimes joked when writing *Rejoice!* and *TUAC* that we were just channelling an album that already exists in another dimension, it certainly felt a bit like that.

'If Never I'm And Ever You' (Gong)

From the longest track Gong have ever recorded to one of the shortest, at just 2:27 (although not THE shortest, which must be the six-second 'Parkin Triumphant' on *Shapeshifter*) and the last to be laid down for the album. Inevitably, some sections originally intended for 'Forever Reoccurring' ended up getting the boot but were too damn good to be ignored. So one of them ended up here – the staccato bass and drum pattern that sits under the repetitive guitar notes that open the track. Another riff migrated over from the following track, 'My Sawtooth Wake'. Kavus had the idea of putting them together to make a short song.

Fabio came up with the three notes of A, E and E flat that open the song, played solo on guitar with a delay pedal before bass, drums, sax and Kavus's guitar come in with the staccato, punching riff, mostly on the offbeat, giving the song the feeling that it's teetering on the edge of collapse. The riff goes up, but the verse melody line goes DOWN before the song dives into F for the glorious chorus of 'they were, they were golden'. The lyrics came quickly – Kavus wrote them on a train to Manchester, where he was DJing, and says: 'The lyrics had a real charge to them, against that tune, so you don't question it.' The melody line is mostly Kavus's but Cheb came up with the answering vocals sung by him and Fabio.

After a short sax riff over descending chords, the song ends fairly abruptly. As Kavus said to the author: 'That's how long it turned out. It didn't need to do any more than that. It made its case and f***ed off!'

'My Sawtooth Wake' (Gong)

As stated in the preceding chapter, Kavus Torabi likes to write songs with a nautical theme and, invariably, they result in the boat going down with all hands. He had just read two books about Donald Crowhurst, the British businessman and amateur sailor who disappeared while taking part in the *Sunday Times* Golden Globe round-the-world yacht race in 1969. Out of his depth in more ways than one, both he and his boat, the Teignmouth Electron, were unsuited to the rigours of the race and he soon found himself in last place. Sadly, his growing desperation encouraged him to create an elaborate deception that involved falsifying his position and attempting to cut out a section of the race before heading home as the apparent leader.

Logbooks found in his boat, which was discovered drifting, unmanned, on July 10, show his increasing mental deterioration and have led to theories that he may have committed suicide by deliberately throwing himself into the sea. His family maintain his death could have been an accident – he tended to fall off his boat quite frequently, and a logbook entry suggests he was planning to climb up his mast to the crow's nest.

However he met his demise, the story of Crowhurst has been made into a documentary and two dramatic films, including 2018's *The Mercy* starring Colin Firth. It also provided the inspiration for this track, which doesn't mention Crowhurst by name but certainly depicts one man pitched against the might of the sea and losing – ' wet vicious pitchpooling, Leviathan rolling knockdown, breathing the ocean in and I'm breathing the ocean into myself'.

The song bears some resemblance to an earlier Gong track, 'Fohat Digs Holes In Space' from 1971's *Camembert Electrique* (and also used on the *Continental Circus* soundtrack as 'What Do You Want'). Opening with some brief glissando from Fabio, it quickly settles into a Fohat-style chugging rhythm in E played by Dave, Cheb and Kavus, while Fabio glisses a cycle of chords underneath and Ian adds squealing and screaming jazz sax. Kavus said: 'I think we all came up with this together while jamming – we all acknowledged it had a Fohat vibe, but we thought, what could be more Gong?'

After the lengthy intro, Kavus sings slightly discordant melody lines for the first verse, his voice frequently slipping a semi-tone above and below the root note of the chord, accompanied by some strange, augmented guitar chords, while the rhythm continues in a more subdued fashion beneath him. After that verse, it crashes back into the Fohat rhythm before further vocal sections pop in and out, slightly different to the first but with the same discordant shifts and slides.

There's some magnificent riffs in there as well; all played against the Fohat rhythm which gets louder and more powerful like a roiling sea, while Ian's sax squeals like a panicked seabird. Kavus said: 'Ian is so good on this track – he legitimises it. He could play a Slayer riff and it would sound like Gong. The minute that guy puts the sax in his mouth it's instant Gong.' And Dave adds: 'He's incredibly well-skilled, possibly the best sax player I have ever worked with. He's kind of inspired and plays in the moment.' At one point it almost sounds like a rushing sea sound effect has been added, while the lyrics allow the band to sing 'Down!' in unison, presumably as our ill-fated vessel begins its final plunge to its watery grave.

Towards the end, we reach what Kavus has called 'the choir of the dead sailors'. Our doomed mariner has descended to Davy Jones's locker, where he is greeted by his fellow drowned seadogs. The tune starts with Ian on sax – in fact, it's a slowed-down version of a riff composed by Dave and played towards the end of 'Forever Reoccurring' in a bit of conceptual continuity – before the sailors croon 'spirit bright from the stars, rustling like dead leaves she falls down ... she falls down…' It's Gong meets *Pirates Of The Caribbean.*

Kavus discussed the song with the author: 'It's my favourite tune to play live. I never ever not want to do this song. I remember trying it out in the soundcheck in Japan and it sounded terrible, we hadn't quite got it. But by the time we recorded it and started playing it live it really found its groove' And what, pray is a sawtooth wake? Well, it started as a wave and then turned into the idea of a wake because, of course, this is another Gong song about death.

'The Elemental' (Gong)

The final song on the album turned out to be the most controversial. It certainly divided opinion when it was released as an internet single, with some fans feeling it was more Kavus than Gong. Perhaps that's because it opens with just his voice and solo acoustic guitar chords – strange ones, because that's the way Kavus rolls. The song wasn't necessarily intended for Gong. He recorded the verse and chorus on his phone and named it '60s Vibe' because it had a Kinksy, Beatley feel. But during rehearsals for *The Universe Also Collapses*, Fabio mentioned how nice it would be to have a song-based number for the album after three tracks constructed on heavy riffing. So Kavus played his recording – there were no lyrics, just the songwriter going 'da-da-da-da' – and the rest of the band said great, let's do it.

It is fairly unusual for a Gong song to be based on acoustic guitar – it happens on *Magick Brother* and *Shapeshifter,* but you will find few other examples, especially on the trilogy. It was written in open chords, which made it just that little bit too high for Kavus to sing it comfortably, so he had to tune his acoustic guitar down a tone. This put the song in the key of G major, with the second chord a very unexpected G flat, and it still sounds ever so slightly out of his comfort zone. After the first verse of just Kavus and acoustic guitar, the song explodes into a rising guitar riff that the band came up within rehearsals.

The second verse sees the whole band powering the song along, with added handclaps, before entering the insanely catchy chorus of 'And the elemental spirits take me for their own'. There's a repeat of the big riff before another verse and chorus repeat.

For me, this screams 'XTC', and maybe that's not so surprising as Andy Partridge's clever little band are Kavus's Beatles. It's the way the unorthodox and unpredictable verses explode into a singalong chorus. And, of course, it's that '60s vibe that XTC embraced so joyously in the latter half of their career. There's even a middle eight that sounds like it could have been a song all of its own, another XTC device. Dave says his bassline is channelling his 'inner Colin Moulding'.

But this is a song of two halves – at the 3:14 point, it enters a short section that will be repeated later, a crash of heavy chords with Ian playing jagged sax riffs over the top. We go back into the chorus, followed by a bit of an acoustic guitar-led minor key lull before a drum break from Cheb returns us to the heavy, crashing chords and the final line of the album 'Remember there is only now'. According to Kavus, it's Gong gone glam rock, but Ian's squealing sax takes it into King Crimson territory, with some great lead guitar from Fabio and the massed Gong choir repeating the final line. On the CD version, the song ends suddenly on 'Remember', but on the vinyl the word was repeated in a never-ending loop on the run-out groove. Kavus told the author:

> I'm still not sure if it was the right song for the album. Dave was really into it, [Planet Gong website guru] Jonny Greene thought it was the single. I'm still not sure if we slightly trod over the line of what was Gong and what wasn't. It's the one song I was ambivalent about. I was really anxious about it and still to this day have not looked at a single comment.

The song, however, works as a 'coming down' from the extraordinary sights and sounds presented by the band over the preceding three tracks – and the final line is a summing up of the band's current philosophy. Kavus said: 'It says where Gong is at. This Gong now.'

Unending Ascending (A Pan-Galactic Suite By Gong) (2023)

Personnel:
Ian East: saxophones and woodwinds
Fabio Golfetti: guitar and singing
Cheb Nettles: drums and singing
Dave Sturt: bass guitar and singing
Kavus Torabi: singing and guitar
Saskia Maxwell: singing on 'Ship of Ishtar', 'Lunar Invocation' and 'Asleep Do We Lay'
Frank Byng: cymbal scrapes on 'Choose Your Goddess'
Recorded and mixed by Frank Byng at Snorkel Studios, London
Saskia's vocals recorded by Silas Wynne
Produced by Frank Byng and Gong
Released: 3 November 2023 on Kscope
Highest chart positions: UK Album Sales: 57, UK Rock and Metal Albums: 8
Running time: 40:02

The Universe Also Collapses was Gong's 'space' record – *Unending Ascending* is the band's 'lunar' album. 'The next one will be our 'aquatic' record', Kavus Torabi told *Prog* magazine. 'We see the whole thing as a pan-galactic suite. Sorry if that sounds like mystical bollocks, but this is Gong.' Don't apologise, Kavus. One of the many things we love about Gong is the mystical bollocks.

When I chatted to the band for the first edition of this book, I cheekily suggested a live album was overdue. Lo and behold, it appeared, recorded during Gong's 2019 tour with the Ozric Tentacles before the first Covid lockdown in the UK. *Pulsing Signals* was released to entirely positive reviews and hit number 16 in the UK rock charts, bridging the gap very nicely between the studio albums.

Lockdown affected Gong just as much as every other touring band, forcing them to postpone and sometimes cancel gigs while looking for other creative outlets that could function remotely. They didn't get back on the road until the end of February 2022, but they already had some new musical ideas that began to slip into the set. Aside from the fact that the 20-minute monster from *The Universe…*, 'Forever Reoccurring', had been promoted to pride of place as the set opener, there appeared a brand-new track with the very Gongish title 'My Guitar Is A Spaceship'. Kavus explained:

> We'd already planned the kind of album we wanted with *The Universe Also Collapses* – we didn't know precisely what we would write, but we did know we wanted a long, substantive piece. With this one, we said we would do shorter pieces – well, short by our standards! Although we didn't necessarily have the tunes, we said, let that be the blueprint. The

> one track that really set this record up was 'My Guitar Is A Spaceship' – when we wrote that, we said, 'F*** me, that's it, that's what the album has to live up to.'

Composed in March 2022, the band imagined what it would be like to debut the track at that year's Glastonbury Festival. If only they were asked to play! Can you imagine?! Two days later, the text invitation came ... Kavus said 'Man, we made that happen with this song!'

Another big influence on the album came from someone who had died in 1971, the year Kavus was born. Virgil Finlay was an American artist who specialised in illustrating pulp fantasy, science-fiction and horror stories for magazines and books. Working in stark black and white, his art managed to be both futuristic and vintage, harking back to the 1920s. Kavus had come across his work and given some of the illustrations to the band's 'photon sculptor', Jasper Johns, to project on screens during the band's gigs. Finlay's monochrome visions helped set the 'pulpy' tone and direction of the album – where *The Universe...* was mathematical and precise, *Unending Ascending* would be a fun trip, an edition of *Amazing Stories* magazine set to music. In fact, some of his illustrations were used as inspiration for the promotion of two singles from the album, 'Tiny Galaxies' and 'All Clocks Reset'.

The other big difference about this album compared to the previous two is that much of it was road-tested before it was recorded, with the exception of 'All Clocks Reset', 'Ship Of Ishtar' and 'Choose Your Goddess'. By September 2022, when Gong embarked on a European tour, the set included many of the songs that would become *Unending Ascending*. Indeed, 'Lunar Invocation' took shape during the concerts, starting life as a drone transition between 'My Guitar Is A Spaceship' and 'Requiem For A Dying Sun', an early title for what became 'O, Arcturus'. The band eventually found the confidence to drop all the 'classic tracks' from the Daevid Allen era to create a performance based solely on the most recent three albums.

For the recording sessions, Gong went back to Snorkel Studios, where they were reunited with Frank Byng, who had produced *The Universe...* and the live album. By now, the band had complete faith in Byng's ability to bring out the best in their performance – also, after nine years and three albums together, this was the most stable lineup in the band's history. Kavus told me:

> It was the most enjoyable album to make. A lot of the decisions as to how the songs should go were agreed by us before we even recorded them because we played a lot of the stuff live and because there were no unknowns. We know how much we enjoy working with Frank; we know how he works and the speed at which he works. He's very considered, very measured – we know he can deliver beautiful results because he is totally committed.

Once again, drummer Cheb Nettles was instrumental (pun intended) in working out several of the arrangements, as well as coming up with many of the riffs that formed the bedrock of the songs, while Ian East plays some of the best saxophone I've ever heard from him. *Unending Ascending* also features the first female vocalist on a Gong album since Gilli Smyth's space whisper was sprinkled over *I See You* in 2014. The band met singer, musician and dancer Saskia Maxwell while touring with the Ozric Tentacles – her partner is Ozrics keyboardist Silas Wynne – and she whirled dervishly on stage to 'Master Builder' and 'Insert Yr Own Prophecy'. There was even talk of Saskia becoming a member of Gong – so by the time you read this, the band may be a six-piece!

With striking artwork by Steve Mitchell of fiftysevendesign, the album was hailed as Gong's most 'classic' sounding release since the 1970s. Melodic, playful and upbeat, with all the tracks segueing into each to create a single suite of music (albeit with a gap in the middle where, back in the mists of time, one would turn the record over), *Unending Ascending*'s combination of jazzy space-rock in tricky-dicky time signatures was compared to *Angel Egg* 50 years earlier. Reviewers hailed the album as 'playful and exploratory, enraptured by the possibilities of the invisible worlds' (*Prog magazine),* 'a marvellous continuation and evolution of their work' (*Distorted Sound*) and 'full of fun and energy' (*Allmusic*). The album was even reviewed in the *Financial Times*, which described it as 'prime psych-rock'. Whatever they are smoking in the FT newsroom, it's doing them some good!

True, there are no Pothead Pixies or Zero the Hero – the new lineup has been careful to avoid plundering Daevid Allen's mischievous mythology – but the combination of crisp guitar riffs, jazzy spontaneity, shimmering glissando, powerful rhythmic precision and quite literally out-of-this-world lyrics makes this album sound fresh and exciting while still being quintessentially Gong. It may also have helped that this is the shortest studio album Gong have released since the vinyl days – and, sometimes, less can be more.

As for the future of Gong, it is in very good hands indeed, with the band already thinking about album number four with the current lineup. Last words from Kavus:

> When we are doing the band, and there's eight of us together, including the crew, we're living Gong really. We are what Gong has always been: an anarcho-collective where there is no one point of view – the division of labour within the band is pretty equally split. We have our team of 'spiritual warriors' – we have Frank, who we love making records with, and Steve, who has done the best artwork he's done for us. We want to keep making these albums with this team; it seems to work. We're very happy with the way everything has gone with this record: the sound, the songs, the artwork, the response and the support from the record label, which has been brilliant, so we're already talking about the next album.

'Tiny Galaxies' (Music by Gong, lyrics by Kavus Torabi)
We open with gentle, shimmering guitar arpeggios as we are invited to 'pick the telescope up, you'll see infinity' before explosive chords herald soaring harmony vocals – a speciality of this incarnation of Gong (every member of the band can sing, apart from Ian, who is busy blowing sax and flute). Fabio came up with the verse and Kavus came up with the middle bit, originally used as the chord sequence of 'O, Arcturus'. There is a big Syd Barrett influence here in the apparent musical simplicity, with Cheb playing muffled beats on his tom-toms like early Nick Mason, followed by a sequence of random-sounding power chords. Kavus said:

> It does sound very Syd, but you know what? Daevid was a huge Syd fan and developed his glissando technique after seeing Barrett do it with a Zippo lighter. Does it sound a bit like Floyd? So what! Let's make some psychedelic pop. And I love playing it and singing it.

'Tiny Galaxies' segues in E major into…

'My Guitar Is A Spaceship' (Music by Gong, lyrics by Kavus Torabi)
Possibly the best Gong anthem since 'You Can't Kill Me'. I compare the two not musically but in aggression and attitude – both of them leave you wanting to jump up and down, punching the air. In fact, they couldn't be more musically different. Where 'You Can't Kill Me' shifts through several different chord sequences, mostly in 4/4, 'My Guitar Is A Spaceship' consists of the same riff in 9/8 played non-stop all the way through. Ian gets a frantic but perfectly played sax solo first, followed by Fabio on glissando guitar. Towards the end, Ian is playing a twisty, descending sax riff over the rising guitar figure, the whole thing colliding together like a rocket soaring into space. There are just five lines of lyrics, sung twice, but they are a joy for any fan of this band and give the album its title – 'Unending, ascending, sending love from Planet Gong'.

'My Guitar…' wasn't the first track to be written for the album – the band had already come up with parts of 'All Clocks Reset' and early tries at what became 'Choose Your Goddess'. However, as Kavus points out earlier, it was the track that set the blueprint for the album and pointed it in the right direction. It began with a drum pattern from Cheb Nettles. Kavus then played a 'Taxman'-like riff over the top, and 20 minutes later, they had the whole tune together. Kavus said, 'It just burst into our ears!' This became the band's opener for their 2023/2024 joint tour with the Ozrics, and it's hard to imagine a Gong gig in which this wouldn't be played. At the end of 'My Guitar…', rhythmic percussion carries on into the following track.

'Ship Of Ishtar' (Music by Gong, lyrics by Kavus Torabi)
The band knew this was to be their lunar album and Ishtar is the lunar goddess (she is also known as Inanna, the Mesopotamian goddess of love,

war, fertility, beauty, sex, divine law and political power, which must keep her pretty busy in the office). The name was also used by US fantasy author Abraham Merritt for his book *The Ship Of Ishtar*, originally illustrated by the aforementioned Virgil Finlay. You see, it's all connected.

The band wanted a contemplative drone piece to break up the noisier songs on the album – the melody hit Kavus as he was going for a walk. He said: 'I had to run back home to start it!' He recorded the vocal melody and put on a bunch of instruments he had at home, including a harmonium, and at that stage, it was quite formless. Then, he passed it on to the rest of the band.

The centrepiece is Dave's e-bow bass, doubled up on two tracks. Cheb put on some lovely cymbal swirls and bells, Fabio injected his glissando guitar, Ian added his gentle mystic flute and then it was given to Frank Byng to sort out. Frank spent a week going through it and tweaking it right through to the very end. Kavus said: 'When I heard the first mix that Frank had done, I cried. It was absolutely so beautiful, I thought, f***ing hell, we've done it! We've now opened another portal of stuff we can do.' Dave added, 'I think it's great where it appears on the album after the poppy excitement of the first two tracks. You suddenly fall into another world.'

In A. Merritt's book, the Ship of Ishtar is a sailing vessel crossing an eternal sea. And so it is in Gong's song, but more of a spaceship sailing serenely through the universe. Kavus's sinuous, melodic chant over an A chord that slips and slides between a major seventh and a sixth channels mysterious eastern scales as he sings in praise of the ship 'onward, guided by Venus' (Venus being Ishtar's planet, you see). The ship carries a 'sacred cargo', a 'hold of many worlds under your sails'. The music swells and builds in intensity until Kavus sings 'Aboard! Aboard now!', and the ship disappears gently into the night with Saskia whispering in our ears. The longest track on the album, it is 8:34 of the most sublime, transcendent Gongness.

'O, Arcturus' (Music by Gong, lyrics by Kavus Torabi)

One of the early songs that was thoroughly road-tested live, it was originally known as 'Requiem For A Dying Sun', and it is indeed a song about a dying star. Arcturus is the brightest star in the northern constellation of Bootes – known to us laypeople as The Herdsman, visible in the northern hemisphere. At 7.1 billion years old, it has used up its core hydrogen and expanded to 25 times the size of our own sun. It is now what is known as a red giant, just one step away from its final evolutionary end.

However, this is not music to die to. Instead, Gong craft a perky, medium-paced pop song introduced by Cheb's bright drums, offering melodic harmonies that follow evenly-paced chord changes. There's a great Kavus lead guitar break in the middle before the harmonies build into something almost triumphant and glorious – perhaps mirroring the star's expansion as it heads towards its fiery demise. It ends with a slow, circular riff in what sounds like 10/8, melting into glissando chords.

There are both musical and lyrical references to other songs on the album. Some of the chord patterns here mirror part of the loud section of 'Tiny Galaxies', particularly the D-B-F-A-Ab-E sequence. There's a lyrical nod to the aforementioned 'Ship Of Ishtar', plus a humorous reference to the telescope the listener was invited to pick up in the opening track. 'Which end did you put your eye?' asks Kavus.

It's something Gong have always delighted in doing – what Frank Zappa referred to as 'conceptual continuity', subtly reprising lyrical and musical elements throughout the album (or, in Zappa's case, unsubtly doing it throughout his entire career). It helps to make the album feel cohesive and interconnected and creates the idea of a complete artwork that should be enjoyed in its entirety.

'All Clocks Reset' (Music by Gong, lyrics by Kavus Torabi)

No segue this time – there's a gap between tracks four and five just like you would have on a vinyl record. In fact, it appeared the segueing was one of the most difficult things to get right during production, harder than it would have been in the old pre-digital days. Dave told me, 'We didn't know how to deal with it when people would be streaming individual tracks; even if you try to listen to the album on certain platforms, they put an automatic gap between them. It might persuade more people to buy the physical product – that's the only way you are going to hear it properly.' The album was released in both CD and LP formats, so there was plenty of physical product available.

'All Clocks Reset' was an early track that started life about six months before the main rehearsals, without Fabio, who was in Brazil. Here are some mystical bollocks from Kavus:

> It's like getting to a moment of pure ecstasy, the peak point of the psychedelic experience at which the physical body falls away, time falls away, everything falls away, and you are at one with the singularity and the eternal, just the ultimate psychedelic moment. It's like the moment of death, returning to everything, leaving your physical body, your thoughts, your ego, leaving the constraints of time and space and having this moment of pure ecstasy while wrapped up in a very knotty XTC-inspired pop song.

Phew! If that hasn't blown your mind, then you probably don't have one.

It opens with what is known as a 'hocket' – alternating notes shared between two or more instruments. In this case, it's a three-way duel between Kavus and Fabio's guitars and Ian's saxophone. The band did it before on 'Rejoice!', the title track of their first album without Daevid Allen, and the technique was also used by Robert Fripp and Adrian Belew during the 1980s incarnation of King Crimson.

The opening hocket rises up, reaches a plateau, drops down a bit, then repeats before a major seventh introduces the first line of the first verse,

'Unending, ascending do we rise'. Hey, that's the album title again. Conceptual continuity, folks! The XTC feeling comes in the relentlessly bright and breezy playing, plus the unexpected chord changes and middle eights that sound like songs all of their own. For me, there are also elements here of the chorus to 'I Never Glid Before'. Perhaps that's why fans thought the track harked back to the *Angel Egg* era when 'All Clocks Reset' dropped as a single. This came as a surprise to the band, who feared the song was too unlike Gong. For Dave Sturt, this reminds him of Gentle Giant and the way in which their many, many instruments link together like cogs in a big musical machine.

'Choose Your Goddess' (Music by Gong, lyrics by Kavus Torabi)
A title that sounds so 70s Gong that it ought to have Gilli Smyth space whispering on it. In fact, this song stole its name from the following track, 'Lunar Invocations', which does indeed invite the listener to select from a multiple-choice list of goddesses. Cheb came up with a powerful, muscular riff in something like 10/4 that's so Led Zeppelin that one expects Robert Plant to bound into the room with his shirt unbuttoned. Think 'Immigrant Song' from *Led Zeppelin III*. The band played around with it at the first writing session, then got back together again when Fabio was over from Brazil six months later. Kavus said:

> We have recordings of us just jamming that riff for five minutes, just dipping down then building it up, and we thought as long as this riff is at the centre, then we've got something. But it was the last one to come together – we had just five days to get it finished for the album, so it was pretty stressful.

From the Led Zep riff, the song moves into a 'Fohat' moment, with glissando guitar over a pounding rhythm, Ian coming in and out with celestial sax phrases. Kavus croons a gentle paeon to the 'ruler of the sky … goddess of the tides, queen of desire'. As the music builds in intensity and volume, we eventually plunge back into the mayhem of the riff, Cheb's drums crashing like a lightning storm on the planet Venus and Ian's sax crying like a Valkyrie.

There are some more vocals over a lighter, major-key section with a melody that is reprised by the sax, punctuated by brief returns to the riff. Eventually, the new band's essential musical trademark – glorious harmony vocals from Kavus, Dave, Fabio and Cheb – brings the song to a close with a final, whimsical solo sax motif that is oh so Bloomdido Bad de Grasse!

'Choose Your Goddess' is undoubtedly one of the most complicated songs that the new lineup has attempted, full of strange time signatures, dramatic dynamic contrasts and a riff so powerful that it could topple civilisations. For Dave, 'Choose Your Goddess' is a 'f***er' to play! For Cheb … well, he's a drumming powerhouse, and he propels this song along as if he's channelling Animal from The Muppets. If the man wasn't so damn mysterious, he'd win awards for this one.

'Lunar Invocation' (Music by Gong, lyrics by Kavus Torabi)
After the musical maelstrom that is 'Choose Your Goddess', we really need to take a bit of time to catch our breath and to think about everything that has come before. We need a beautiful drone piece, and this is it. As I mentioned above, it took shape on the road as a moment of respite between 'My Guitar Is A Spaceship' and 'O, Arcturus'. As the tour went on, the moment expanded into a standalone track that reached its final form on stage. Kavus said: 'We'd never really done anything like that where it was just this swell of sound, and we got such a vibe off the audience that, each night, it was expanding. I don't think we could have come up with that in rehearsal.' Initially titled 'Choose Your Goddess', the chanting lyrics do indeed offer a list of ancient deities – Lucina, Europa, Artemis, Diana, Isis, Phoebe and, of course, Ishtar. In the liner notes on the CD and LP, the list is presented with little boxes that you could indeed tick if you wished to deface the artwork. Another reason to buy the physical product.

'Asleep Do We Lay' (Music by Gong, lyrics by Kavus Torabi)
The drone melts into gentle, atmospheric drums by Cheb and watery flute from Ian. There is some flute and percussion interplay that harks back to 'Thought For Naught' from *You* and subtle vocal contributions from Saskia that recall Gilli's space whisper. After the key-shifting, shape-churning acrobatics of previous tracks, 'Asleep…' stays in F# throughout (although ethereal guitar chords move about a bit). This is a suitably low-key ending to the album – we have travelled the cosmos, we have paid our respects to the Moon and we are now relaxing, probably sipping a Pan-Galactic Gargle-Blaster. Said Kavus:

> The last song on the album is a really important one. You can either do the big epic here or sometimes you want to end with something really short. Each position on an album has a weight to it. 'Asleep Do We Lay' is setting up the next album, which is going to be aqua. We've got the galaxy, the Moon and then water, although these themes occur in all of them. That's going to be the third part of our trilogy.
>
> The image in mind was being sat on a beach at about six in the evening, feeling the waves coming in, looking at the mermaids flipping in and out of the water. We wanted it to be really sensual, erotic and sexy but also strange, other-worldly and dreamlike.

This is one of the earliest songs to be worked on and features Dave on upright bass – the bassline actually came together quite late in the recording process and displays a certain Talk Talk influence. As 'Asleep Do We Lay' fades away, we are left with one foot in the past and one in the future (which is always Gong's fate, whatever the lineup).

Gong: Live Etc

There are live Gong albums covering pretty much every incarnation of the band and, while most of them draw from the classic trilogy, they still have plenty to offer thanks to changing lineups and the fact that, during any given concert, at least one member is doing something completely amazing. This round-up concentrates on officially-released albums that are available at the time of writing – your first point of call should be the Planet Gong website, wherein you will find many of these treasures.

So, moving chronologically, let's start with *Glastonbury Fayre '71* (GAS ARC CD001), a digitally-remastered mini-album containing Gong's contribution to the early incarnation of the Glastonbury festival. It contains tracks that never made it on to any studio albums, including 'It's Only The World Said The Girl', the 'Fun Gods' medley and 'Divine Mother'. The current CD packaging credits Laurie Allan on drums, despite the fact he didn't join until later in the year and Pip Pyle drummed at Glastonbury. In fact, they are both on the album because some of the recordings come from a concert in Nanterre the following year.

There is further confusion to be had with a live release from French label LMLR. *Live In Lyon* is supposed to be from an 'iconic' concert on 14 December 1972, but the ever-helpful Discogs will tell you that Gong played elsewhere on that day, and the recording actually dates to 17 or 19 January 1973. It contains rare outings for 'Dreaming It', 'I Feel So Lazy' and the Soft Machine track 'Why Are We Sleeping'. The quality is a bit ropey as it's a straight copy of an earlier GAS tape, but it's fascinating, nonetheless.

In 2019 a beautiful box set called *Love From The Planet Gong* (UMC) was released containing the classic trilogy albums and *Shamal*, plus associated live recordings from the period. So you get what seems to be the complete recording of the *Angels Egg* and *You* band at The Bataclan in Paris in May 1973, including a fascinating early version of 'Oily Way'; the Club Arc En Ciel in Roanne in August the same year, containing a rare live rendition of 'Ooby-Scooby Doomsday'; the Hyde Park concert in June 1974, shortly after the band completed *You*; and a composite set created out of two nights at London's Marquee Club in September 1975, post-Daevid but with Steve Hillage and Miquette Giraudy and the rest of the band playing tracks from *Fish Rising* and *Shamal*.

There is also a CD of BBC Radio 1 sessions from 1973 and 1974 – the latter including rare appearances by Ron Tait on drums and Diane Bond replacing Gilli. Those tracks also appear on *Pre-Modernist Wireless: The Peel Sessions* (Strange Fruit, 1997), which breaks my own rules by being out of pressing at the time of writing but is worth seeking out because it also features a rare live-in-the-studio version of 'Magick Brother' and three tracks with Kevin Ayers as part of the band.

If you don't fancy splashing out three figures on the box set (although you could spend your money on worse things) the four studio albums were also released as double CDs containing extracts from Bataclan, Roanne, Hyde Park and The Marquee Club.

Another 1974 gig, recorded at La Salle Elsa Triolet in Longlaville, France, has been rescued from the archives by Madfish and is available in both CD and LP formats with an A2 poster.

A further concert from 1975 – in fact, Hillage's last before quitting Gong for a successful solo career – is available on *Live In Sherwood Forest '75* (Mlp).

In 1977 Virgin released *Live Etc* featuring tracks from 1973 to 1975 – most come from the concerts mentioned above. It was re-released on CD in 2015. *Gong Est Mort – Vive Gong* (Belle Antique JPN [CD], Tiger Bay [VINYL]), the 1977 reunion concert in France, can still be found at not too silly prices, as can the *25th Birthday Party* (Voiceprint), recorded live at the London Forum in 1994 with Steffe Sharpstrings and Shyamal Maitra replacing Hillage and Pierre Moerlen.

The 1990 concert recorded for Central TV with Steffe on guitar, Paul Noble on keyboards and Pip back on drums is available as a CD/DVD set called *Access All Areas* (Edsel). Fast-forward to 2000 and *Live 2 Infinitea* (Snapper) captures the *Zero To Infinity* lineup on its Spring tour – at one stage the two albums were bundled together as one package called *From Here To Eternitea* (Recall), but my investigations suggest buying the two albums separately may be easier on your wallet. A DVD is also available from the same tour called *High Above The Subterranea Club* (Snapper).

The Planet Gong website has very reasonably-priced copies of *Gong Global Family – Live in Brazil* (Voiceprint, 2009), recorded on 10 November 1997 and featuring Daevid Allen and Josh Pollock in Sao Paulo with members of the Brazilian IOCT. It draws from the early albums and includes a well-shot DVD.

Finally, we have a live album of the current Gong lineup. *Pulsing Signals* (Kscope) was recorded in 2019 on the tour to promote *The Universe Also Collapses* (or do albums now promote the tours? Discuss). It features all but one of the tracks from that album, along with selections from *Rejoice! I'm Dead!* and two Gong classics, a punky version of 'You Can't Kill Me' and a roof-raising 'Master Builder'. It illustrates what a powerful and exciting live lineup this is.

When it comes to compilations, I'm going to assume true Gong lovers possess all the studio albums – at the very least you should have the classic trilogy, from which most straightforward round-ups draw their material. But there are still a few collections that deserve to be mentioned. First off, I recommend *Je Ne Fum' Pas De Bananes* (Gonzo), a collection of demos by Daevid Allen and the Banana Moon Band but containing original versions of Gong single 'Est-ce-que Je Suis (Garcon Ou Fille)' and 'Hyp Hypnotise You'. There are alternate versions of those tracks, plus a wealth of other unreleased Gong treasures, on *Camembert Eclectique* (GAS CD 001), which contains rehearsals and demos from Gong in 1970.

Another compilation that also delves back into the roots of the band is *Histories And Mysteries Of Planet Gong* (Voiceprint VP279CD) that offers rare live and radio recordings from 1971 and 1972, as well as solo Allen and Mother Gong tracks. Here you will find 'Dreaming It', a rare live Gong track from 1970, plus 'Clarence In Wonderland' from 1971 with Kevin Ayers. *Gong In The 70s* (Voiceprint) is an interesting collection of live tracks and out-takes, put together as a benefit album for Tim Blake. It includes a stonking live version of 'Where Have All The Flowers Gone?', an abortive single. *Family Jewels* (GAS CD008) has some live Gong tracks from 1997 with Steffe on guitar.

Between 2004 and 2006 Daevid Allen released a series of rare recordings on his own Bananamoon Obscura label through Voiceprint. Most of them do not concern us here, but I would point you in the direction of volume 16, *Gong On Acid 73*, featuring a tape collage of out-takes recorded during the *Angels Egg* sessions.

Just to tidy up any loose ends, the three post-trilogy albums were sampled on *Wingful Of Eyes (A Retrospective '75-'78)* (1986, Virgin) and *Time Is The Key*, *Live* and *Leave It Open* were packaged together as a 2CD set entitled *Arista Years* (2008, Arista), inaccurately credited to Gong.

Pierre Moerlen's Gong

Downwind (1979, Arista)

Personnel: Pierre Moerlen drums, Hammond organ, Yamaha piano, lead vocal, Oberheim polyphonic synthesiser, vibraphone, xylo-marimba, concert toms, timpani, glockenspiel, assorted percussion, Korg synthesisers, cowbell, timbales. Benoit Moerlen vibraphone. Hansford Rowe bass, vocal. Francois Causse xylo-marimba, congas. Ross Record guitar, back-up vocals.
Additional personnel: Didier Lockwood violin on 2,6&7. Mike Oldfield guitar, bass, Irish drum on 3. Steve Winwood Mini Moog, Korg synthesisers on 3. Didier Malherbe sax on 3. Terry Oldfield flute on 3. Mick Taylor lead guitar on 5.

Tracks: 1. 'Aeroplane' (Moerlen, O'Lochlainn) 2. 'Crosscurrents' (Moerlen) 3. 'Downwind' (Moerlen) 4. 'Jin-Go-Lo-Ba' (M. Olatunji) 5. 'What You Know' (Moerlen, O'Lochlainn) 6. 'Emotions' (Moerlen) 7. 'Xtasea' (Moerlen)

AFTER releasing *Expresso II* in 1978, the band that still called itself Gong changed its name and record label. It became Pierre Moerlen's Gong, or PMG, as it had been really since *Gazeuse!*, and a new deal was signed with Arista (Pierre's record company friend had moved there from Virgin). Bon Lozaga joined officially but soon quit, replaced by young American guitarist Ross Record from the Pat Travers band, and Mireille Bauer left to join French jazz fusion group Editions Speciale.

PMG recorded most of the tunes at Matrix Studios, London, in August 1978 but the centrepiece of the album, the title track, was laid down earlier in June while Pierre was working on Mike Oldfield's album *Incantations*. It certainly sounds like a collision between Moerlen and Oldfield, with the former's interlocking tuned percussion providing the backbone of the tune and the latter's unmistakable lead guitar swirling around over the top.

Mike's brother Terry plays high-pitched flute that's almost an Irish tin whistle while Didier returns with some saxophone flourishes towards the end. Oldfield also plays bass from the concert tom solo to the end of the middle section, with Hansford Rowe providing the low notes at the front and end, where it gets a bit funky.

Elsewhere, we see the return of vocals to a Moerlen Gong album with the rather pedestrian AOR rock of 'Aeroplane' and 'What You Know', sung by PM himself with assistance from Hansford Rowe. The latter features ex-Rolling Stone Mick Taylor on guitar – Moerlen had recently drummed on his first solo album. 'Jin-Go-Lo-Ba' is a 1959 song by Nigerian percussionist Babatunde Olatunji that has been covered by several artists, most notably Santana on their 1969 debut album. 'Crosscurrents' mines the same seam as 'Downwind' of blended percussion instruments in tricky time signatures, although it features the inspired jazz violin of former Magma member Didier Lockwood. His work is particularly impressive on the slower, more reflective final two tracks, 'Emotions' and 'Xtasea'.

Time Is The Key (1979, Arista)
Personnel: Pierre Moerlen vibraphone, electric vibe, marimba, glockenspiel, timpani, darbourka, drums, gongs, string synthesiser. Hansford Rowe bass. Bon Lozaga guitar. Additional personnel: Darryl Way violin on 1. Joe Kirby acoustic bass on 1&2. Peter Lemer keyboards on 2-11. Nico Ramsden rhythm guitar, lead guitar on 8. Allan Holdsworth lead guitar on 9-11.

Tracks: 1. 'Ard Na Greine' (Moerlen) 2. 'Earthrise' (Moerlen) 3. 'Supermarket' (Moerlen) 4. 'Faerie Steps' (Moerlen) 5. 'An American In England' (Rowe) 6. 'The Organ Grinder' (Moerlen) 7. 'Sugar Street' (Moerlen) 8. 'The Bender' (Moerlen) 9. 'Arabesque Intro' & 'Arabesque' (Moerlen) 10. 'Esnuria Two' (Moerlen) 11. 'Time Is The Key' (Moerlen).

By the end of 1978, Didier Lockwood had both joined and then left PMG, along with Ross Record, who suffered from severe stage fright. Brother Benoit also quit the following year, but Bon Lozaga came back, playing on a European tour that would provide most of the recordings for *Live* (1980, Arista). In June Pierre holidayed in Ireland with his wife and son, where he composed most of the material for *Time Is The Key*. He said in an interview with *Big Bang* magazine in 1985: 'We stayed in Skull, on the south coast of Ireland, near a small village on the edge of a beautiful bay, 300 metres from the house of the father of Rick Laird, the bassist of Mahavishnu Orchestra ... Far from cities, noise, neurosis ... I could live in such a place, isolated in the middle of nature .. We spent eight unforgettable weeks, and that's where I composed *Time Is The Key*.' The core trio of PM, Bon and Hansford Rowe then went into Konk Studios in London, in August. They were helped out by former Gong guitarist Allan Holdsworth; former Curved Air violinist Darryl Way; and Peter Lemer, Nico Ramsden and Joe Kirby from Mike Oldfield's touring band.

The result is an album that could be renamed Timing Is The Key, as most of the tracks are created using various tuned percussion instruments that interlock in intricate and tightly-controlled ways. The first four make up something like a mini-symphony – they segue into each other, building up the instrumentation as they go along, starting with a glockenspiel playing two repetitive notes on 'Ard Na Greine' and finishing with drums, bass, keyboards and assorted percussion on 'Faerie Steps'.

'An American In England' is a Hansford Rowe composition in a mixture of time signatures (but mostly 6/8) in which Rowe plays lead bass over drums and repetitive acoustic guitar figures. 'The Organ Grinder' is a funky little number with slap bass and Peter and Bon taking the melody. Tracks 7-10 segue into each other again as another mini-symphony. 'Sugar Street' and 'The Bender' are slower-paced and swampier – the former relies heavily on Rowe's funky bass, while Bon stretches out on the latter. 'Arabesque' sees the first appearance of Holdsworth over a sinuous 'belly-dancing' melody played on keyboards – his signature guitar sound of lightning-fast phrases dances around for an entertaining five minutes, seemingly taking absolutely no notice of what is going on around him.

Like 'Esnuria' on *Gazeuse!*, 'Esnuria Two' again features Allan Holdsworth, although pride of place is given to Peter Lemer on keyboards, who holds this rocking track together and provides an excellent jazz fusion solo. Holdsworth comes in around the halfway mark with some suitably bewildering guitar runs that sound like he's using his SynthAxe. After three and a half minutes the track suddenly pauses and goes into a more contemplative section based on Moerlen's vibraphone.

Finally, the title track once again shows Lemer off with some slightly funky keyboard chords and a violin-like solo. Holdsworth is apparently on there somewhere but, if so, he is criminally under-used.

Leave It Open (1981, Arista)

Personnel: Pierre Moerlen drums, vibraphone, synthesiser, rhythm guitar, keyboards, gongs. Hansford Rowe bass, rhythm guitar, vocals. Bon Lozaga guitar. Francois Causse congas, timbales, percussion.
Additional personnel: Demelza Val Baker congas on 1. Charlie Mariano sax on 1,3&4. Brian Holloway rhythm guitar on 2.

Tracks: 1. 'Leave It Open' (Moerlen) 2. 'How Much Better It Has Become' (Moerlen) 3.' I Woke Up That Morning Felt Like Playing Guitar' (Moerlen) 4. 'It's About Time' (Rowe) 5. 'Stok Stok Stok Sto-gak' (Rowe) 6. 'Adrien' (Moerlen)

The core PMG lineup of Moerlen, Rowe, Lozaga and Causse toured to promote *Time Is The Key* with Steely Dan keyboardist Jeff Young in late 1979 before entering Stars And Stripes studio in London in early 1980 to record *Leave It Open*. Once again, the majority of the tracks were written by Moerlen with a couple of contributions from Rowe. Young had quit before the sessions, so the band called in veteran US jazz saxophonist Charlie Mariano, who had played with Stan Kenton and Charles Mingus, as well as having a solo career that stretched from 1956 to 2003. Also joining the sessions were Australian guitarist Brian Holloway and British percussionist Demelza Val Baker.

Dominating the album is the 17-minute title track, very much in the same vein as the first four tunes on *Time Is The Key*, with increasing amounts of repetitive, interlocking tuned percussion. Mariano provides bursts of improvised sax, Rowe an expressive, powerful bass sound and there's some impressive soloing from Lozaga. The track follows a fairly predictable pattern of alternating solos and quiet passages, and the whole thing manages to stay in pretty much the same chord most of the way through, fading out on Moerlen's drumming and Causse's congas. The playing is, as usual, exemplary but the composition is a little too drawn out and lacking in variety for me.

'How Much Better It Has Become' has a bit more pace and urgency about it – the vibraphone and marimba kick off proceedings again but it powers along with Lozaga's guitar chords and Rowe's pounding bass. Moerlen's percussion here is particularly wild and unrestrained.

Unusually for a Moerlen song, 'I Woke Up That Morning Felt Like Playing Guitar' opens with, um, guitar – nice open, strumming chords from Pierre overlaid with Lozaga's lead and Mariano's sax. Rowe's 'It's About Time' is a funky little number in 6/8 which his busy bass is matched by frantic percussion from Pierre and guitar chords from Lozaga. After about two minutes the track stops, there's the creak of an opening door and a voice speaks the title of the track. Sounds like Francoise has just entered because there are now some congas. A minute later Mariano's bursts in with some enthusiastic sax. It's the jazziest track on the album and doesn't really sound like PMG at all.

Another Rowe composition, 'Stok Stok Stok Sto-Gak' again eschews tuned percussion for a more standard rock format, propelled by a lurching, rising bass and adorned with sparkling guitar work from Lozaga. Finally, 'Adrien' is a gentle, quintessential PMG tune led by Pierre's tuned percussion with added baby noises – it's dedicated to his newborn son who later became a musician in his own right.

Leave It Open marked another end of an era for PMG. Rowe said to Anil Prasad in 2017: 'I think it was probably a natural conclusion. Arista dropped us. We did the *Leave it Open* album, which was the final record on the contract. We recorded it pretty much ourselves. It sounds okay to me, but it wasn't of the audiophile quality of the earlier records. I love the music. It was our final statement together. Francois plays a lot of drums on it. Pierre also played a lot of keyboards and vibes on it, which gave it a special flavour. There were no further record deals to be had. It was the end of 1980 and the labels were doing a lot of house cleaning and we were part of that.'

Breakthrough (1986, Arc Music)

Personnel: Pierre Moerlen (drums, vibraphone, timpani, gong, synthesiser, vocals, xylophone. Hansford Rowe bass. Lena Andersson: vocals. Nina Andersson sax, vocals. Christer Rhedin Moog solos. Dag Westling acoustic guitar. Michael Zylka Chapman stick. Ake Zeiden guitar.

Tracks: 1. 'Breakthrough' (Moerlen) 2. 'Spaceship Disco' (Moerlen) 3. 'Rock In Seven' (Moerlen) 4. 'Sic 8' (Moerlen) 5. 'Poitou' (Moerlen) 6. 'Children's Dream' (Moerlen) 7. 'Portrait' (Moerlen, Kopf) 8. 'Road Out' (Moerlen, L. Ron Hubbard) 9. 'Romantic Punk' (Moerlen) 10. 'Far East' (Moerlen)

Leave It Open was the last PMG album on the Arista label. From this point on, Pierre's declining financial position forced him to take other, more lucrative, jobs, so he spent 1981 to 1983 working with Magma and Mike Oldfield. He told *Big Bang* magazine in 1985: 'I saw everything crumble around me. It was obviously a bad time, the beginning of the decade. For several months, I struggled, trying unsuccessfully to integrate myself into the Parisian musical world. auditioned for [French singer/songwriter] Maxime Le Forestier – but it didn't work!' In 1985 he joined Tribute, a Swedish art-rock group founded in 1982 by Per Gideon Andersson and Christer Josef Hedin, who sent him a copy of their debut album when their own drummer quit during a tour. He appeared on their second album, *Breaking Barriers*, and then the same lineup – but with Rowe overdubbing his bass – recorded *Breakthrough* in September 1986, released on the ARC Music label.

The result is possibly the band's least-favoured album, an unremarkable and somewhat bland offering dominated by repetitive, synth-led instruments all recorded with a typically soft, glossy 1980s sound. Chord sequences and grooves are set up, but the compositions seemingly go nowhere, relying instead on Rhedin's Moog solos and wordless female voices. Moerlen's trademark tuned percussion is still there, but it's fighting a losing battle.

There are two tracks sung by Moerlen – 'Portrait', with French lyrics by Joelle Kopf, and 'Road Out', which quotes excerpts from a poem by science-fiction writer and Scientology founder L. Ron Hubbard. You will not be humming them in the shower. Zeiden's guitar work is not bad at all, but the poor fellow is trying to follow in the footsteps of Allan Holdsworth and Bon Lozaga. What chance does he have?

Breakthrough didn't break through, and is generally regarded as the weakest PMG offering so far.

Second Wind (1989, Line Records)

Personnel: Pierre Moerlen drums, synthesiser. Hansford Rowe bass. Benoit Moerlen vibraphone, synthesizer, marimba. Ake Zieden guitars. Alex Sanguinetti drums on 9-11. Simon Pomara percussion. Frank Fischer synthesiser, piano. Stefan Traub vibraphone, synthesiser.

Tracks: 1. 'Second Wind' (Moerlen) 2. 'Time And Space' (Traub) 3. 'Say No More' (Moerlen) 4. 'Deep End' (Moerlen) 5. 'Crystal Funk' (Fischer, Mobus) 6. 'Exotic' (Moerlen) 7. 'Beton' (Moerlen) 8. 'Alan Key' (Rowe) 9. 'Crash And Co, The First' (Moerlen, Sanguinetti) 10. 'Crash And Co, The Second' (Moerlen, Sanguinetti) 11. 'Crash And Co, The Third' (Moerlen, Sanguinetti)

Tribute ran out of puff in 1987, but Moerlen found his *Second Wind* back in France with the help of Hanny, Benoit and Ake Zieden. They did two tours of Germany (which may explain why they were now signed to a German record label), recording *'Full Circle' Live 1988* that didn't see the light of day until ten years later on Outer Music, then produced the PMG's fifth album with the help of a few friends. It includes a three-part drum duet recorded with Argentinean stickman Alex Sanguinetti (Alex is coming at you through the left speaker, Pierre through the right). How successful this really is, depends on how much you enjoy hearing nearly half an hour of drumming, and nothing else. But the remaining tracks are all superior to the offerings on *Breakthrough*, an Eighties updating of the PMG sounds but with enough variety in the compositions to maintain interest.

Standouts are the nippy title track, which sounds like it could have come from Downwind; German vibes player Stefan Traub's ballad 'Time And Space', which gives Ake Zieden a chance to stretch out a bit on guitar, and Rowe's equally affecting 'Alan Key'. True, some of the tracks do sound a bit like 'hold music' when ringing a call centre but this is still a step up from its predecessor.

However, this improvement did not translate into better sales, and financial pressures forced the PMG to break up later in 1989. Rowe discussed his view of the albums recorded during this period with the *Innerviews* website in 2017: 'They have a few good moments, but most of it is kind of patched together and not very well recorded. It was hard for Pierre to realise a vision with these albums because he was completely distracted by his own problems and budget constraints. He would get together with a group of guys and fly me in to overdub bass on top of what they did. I'm not very proud of those records. They aren't horribly embarrassing but they're not particularly good, either.'

Pentanine (2005, Musea)

Personnel: Pierre Moerlen drums, vibraphone, xylophone. Alexei Pleschunov bass. Arkady Kuznetsov electric guitar. Meehail Ogorodov keyboards, drums, percussion, underwater voice.

Tracks: 1. 'Flyin' High' (Ogorodov) 2. 'Airway To Seven' (Moerlen) 3. 'Pentanine Part One' (Moerlen) 4. 'Au Chalet' (Moerlen) 5. 'Trip A La Mode' (Moerlen) 6. 'Reminiscence' (Moerlen) 7. 'Interlude' (Ogorodov) 8. 'Classique' (Moerlen) 9. 'Lacheur' (Moerlen) 10. 'Bleu Nuit' (Moerlen) 11. 'Pentanine Part Two' (Moerlen) 12. 'Montagnes Russes' (Moerlen) 13. 'Troyka' (Moerlen)

In the 16-year gap between *Second Wind* and *Pentanine*, the Moerlen brothers returned to Strasbourg to teach percussion before Pierre found a job drumming in the orchestra pit for major touring stage musicals including *Evita* and *Les Miserables*. In 1994 a plan to revive the band resulted in the formation of Gongzilla, without Pierre who went on to replace Frank Katz in Brand X and then return to Gong for a few years. That continued until 1999, when he quit the band after just two dates into a tour, leaving Keith 'Missile Bass' Bailey to fill in.

In 2001 Pierre went to St Petersburg to perform his music with Russian musicians and while there he recorded the tracks that constituted *Pentanine*, masterminded by producer and synth player Meehail Ogorodov. The result is the best PMG album since *Leave It Open*, packed full of interesting and entertaining tunes featuring Moerlen's trademark mix of polyrhythmic tuned percussion and synthesiser. There are moments that remind me of the old, classic Gong – particularly on the dreamy, bubbly opening track, 'Flyin' High', written not by Moerlen but by Ogorodov, complete with propeller plane noises. 'Trip A La Mode' is almost 'The Isle of Everywhere', with a similar pace and circle of chords, while the title track is, as the name suggests, a dense, almost sinister chug-along in 5/4.

Moerlen is well-served by his Russian musicians – Kuznetsoz's electric guitar is a little under-used, but Pleschunov provides solid, funky bass and Ogorodov's keyboards have a jazzy, perky feel to them, resulting in thirteen very pleasing tracks. It bodes well for the future – but, alas, it wasn't to be. The album took a few years to get a release and was finally put on the market in 2005, the same year Moerlen died suddenly aged 52.

Tribute (2010, Association Pierre Moerlen's Gong Tribute)
Personnel: Pierre Moerlen drums on 14. Samuel Klein drums on 1-13. Marc-Antoine Schmitt bass. Sebastien Kohler guitar on 1-13. Matias Canobra vibraphone, marimba on 14. Bubu percussion on 1-13.

Tracks: 1. 'Un Patient' (Moerlen) 2. 'Septembre 02' (Moerlen). 3. 'Contempop' (Moerlen). 4. 'Construction Metallique' (Canobra) 5. 'A Pierre Moerlen' (Canobra) 6. 'Le Duel Massam' (Schmitt, Klein). 7. 'Don Jungle' (Schmitt, Canobra, Klein). 8. 'Back Stage' 9. '28 Fevrier' (Canobra, Moerlen). 10. 'La Valse Du CRS' (Canobra) 11. 'Mister Marco' 12. '05 01 03' (Moerlen) 13. 'Mon Ami Bubu' (Canobra) 14. 'Contempop' [demo version] (Moerlen)

When Pierre Moerlen died in his sleep in the early hours of May 3, 2005, he was busy rehearsing a new PMG lineup with a group of young French musicians. As a tribute to him, they decided to continue working on his compositions, plus their own tracks, eventually releasing the result under the PMG moniker in 2010. A message in the liner notes translates as: 'This album is dedicated to the memory of a great musician, an outstanding and endearing person with whom we had the privilege of sharing his music and a bit of life. Thank you Pierre.'

Moerlen himself only plays on one tune, the demo version of 'Contempop' which opens with Daevid Allen introducing him on drums, taken from a recording of a late 1990s Gong gig. But he composed four additional tracks and the band do a good job with them, opening with the steady, upbeat 'Un Patient' – graced with some nice slide guitar from Kohler – continuing with the darker, denser 'Septembre 2' and the stately and intricate 'Contempop'.

Later, the funky '28 Fevrier' is a collaboration between Moerlen and Matias Canobra, while his solo composition '05 01 03' could have come from *Time Is The Key*. Elsewhere there is tribute to Moerlen from Canobra, a drum 'n' bass duel between Klein and Schmitt and a few tracks that are a bit more experimental in nature, such as the unpredictable 'Construction Metallique' and Canobra's vibraphone solo 'Back Stage'.

Unpredictable and mercurial, Moerlen probably could have had a more successful and stable solo career than he did. But at his best, he was a brilliant percussionist and drummer who added flair and excitement to everything he did. Daevid Allen said: 'I never played with a better drummer – at his peak, no one could touch him. Standing on stage with Pierre behind you in '73 and '74 was unbelievable.'

Mother Gong

Fairy Tales (1979, Charly Records)
Personnel: Gilli Smyth vocals. Harry Williamson guitar. Mo Vicarage keyboards. Didier Malherbe woodwind, reeds. Trevor Darks bass. Ermano Ghisio Erba percussion, drums. Additional personnel: Eduardo Niebla guitar. Ronnie Walthen Uilleann pipes. Marianne Oberasher harp. Nicholas Turner muzma, oboe. Corrina voices.

Tracks: Wassilissa – 1. 'Three Riders' (Smyth, Williamson) 2. 'The Baba-Yaga's Cottage' (Smyth, Williamson) 3. 'The Forbidden Room' (Smyth, Williamson) 4. 'Time Machine' (Smyth, Williamson) 5. 'Flying' (Smyth, Williamson) 6. 'Wassilissa Returns Home' (Smyth, Williamson) 7. 'Through the Machine Again' (Smyth, Williamson) 8. 'The Baba Yaga' (Smyth, Williamson); The Three Tongues – 9. 'The Shoemaker's Son' (Smyth, Williamson) 10. 'Land of Dogs' (Smyth, Williamson) 11. 'The Frog' (Smyth, Williamson) 12. 'An Irish Inn in Rome' (Smyth, Williamson) 13. 'The Arena' (Smyth, Williamson) 14. 'Turtles' (Smyth, Williamson) 15. 'Birds' (Smyth, Williamson) 16. 'The Feast' (Smyth, Williamson); The Pied Piper – 17. 'Hamelin' (Smyth, Williamson) 18. 'Rats Amok' (Smyth, Williamson) 19. 'An Angry Crowd' (Smyth, Williamson) 20. 'Rat Rock' (Smyth, Williamson) 21. 'A Thousand Guilders?' (Smyth, Williamson) 22. 'Children!' (Smyth, Williamson) 23. 'Magic Land' (Smyth, Williamson)

Gilli Smyth left Gong in 1974 because she wanted to spend more time caring for her children and felt the band had abandoned its political and spiritual roots to concentrate on grooves and improvisation. With Daevid Allen's help, she put together a solo album, *Mother*, released in 1978 that explored the themes that would run throughout the Mother Gong albums – the joys and sorrows of motherhood, feminism and the injustice of gender stereotyping, and her belief in the gods and goddesses that guided her. *Mother* is technically a solo album so outside the remit of this book but is worth investigating as it also contains 'lost' Gong recordings from 1971 and 1973.

In 1979 Harry Williamson arrived in Deya, Majorca, to help Gilli compose a follow-up. The son of *Tarka The Otter* writer Henry, Williamson had worked with Anthony Phillips through school pal Richard MacPhail and became a member of Nik Turner's Sphynx. Harry wrote a single 'Nuclear Waste' which was recorded by The Radio Actors, a one-off band that included Sting, Steve Hillage and Mike Howlett, which was released by Virgin and later by DB Records. Daevid and Gilli were going through a rough patch in their relationship, and Williamson fell in love with Smyth as they worked together in the sultry Mediterranean sunshine.

Gilli had already created the concept of a Mother Gong band to promote her solo album, and this became the name for an ever-changing cast of musicians that had Williamson and Smyth at its heart. For *Fairy Tales,* they were ably assisted by Didier Malherbe – under the pseudonym of Pipo Bal de Glass – and pulled in guests including Nik Turner.

Recorded at Foel Studios in Wales during a snowy winter, *Fairy Tales* was designed to be an album parents could listen to with their children, featuring three classic fairy tales set to music. 'Wassilissa' is a Russian story reminiscent of Cinderella – a beautiful girl lives with a cruel witch, who makes her do all the work. The witch is an incarnation of Kali, who fiercely tests the intentions of the young girl and sends her through a time machine to see her future. When she understands the causal relationship of existence, she travels back through the machine, more aware of life in the alternate present.

In 'The Three Tongues', a shoemaker sends his lazy son to be tutored by three masters, only for them to teach the lad how to talk to animals, birds and frogs. Viewing these Dolittle skills as practically useless in the cobbling trade, the father sends his son out into the world where, thanks to his talents, he resolves disputes, passes seemingly impossible tests and is rewarded with a magic flute.

'The Pied Piper' is, perhaps, the most famous story – a German town plagued with rats hires a young man (maybe the shoemaker's son mentioned above) to lead the rodents away with his magic flute. But they renege on his payment, so he also leads all the town's children away into the side of a mountain.

The music accompanying Gilli's spoken-word narration is slightly medieval, sometimes gentle and acoustic, sometimes angry and dramatic, with Didier's woodwind weaving its magic throughout, at one time providing what can only be described as 'rat sax' – sinister, squeaky multi-tracked saxophone sounds that create a sense of real menace. It's probably the kind of album you listen to once and then put away in the rack, but it does repay repeated listenings.

Battle Of The Birds (1981, Otter Songs/2003, Blueprint)

Personnel: Gilli Smyth voice. Anthony Phillips guitars. Harry Williamson guitars, voices. Robin Phillips oboe. Carl & Dorothy violin & cello. Didier Malherbe flutes, piccolo, saxophones. Jan Emerick guitar. Hugh Hopper bass. Guy Evans percussion. Tasmin Smyth, Orlando Allen, Bee Williamson, Aardvark, Helen, Dave the Wave, Claire Jones various voices.

Tracks: 1. 'The Wren & The Raven' (Phillips, Williamson, Smyth) 2. 'Raven Flight' (Phillips, Williamson, Smyth) 3. 'The Magic Bundle' (Phillips, Williamson, Smyth) 4. 'The Promise' (Phillips, Williamson, Smyth) 5. 'The First Test' (Phillips, Williamson, Smyth) 6. 'The Second Test' (Phillips, Williamson, Smyth) 7. 'Wed The Giants Daughter' (Phillips, Williamson, Smyth) 8. 'The First Spell' (Phillips, Williamson, Smyth) 9. 'The Last Spell' (Phillips, Williamson, Smyth) 10. 'From Rags To Riches' (Phillips, Williamson, Smyth) 11. 'Auburn Mary' (Phillips, Williamson, Smyth) 12. 'The Choice' (Phillips, Williamson, Smyth) 13. 'Sombre'

(Phillips, Williamson, Smyth) 14. 'Flight' (Phillips, Williamson, Smyth) 15. 'Twilight' (Phillips, Williamson, Smyth)

Originally released as a limited edition cassette by Mother Gong/Anthony Phillips, this recording was intended as the follow-up to *Fairy Tales* but didn't get a proper release until 22 years later, when it was credited to Williamson, Smyth and Phillips. The music comes from Phillips and Williamson's 1978 *Gypsy Suite*, with overdubs by the 1981 Mother Gong lineup, and Gilli telling a traditional Celtic tale involving magical birds, giants and magical enchantments. The music is a little sparser and more pastoral than on *Fairy Tales,* but the acoustic guitar interplay between Phillips and Williamson is exquisite, while Didier adds magic to every track. 'Auburn Mary' is the only song on the album, sung quite beautifully by Claire Jones with Didier contributing both sax and flute. The final three tracks are instrumental mixes of some of the music used under the narrations.

Robot Woman (1981, Butt)

Personnel: Gilli Smyth vocals, Harry Williamson acoustic, rhythm & glissando guitars, synth on 2 & 5, piano on 3, vocals. Yan Emeric Vagh acoustic, rhythm, lead & slide guitars, scat on 6. Didier Malherbe saxophone, piccolo & bamboo flutes. Dane Kronenberg bass. Guy Evans drums, percussion on 11. Additional personnel: 'Big Al' Mitchell vocals on 10. John Newsham backing vocals on 12. Steve Hillage guitar on 3. Mo Vicarage synth on 5. Nicholas Turner sax on 3. Mike Howlett bass on 3. Hugh Hopper bass on 8 & 11. Steve Broughton drums on 3. Dave Sawyer paper drum on 4.

Tracks: 1. 'Disco At The End Of The World' (Smyth, Williamson) 2. 'Robot Woman' (Smyth, Williamson) 3. 'Machine Song' (Smyth, Williamson) 4. 'The Sea' (Smyth, Malherbe, Williamson) 5. 'Searching The Airwaves' (Smyth, Williamson) 6. 'Billli Bunker's Blues' (Williamson) 7. 'Military Procession' (Smyth, Malherbe) 8. 'Customs Man – Rapist' (Smyth, Williamson, Hopper) 9. 'Fire' (Mother Gong) 10. 'Red Alert' (Williamson, Vicarage) 11. 'Stars' (Mother Gong) 12. 'Australia' (Williamson)

The *Robot Woman* trilogy attained almost legendary status, partly because there were only ever 3,000 pressings on vinyl until 2019 when, to the great joy of everyone in the Gong community, it was issued as a box set with a fourth disc of unreleased material. For many fans, this is the pinnacle of the band's achievement, when Gilli's personal vision and idiosyncratic vocal approach were perfectly balanced by Williamson's songwriting ability and musical chops.

By mid-1979 Gilli and Harry were living together and, inspired by the movie *The Stepford Wives,* plus a science fiction story Williamson had written and recorded a few years earlier called 'A Journey To Atlantis' and the

Douglas Adams radio series *The Hitch-hiker's Guide To The Galaxy*, had put together a small show based on the concept of a cloned woman, touring the US in 1980. This slowly morphed into *Robot Woman* as the tracks and ideas took shape. With the gift of an eight-track recording studio from Daevid Allen, which Williamson installed into a writing studio his father had constructed in North Devon, the album was recorded in the summer of 1981 with the help of Van Der Graaf Generator drummer Evans, Ilfracombe bassist Kronenberg and Didier and Yan, who recorded their 'lost album' *Melodic Destiny* around the same time.

In the box set liner notes, Williamson says: 'The new band arranged, rehearsed and recorded every day for a month. During that time we were visited by several old friends including Hugh Hopper, who guested on some of the recordings. After rehearsals, we would often walk to the sea and revel in the wonderful ancient landscape.'

The result is an album that could almost be the soundtrack to a stage show, mixing disco, jazz, reggae and narrated dialogue into a rich musical melange. Yes, it deals with serious issues but, like the best Gong material, does so with its tongue firmly in its cheek. It tells the story of a dystopian society in which mechanical women serve men's every needs – except one of them has developed consciousness and become fully aware of her subservient role in society. In many ways, it's ahead of its time, foreshadowing the TV dramatisation of *The Handmaid's Tale* and films such as *Ex-Machina* (2014).

It's a bit of a soapbox, but that doesn't detract from the quality of the music. 'Disco At The End Of The World' – originally composed by Williamson in 1978 when he was with Nik Turner's Sphynx – is a funky opening number with hilarious lyrics, cheeky sax from Didier and great guitar licks from Yan Emeric. The slower, lurching title song is full of unpredictable little sax breaks and sassy dialogue, 'Machine Song' features Hillage's soaring lead guitar to a slight reggae backing while 'Searching The Airwaves' is six and a half minutes of pounding instrumental wonderment showcasing Didier's sax. Add 'Billi Bunker's Blues', an amusing cod cowboy song, the sinister 'Customs Man – Rapist' and the terrifying 'Red Alert' and you have an album that every Gong fan should adore.

Robot Woman 2 (1982, Shanghai)

Personnel: Gilli Smyth vocals. Harry Williamson guitar, synth, bass on 6-8, 10, 12, bells & windchimes on 6, piano on 1, 12), vocals. Didier Malherbe saxophone on 1-3, 8,9, flute on 2, 6, 8, 11. Dane Kronenberg bass. Guy Evans drums, timpani on 1, 8, scraper on 6, Flexitone on 6, 9, tube drums on 7, percussion & Fx on 8, paper drum on 9, 13, Chinese cymbal on 13. Additional personnel: Giles Perring guitar & vocals on 2, 9, Fx on 9. Mo Vicarage synth on 4. Andy Anderson drums on 4. Ermanno Ghizio-Erba drums on 4. Sadak drums on 4. Dave The Wave vocals on 5. Paul Sanchez bass on 5. Chris Kerridge lead guitar on 10, 11, conch on 6. Hugo The Gander performer on 6. Claire Jones backing vocals on 7, 11. Toni vocals on 8, 12. Dave Sawyer percussion on 10, paper drum 13.

Tracks: 1. 'Suggestive Station' 2. 'This Train' 3. 'I Wanna Be With You' 4. 'The Moving Walkway' 5. 'The Upwardly Mobile Song' 6. 'Tigers Or Elephants' 7. 'Mirror' 8. 'You Can Touch The Sky (All Work No Play)' 9. '1999' 10. 'Crazy Town' 11. 'The Angry Song' 12. 'My Life' 13. 'Leotards' (all tracks Smyth, Williamson)

The second part of the trilogy doesn't continue the story so much as envisage a parallel narrative, focussing on the adventures of Beta, the Robot Woman, and Mr Kumkwik, her repairman. Recorded between November 1981 and September 1982, it features many of the musicians who contributed to *Robot Woman*, including Guy Evans on drums, Dave Kronenberg back on bass and, of course, trusty Didier Malherbe. During the recording process, Dave Sawyer turned up with home-made instruments he had made and had fun with Williamson and Evans trying to play them. Some of the results of this experimentation were released on a limited-edition cassette tape called *W.F.M* (the letters stand for Words Fail Me) in 1981 but were also used on this album and on a collection mentioned earlier in the book, *The History & Mystery of Planet Gong*.

Robot Woman 2 is a denser, more subdued album than its predecessor – only a few of the tracks immediately jump out at you and grab you by the ears. 'I Wanna Be With You' develops into a catchy pop song, while 'You Can Touch The Sky' has an appealing Latin rhythm and smoochy major seventh chords. '1999' was later reworked as '1989' on the *Gongmaison* album and 'Angry Song' seems anything but, a swaying ballad sung very nicely by Claire Jones.

If you like your Mother Gong with plenty of weird sax sounds, narrative-forwarding dialogue, commanding bass and abrupt changes in mood and musical direction, there's plenty of that, too, plus another (less successful) attempt at a funky disco song in 'This Train'. There's a lot of Didier on the album, which is always a good thing, but it suffers a bit through the lack of a lead guitarist. Having said that, it repays repeated listens and still contains enough good music and good humour to make it an essential part of your Mother Gong collection.

Robot Woman 3 (1986, Shanghai)
Personnel (box set listing): Gilli Smyth vocals. Harry Williamson synth, piano, drums, Fx, bass, guitar on 4, vocals. Additional personnel: Michael tabla on 1. Orlando Allen vocals on 2iii. Matt Arnold violin on 2iii. Tony Norris horns on 3. Tom The Poet voice on 5, backing vocals. Nimbin Silly Symphony (Lisa Yeates, Soozah Clark, Bruce McNicol) vocals on 1, 3. Lee, Bee, Alicia, John vocals on 4. Nadine Honey vocal on 6ii.

Tracks (original vinyl listing): 1. 'It's You And Me Baby' (Williamson, Smyth) 2. 'Faces Of Woman'. i 'Faces Of Woman' (Williamson, Smyth, Allen) ii. 'Desire.

War.' (Williamson, Smyth, Tom The Poet) iii. 'Children's Song' (Smyth, Williamson) 3. 'Lady's Song' (Hanley, Oliver) 4. 'Woman Of Streams' (Williamson) 5. 'I'm Sorry' (Smyth, Tom The Poet) 6. 'Men Cry i. Men Cry' (Williamson, Smyth) ii. 'Solutions' (Williamson, Smyth, Tom The Poet) iii. 'Magenta Part One' (Williamson, Smyth, Allen)

In 1983 Gilli and Harry went to live in Australia, setting up a studio and home in Melbourne. While there they got to know a political comedy trio called Silly Symphony, who subsequently appeared on the third and last *Robot Woman* album, recording their tracks at Richmond Studios where Williamson worked part-time. He says of this period: 'This was the era of drum machines and synths, and we enjoyed the relative luxury of 24 tracks, a Fairlight, MIDI, gold foil reverbs and AMS outboards.' It's the lack of 'proper' drums that makes *Robot Woman 3* sound the most dated of the trilogy – that and the preponderance of recitation over electronic beats, and the consequent reduction in the number of memorable melodies. Having said that, 'Lady's Song' is a fun calypso with convincing horns from Tony Norris, and 'Woman Of Streams' is a hypnotic chant combining acoustic guitar, synth and muted electronic percussion. The best song on the album is probably 'Solutions', sung by Harry and Nadine Honey – it's marred a bit by the ever-present synth and electronic drums but has some lovely melodies in it.

Various sources list Daevid Allen as being present on two of the tracks, although the 2019 box set doesn't mention him and, indeed, it's hard to spot his presence. His young son Orlando is there, however, taking lead vocals on 'Children's Song'.

Mother Gong albums frequently tread a tightrope between musical entertainment and soapbox – *Robot Woman 3*, which explores 'unfolding female consciousness in various forms', is the most soapbox-y of the trilogy and, in my humble opinion, suffers as a result. Yes, the message is important – and still is, 40 years later – but the delivery is not as effective as on the previous two albums.

The Owl And The Tree (1989, Demi Monde)

Personnel: Gilli Smyth speaking voice, space whisper. Harry Williamson everything imaginable plus synths, keyboards, vocals, craziness. Fretless Fred (Conrad Henderson) bass. Tim Ayres bass. Robert George drums, percussion. Wandana Arrowheart harmonium. Robert Calvert sax, vocals. Georgia O'Hara vocals. Daevid Allen vocals, acoustic guitar, glissando.

Tracks (original vinyl listing): 1. 'The Owly Song' (Allen) 2. 'I Am My Own Lover' (Allen). 3. 'I Am A Tree' (Williamson, Smyth) 4. 'Lament For The Future Of The Forest' (Williamson, Smyth) 5. 'Hands' (Williamson, Smyth) 6. 'Unseen Alley' (Williamson, Smyth) 7. 'La Dea Madri' (Williamson, Smyth) CD bonus tracks: 8. 'Love Poem'. 9. 'Coda Wave'

The first collaboration between Mother Gong and Daevid Allen (unless he really does appear on *Robot Woman 3*) is this album, also mistakenly credited to Gong on a CD release. I say collaboration – in fact, they each occupy one side of the original vinyl and are clearly doing their own thing here, although all the tracks were recorded together at Harry Williamson's studios in Melbourne during Allen's Australian self-exile. It features the new Oz lineup of Mother Gong – Henderson is of Sri Lankan origin but moved to Australia in 1981, Robert Calvert cut his teeth in early 1970s British prog band Catapilla, followed by improvising band John Stevens Away and is not to be confused with Hawkwind's Robert Calvert, and Robert George is an accomplished improvising jazz drummer.

Side one of the vinyl is occupied by two of Allen's most engaging and entertaining compositions – the delightfully playful 'The Owly Song' is a charming ditty based on Allen's acoustic guitar and then partner Wandana's harmonium, while 'I Am My Own Lover' is a 15-minute philosophical statement in which Allen sets his lovers and teachers free with the help of the Mother Gong backing band.

The second side is Mother Gong alone, five brooding and mournful compositions with an ecological bent and a heavier jazz influence provided by Calvert's lyrical sax and George's light-touch drumming. 'I Am A Tree' is Gilli talking over a synth backing, 'Lament For The Future Of The Forest' a gently swinging instrumental, 'Hands' and 'Unseen Ally' are Gilli poems intoned over slow synth chords, occasional percussion and expressive sax. Final track (on the vinyl at least) is 'La Dea Madri', a more upbeat, jazzy backing to Gilli's poetry in which the Mother Goddess journeys through our world meeting indifference and rejection.

The CD release of the album rather bizarrely credited the recording to Gong and, despite having the same tracklisting as the vinyl (with 'Tudor Love Poem' as an extra song), it swaps the sides round, opening with the Mother Gong tracks instead. A 2004 release on Voiceprint keeps the new order, adding 'Love Poem' and 'Coda Wave' as extra tracks. Now, 'Tudor Love Poem' and 'Love Poem' are the same compositions but seem to be slightly different mixes – the acoustic guitar is more prominent in the latter – and both originate from a 1988 limited-edition cassette tape called *Fish In The Sky*. Finally, 'Coda Wave' sounds like a two-minute instrumental collage or out-take from the recordings, dominated by Calvert's sax and some frantic drumming from George. It could be the same track as 'Codawave' on the 1989 limited edition cassette *Buddha's Birthday,* but it was so limited even I don't have it!

She Made The World – Magenta (1993, Voiceprint)

Personnel: Gilli Smyth words and vocals, Robert Calvert tenor & soprano saxophones. Robert George drums & percussion. Conrad Henderson bass guitar. Harry Williamson synth, guitar, glissando, vocals on 3 Daevid Allen drone on 1.

Tracks: 1. 'Magenta' 2. 'Water' 3. 'She Made The World' 4. 'The Weather' 5. 'Malicious Sausage' 6. 'Sea Horse' 7. 'Spirit Calling' 8. 'Tattered Jacket' 9. 'Waipu' 10. 'When The Show Is Over' 11. 'I Am A Witch' 12. 'The Spirit Of The Bush' 13. 'Blessed Be'. All lyrics by Gilli Smyth except 'Tattered Jacket' co-written with Daevid Allen, and 'Water' by Harry Williamson. Music improvised by the whole band, except 'Waipu' written by Harry Williamson and 'She Made The World' by Harry Williamson and Robert Calvert

The years 1988 to 1993 were very productive ones for Mother Gong. With their own studio at their disposal, the band could spend hours improvising under Gilli's lyrics. Paradoxically, however, it was getting harder to release their music as sales were never high enough to keep record companies interested. So the next three albums that turned up in the early to mid-90s were recorded some years previously. Before that there was a live album – called, with splendid lack of imagination, *Live '91* – recorded on a US tour with Tom The Poet but without Henderson or George, so their parts were pre-programmed into Williamson's keyboards. The result is a set that was heavy on the atmospheric tracks, while the faster numbers show their limitations, especially with the tinny electronic drums.

Live 91 was intended to promote what should have been the band's next album, *Wild Child*. But that was pushed back ... and back ... until 1994. Instead, a year earlier, Voiceprint released *She Made The World – Magenta*, consisting of improvised tracks recorded from 1986 onwards. The reason for the double-barrelled title isn't entirely clear, except that 'Magenta' is the only track featuring Daevid Allen and it's a whopping 32 minutes long. You will recognise it from a much shorter sample that closed 1986's *Robot Woman 3* – Harry and Daevid provide a single-key drone under Gilli's spoken word recitation. 'She Made The World' features beautiful, finger-picked acoustic guitar from Williamson, who also contributes roaring vocal noises and some rare singing on the album as the song picks up speed and heavier instrumentation in its second half.

For the rest of the album, the tracks pretty much follow the same pattern of instrumentals supporting Gilli's poetry – sometimes gentle and contemplative, sometimes a little discordant and disjointed. Unlike the *Robot Woman* trilogy, there are no songs to break up the poetry, with the result that the album becomes somewhat samey after a while. But there is no denying the beauty and power of the music this band can create.

Tree In Fish (1994, Tapestry/2004, Voiceprint)

Personnel: Gilli Smyth words & vocals. Harry Williamson keys, guitars & production. Robert Calvert saxophones & philosophy. Robert George drums & repercussions. Conrad Henderson basses. Tom The Poet vocals on 4 (2004 version). Didier Malherbe sax on 8 (2004 version). Shyamal Maitra percussion on 8 (2004 version).

Tracks (1994 version): 1. 'The Ally' (Williamson, Calvert, George) 2. 'Love Poems' (Smyth, Williamson, Calvert, George) 3. 'Lament' (Smyth, Williamson, Calvert, George) 4. 'Between Us' (Henderson, Smyth, Williamson, Calvert, George, Allen) 5. 'She Smiled' (Smyth, Williamson, Calvert, George) 6. 'The Mother Goddess' (Smyth, Williamson, Calvert, George) 7. 'Cafe Reflections' (Smyth, Williamson, Calvert, George) 8. 'The House Is Not The Same' (Henderson, Smyth, Williamson, Calvert, George, Normal) 9. 'Space Tango' (Smyth, Williamson, Calvert, George) 10. 'The Beach Is Hot' (Smyth, Williamson, Calvert, George) 11. 'Balein' (Henderson, Smyth, Williamson, Calvert, George) 12. 'Touch' (Smyth, Williamson, Calvert, George) 13. 'Tree I' (Smyth, Williamson, Calvert, George) 14. 'Tree II' (Smyth, Williamson, Calvert) 15. 'Wilful Housewife' (Smyth, Williamson, Calvert) 16. 'Crying' (Smyth, Williamson, Calvert) 17. 'Man/Woman' (Smyth, Williamson, Calvert).

Tracks (2004 version): 1. 'Simple' 1 (Smyth, Williamson, Calvert, George) 2. 'Four Horsemen' (Smyth, Williamson, Calvert, George) 3. 'Buddha's Birthday' (Smyth, Williamson, Calvert, George) 4. 'Faces' (Smyth, Williamson, Calvert, George) 5. 'Cafe Reflections' (Smyth, Williamson, Calvert, George) 6. 'The House Is Not The Same' (Smyth, Williamson, Calvert, George, Normal) 7. 'Tree II' (Smyth, Williamson, Calvert) 8. 'Greenfields' 9. 'Wilful Housewife' (Smyth, Williamson, Calvert, George) 10. 'Song Of Skye' (Smyth, Williamson, Calvert, George) 11. 'Simple 2/La Dea Madri Edit' (Smyth, Williamson, Calvert, George) 12. 'She Smiled' (Smyth, Williamson, Calvert, George) 13. 'Crying' (Smyth, Williamson, Calvert) 14 'Medicine Woman' (Smyth, Williamson, Calvert, George) 15. 'Aere' (Smyth, Williamson, Calvert, George)

Now, this is a strange one. Not only have there been two issues of *Tree In Fish* but they are pretty much different albums, sharing only five songs. The original, a limited US edition, repeats most of the tracks from The Owl And The Tree – 'Ally' is 'Unseen Ally', 'Lament' is 'Lament For The Future Of The Forest', 'The Mother Goddess' is 'Le Dea Madri' and 'Tree I' is 'I Am A Tree'. In fact, so is 'Tree II' but with a different instrumental backing. Of the rest on the 1994 release, 'Between Us' 'The Beach Is Hot' and 'Balein' will turn up on a later version of *Wild Child*. Anyway, your chances of getting hold of a copy are slim (although many of the tracks have been put on YouTube) so we will concentrate on Voiceprint's 2004 issue.

It opens with 'Simple I', a short instrumental with similarities to the original backing to 'I Am A Tree'. 'Four Horseman', a pounding, driving track with great drum work by George and dramatic, doom-laden words, was first introduced on *Live 91*, the Calvert sax showcase 'Buddha's Birthday' comes originally from a cassette release, as does 'She Smiled', and 'Cafe Reflections' was originally on the *Fish In The Sky* tape. 'The House Is Not The Same' is an unusual little number featuring Harry's discordant guitar chords and random sax noises under Gilli speaking a poem by Henry Normal.

There are a couple of other oddities. 'Greenfields' comes from Glastonbury Festival in 1991 and features Didier Malherbe on sax and Shyamal Maitra on tablas, while 'Medicine Woman' was recorded live at the Bellingen Festival in Australia with the help of Kangaroo Moon.

Wild Child (1994, Demi Monde/2004, Voiceprint)
Personnel: Gilli Smyth vocals, space whisper. Harry Williamson synths, guitars, vocals. Robert Calvert tenor & soprano saxophones. Robert George drums, percussion. Conrad Henderson fretless and fretted bass.

Tracks (2004 version): 1. 'Today Is Beautiful' 2. 'Augment/Lady' 3. 'Time' 4. 'Between Us' 5. 'Child' 6. 'Room I' 7. 'We Women' 8. 'The Beach Is Hot' 9. 'Superboots' 10. 'Balein'. All tracks by Mother Gong.

Five years after the tracks were recorded, *Wild Child* finally saw the light of day through Demi Monde – it is generally regarded as Mother Gong's best album since *Robot Woman*. All the previous releases of material from the sessions at Spring Studios tend to follow the same pattern of somewhat formless improvised instrumentals under Gilli's poetry – the tracks on *Wild Child*, recorded at Foal Studios in Wales in 1989, seem to have a bit more structure and purpose to them. Having said that, the liner notes make a point of saying that some of the tracks 'employ a technique we call spontaneous composition method (SCM). We have developed this over the past two years by continuously recording live in the studio in Australia. The music is created spontaneously with only the most basic prior agreements on form + tonality; the end result is dependent on the moment by moment reaction of all of us to the lyrical images presented by Gilli.'

The album was recorded in just a few weeks before a tour (and after the death of Gilli's mother). Harry Williamson says the first eventual release saw the tracks re-ordered and other tracks added, against the band's wishes. I have the Voiceprint version which opens with 'Today Is Beautiful' rather than 'Time', and this is the version that seems to be most widely available. Which is a shame, really, as 'Time' is a lovely number in 6/8, that sounds like a proper song, with Gilli almost singing, helped by Harry's backing vocals, enriched by a lovely, warm band sound and production. It is inspired by 'Time Is The Simplest Thing', a sci-fi novel by Clifford D. Simak, which explores the theme of the intolerance of ordinary people towards those with unusual abilities.

The first part of 'Augment/Lady' is a pounding, brooding instrumental, powered along by Henderson's bass. 'Between Us', originally released on *Tree In Fish*, is playful and quirky, while the almost title track is a superb piece of minor-key drama as Gilli cries out for her mother. 'We Women' is another quirky, bouncy tune with lovely little soprano sax interjections by Calvert, and 'Superboots' is a seven-minute funky workout. The Voiceprint album ends on the 11-minute 'Balein', a steady, hypnotic piece founded on Henderson's bubbly bass.

What are we missing from the original *Wild Child* release? Well, the vinyl included 'Crazy Town/Fire', which I can confirm is the *Robot Woman 2* track reworked in superfast style just like on *Live 91*. Personally, I don't think it fits the album at all. Then there's 'Room II' and 'Aere' from the Demi Monde CD – the former is simply a continuation of the improvised 'Room I' but with more keyboards, while the latter you'll find on the 2004 *Tree In Fish* release. Clear as mud? Personally, I think the Voiceprint version is the one to get, that sounds like a more cohesive album.

Eye (1994, Voiceprint)

Personnel: Gilli Smyth spoken word, space whisper. Harry Williamson keyboards, percussion Doug Kerr bass. Robert George drums. Robert Calvert saxophone, keyboards. Tom The Poet vocals on 11, 12, 14. Alicia Gardiner, Bee Williamson, Claire Avent, Lisa Maree Faulkner vocals on 2. Liz van Dort vocals on 2. Tarnia Gzatska percussion on 6. Orlando Allen percussion, didgeridoo on 6, drum on 9. Taliesin Allen drum on 9.

Tracks: 1. 'Fanfare' (Calvert, George, Kerr, Smyth) 2. 'She's The Mother Of ...' (Smyth, Williamson, T. Allen) 3. 'Sun Day' (Calvert, George, Kerr, Smyth) 4. 'Beds' (Williamson, Smyth) 5. 'Time Is A Hurrying Dog' (Calvert, George, Kerr, Smyth) 6. 'Ancient' 7. 'Zen' (Williamson) 8. 'Quantam' (Calvert, George, Kerr, Smyth) 9. 'Spirit Canoe' (Mother Gong) 10. 'What If We Were Gods And Goddesses' (Calvert, George, Kerr, Smyth) 11. 'Auction' (Mother Gong) 12. 'Little Boy' (Williamson, Smyth) 13. 'Magic Stories' (Calvert, George, Kerr, Smyth) 14. 'Excuses' (Williamson) 15. 'Sax Canoe' (Mother Gong) 16. 'Fairy Laughter' (Calvert, George, Kerr, Smyth) 17. 'Virtual Reality' (Calvert, George, Kerr, Smyth)

By the time Mother Gong came to record their final studio album, Conrad Henderson had gone and was replaced on bass by Doug Kerr. Recorded once again at Spring Studios in Melbourne, *Eye* also heralded the break-up of the band, not to perform together until the first Gong Unconventional gathering in 2005. It also saw the end of Gilli and Harry's marriage – they divorced in 1992. Gilli would rejoin Gong for two more albums, while Harry concentrated on composing and producing.

Their swansong album doesn't quite have the energy and cohesiveness of *Wild Child* but in my view ranks higher than much of the post-*Robot Woman* material. There are quite a few standout tracks – the gospel soul of 'She's The Mother Of...', the playful jazz of 'Sun Day' and 'Time Is A Hurrying Dog', the hypnotic ethnic rhythm of 'Ancient', the funky bubble of 'Quantum'. Many of the tracks – some just a few minutes long – grew out of jam sessions involving Calvert, George, Kerr and Gilli, with Harry Williamson putting the finishing touches to them in the mixing process.

The only new Mother Gong compositions to appear after *Eye* are two tracks – 'The Whisperer' and 'Honeypath' – on *Mother Gong 2006* (2006, Voiceprint), which mostly consists of recordings from the Unconventional Gong Gathering in Glastonbury in 2005. If you want more live Mother Gong, try *Glastonbury 1979-1981* (2005, Voiceprint), which is pretty self-explanatory, and *O Amsterdam* (2007, Voiceprint) the band's contribution to the 2006 Unconventional. And, finally, *The Best Of Mother Gong* was released by Voiceprint in 1997.

Other Gong

There is a video on YouTube of Daevid Allen trying to list all the Gong offshoots – and even he can't remember them all. So what chance, dear reader, do we have? Trouble is, the Gong universe has grown so much over the last 50 years that it would be nigh on impossible to include every band and every musician within it.

So, we have to lay down some ground rules. This section will include bands directly created by members of Gong – but only after they have been connected to the band. It will not contain bands that existed before being associated with Gong. Neither will it feature bands that were just inspired by Gong or wanted to sound like them. So we include Planet Gong but not Here & Now nor Kangaroo Moon.

Same goes for bands that didn't release any recorded material – this is primarily a discography, after all. Oh, and you won't find any solo albums here, including Steve Hillage's System 7. They are for another book and another day. And truth be told, I'm not a System 7 fan, so that is best left to someone with more enthusiasm for that kind of music than I. And there's no Crystal Machine, because Tim Blake's recordings were released under his own name.

Some Gong offshoots only released live albums, so I've listed those if there are no studio recordings. Otherwise, they are mentioned in passing. And there are some bands that involve former Gong members but, to me, don't feel like part of the universe, such as Bon Lozaga's Soften The Glare.

There will undoubtedly be some readers who disagree with this arbitrary boundary.

Dashiell Hedayat

Obsolete (1971, Shandar/ 2016, Replica)

1-3 'Eh, Mushroom, Will You Mush My Room?: Chrysler; Fillet de l'Ombre; Long Song For Zelda' 4. 'Cielo Drive' All tracks written by Dashiell Hedayat

There are some who view this as a great almost-lost Gong album. I don't, because it's clearly a Dashiell Hedayat (real name Jack-Alain 'Melmoth' Leger) project with Gong as the backing band – he wrote the songs, sings them and plays the lead guitar on 'Chrysler' and 'Cielo Drive'. It is difficult to say how much songwriting input the band had – in her publication *Gong: Politico Historico Spirito* Gilli Smyth says: 'Dashiell Hedayat comes to Sens to work on album *Obsolete* with his vocals, music by Gong', which doesn't really nail it down for us. This is not to say that *Obsolete* is not worth the attention of the Gong completist, and is not an entertaining album in its own right. In fact, it helps us to plot the development of the band from the hippy whimsy of *Magick Brother* to the proto-punk of *Camembert Electrique*.

For a start, it features the entire mid-1971 Gong lineup of Daevid Allen, Gilli Smyth, Didier Malherbe, Christian Tritsch and Pip Pyle, with Beat author

William Burroughs on 'Long Song for Zelda' and Robert Wyatt's then five-year-old son Sam contributing to 'Cielo Drive'. Stylistically, this has a lot in common with 'Blues For Findlay' on *Continental Circus*, being mostly hard, driving, repetitive riffs and chord sequences with Hedayat's spoken poetry over the top. 'Chrysler', for example, consists of just two alternating chords, E9 and D9, throughout its 6:40 length.

Pip Pyle's drumming is particularly powerful here (and he plays guitar on 'Cielo Drive'), while Hedayat provides almost non-stop lead guitar through 'Long Song' and Didier contributes very watery percussion to 'Fille de l'Ombre'. 'Cielo Drive' – it's where the Manson family house stood in Los Angeles – is a 21-minute epic driven by Tritsch's bass, and at times he's playing a riff that comes very close to 'Flying Teapot'. Perhaps this is where the inspiration comes from. The track is thoroughly washed by Allen's glissando guitar, with sax improv by Didier and wah-wah lead guitar from Allen.

Some listeners may find this album somewhat repetitive and simplistic, certainly compared to the twists and turns that take place on *Camembert Electrique*, but it does occupy an important place in the story, and one could argue that this is a band in itself, Obsolete-Gong, and deserves to be in this book. The 2016 official reissue includes a 12-page booklet. However, when I last looked, CDs were going for silly money so you may have to make do with a download.

Planet Gong
Live Floating Anarchy '77 (Charly, 1978/Charly. 1996)

1. 'Psychological Overture' 2. 'Floating Anarchy' 3. 'Stoned Innocent Frankenstein' 4. 'New Age Transformation Try: No More Sages' 5. 'Opium For The People' 6. 'Allez Ali Baba Black Sheep Have You Any Bullshit: Mama Maya Mantram' (all tracks by Daevid Allen)

Live Floating Anarchy 1991 (2005, GAS Records)

1. 'Psychological Overture/Floatin' Anarchy' (Planet Gong) 2. 'It's The Time Of Your Life' (credited on album to Daevid Allen but actually Christian Tritsch) 3. 'Stoned Innocent Frankenstein' (Allen) 4. 'New Age Transformation Try: No More Sages' (Planet Gong) 5. 'Poet For Sale' (Allen) 6. 'Pot Head Pixies' (Allen) 7. 'Astral Alien' (Allen) 8. 'Much Too Old' (credited on album to Allen but actually Allen, Laswell) 9. 'Change The World' (credited on album to Allen but originally credited to Gilli Smyth) 10. 'Teeth' (Planet Gong) 11. 'Allez Ali Baba Blacksheep Have You Any Bullshit: Mama Maya Mantram' (Planet Gong) 12. 'Opium For The People' (Planet Gong) 13. 'Astral Alien' (soundcheck version) (Allen)

When Daevid Allen left Gong, one of the many projects in his head was the idea of a 'space-punk' band to combine the other-worldliness of Gong with the aggression of punk rock. Mike Howlett spotted Here & Now playing a gig in London and thought their brand of 'unpredictable musical anarchy' would be perfect. Formed in 1974, Here & Now were a kind of hippie/punk crossover with more hair but less spitting, who famously would play for free but have a whip-round to cover the cost of petrol. They heard that Allen wanted to meet them and together they created a touring show called Planet Gong, inspired by the philosophy of 'floating anarchy'. Daevid said in 2010 in an article, 'The Gong Remains The Same', by Jack Barron, in *Record Collector* magazine:

> Floating Anarchy was pretty much my response to Johnny Rotten. I totally agreed with him. I thought the prog rock thing was getting nauseatingly middle class. And as a middle-class revolutionary, I couldn't really sit with it for too long. And even Gong was getting a bit that way.

The lineup included Daevid and Gill, Stephan Lewry (Prof Steffe Sharpstrings PA) on guitar and vocals, Keith Dobson (Kif Kif Le Batteur) on drums, Keith Bailey (Keith da Missile Bass) on bass, Gavin Allardyce (Gavin Da Blitz) on synthesiser and Suze Da Blooz and Annie Wombat on backing vocals. The first album was taped at a gig in Toulouse during a short tour of France and, despite the lousy recording conditions, is a powerful and joyous record of a group of musicians teetering on the edge of anarchy. It includes a single, 'Opium For The People', made in a French studio during the tour.

Here & Now broke up in early 1986 but reformed for occasional gigs less than 18 months later, eventually joining up with Allen once again for a short Planet Gong tour at the end of 1991. The second live album was recorded at gigs in Sheffield, Preston and Norwich and, thanks to the CD format, offered up a fuller selection of tracks. Everything is there from the original album, with the addition of tracks from the debut Gong album, Allen's first solo release and a New York Gong song, 'Much Too Old'. Both albums are worthy of your attention and your hard-earned.

Strontium 90

Strontium 90: Police Academy (Ark 21 Records, 1997/Gonzo Media Group, 2010)

1. 'Visions Of The Night' (Sting) 2. 'New World Blues' (Mike Howlett) 3. '3 O'Clock Shit' (Sting) 4. 'Lady Of Delight' (Howlett) 5. 'Electron Romance' (Howlett) 6. 'Every Little Thing She Does Is Magic' (Sting) 7. 'Towers Tumbled' (Howlett) 8. 'Electron Romance' [live] (Howlett) 9. 'Lady Of Delight' (live) (Howlett)

A very short-lived band formed by bassist Mike Howlett after leaving Gong. He first met guitarist Andy Summers when he was playing with Kevin Coyne, who supported Gong on a UK tour in 1974, then bumped into him again in January 1977 at a party held by Lady June, longtime Gong and Soft Machine friend and poet. Mike explained to the author:

> I had made a demo of my own material for Virgin in my home studio and Simon Draper suggested they pay to make a better quality recording because it was my first attempt. So I asked Andy if he would play guitar – he had just returned from two years in California studying classical guitar and was confused about the exploding punk scene in the UK. I had met Sting when I went with my then-girlfriend, Carol Wilson, who was manager of Virgin Music Publishing, to check out a band called Last Exit in Newcastle. She signed Sting as a songwriter and persuaded him to come to London, where she could introduce him to other artists. I helped him move into his flat in Westbourne Grove and asked him to sing on my demo. When the drummer I had lined up couldn't make it – Chris Cutler from Henry Cow – he suggested bringing Stuart Copeland along. So they all met for the first time in a small 8-track studio in Swiss Cottage playing my songs and played together for the first time at the 1977 Gong reunion in Paris. In the end, Virgin decided not to sign us, we did a couple of more gigs around London, but I wasn't enjoying it, so I broke up the band. Stuart likes to think he stole Andy from me and that I was trying to steal Sting from him, but that is simply not true. I had had enough of bands – I had been in bands since I was 12 years old.

The demos and two live tracks were eventually released twenty years later, more for their interest to Police fans than Gong followers. Sting's solo demo of 'Every Little Thing She Does Is Magic' is certainly the standout track.

Bloom

Bloom [credited to Didier Malherbe] (Sonopresse, 1979/Charly Records, 1980/Voiceprint, 2001)

1. 'Bateau-Bole' (Didier Malherbe) 2. 'Whiskers' (Malherbe) 3. 'Give A Chance To To-Morrow' (Malherbe) 4. 'Dan-Dan' (Yan Vagh) 5. 'Suite A Tout De Sweet' (Malherbe)

Yes, I know I'm bending my own rules here. There WAS a band called Bloom, led by the master of all things wind-driven and including Yan Emeric on guitar, Peter Kimberley vocals, Winston Berkeley bass and Jean Padovani on drums. But the album they recorded – and a very rare single coupling 'Danskoria' with 'Bong' – ended up being credited to Didier alone. Perhaps the record company thought Gong fans would not realise the band was inspired by Malherbe's alter-ego Bloomdido Bad de Grasse. In any case, it was a short-lived formation that broke up in 1982. The music is superb jazz fusion tinged with Didier's own particular brand of pixie mischief.

New York Gong

About Time (Charly, 1980/Spalax, 1998)

1. 'Preface' (Daevid Allen, Michael Beinhorn) 2. 'Much Too Old' (Allen, Bill Laswell) 3. 'Black September' (Allen, Chris Cultreri) 4. 'Materialism; (Laswell,

Cultreri) 5. 'Strong Woman' (Allen, Bill Bacon) 6. 'I Am A Freud' (Allen) 7. 'O My Photograph' (Allen) 8. 'Jungle Windo(w)' (Allen) 9. 'Hours Gone' (Allen)

Allen's stint with Here & Now was short-lived – he bowed out before a tour in 1978 with various illnesses reported as a bad back, exhaustion and Russian flu. A few months later he went to New York, where he formed a one-off 'American Gong' lineup for Giorgio Gomelsky's Zu Manifestival that included future members of Materiel plus Chris Cutler from Henry Cow on drums. Returning in early 1979, the same lineup of Bill Laswell on bass, Cliff Cultreri guitar, Michael Beinhorn synth, Don Davis sax & flute, Mark Kramer keys/trombone and Bill Bacon on drums, toured the USA as New York Gong, stopping off in Willow, NY, to record an album. The result is a much harder-edged collection than anything Allen had made since *Camembert Electrique*, a mixture of punk, new wave and hippie whimsy. Most of the tracks are short and snappy, with the exception of the nine-minute 'O My Photograph' and 'Jungle Windo(w)', which features saxophonist Gary Windo improvising furiously. Keen-eared fans will recognise 'Hours Gone' as a reworking of the 1974 abortive Gong single 'Where Have All The Flowers Gone'. The group fell apart after a European tour and Allen cut up some of the tracks to create a number of solo albums.

The Invisible Opera Company Of Tibet [Oz Version]
Invisible Opera Company Of Tibet (Voice Print, 1991)

1. 'Marpa's Entrance' (Chandrabhanu) 2. 'G'Day' (Russell Hibbs) 3. 'Hungry Ghosts' (Chandrabhanu) 4. 'Away, Away' (Daevid Allen) 5. 'Trial By Headline' (Allen) 6. 'Chernobyl Rain' (Hibbs) 7. 'Gorilla' (Harry Williamson) 8. 'Milarepa's Journey' (Chandrabhanu) 9. 'The Other Side Of Me' (Hibbs) 10. 'Man And Woman' (Hibbs) 11. 'The Family' (Hibbs) 12. 'Stormbirds' (Hibbs) 13. 'The Actor' (Hibbs).

The Invisible Opera Company of Tibet story is a tad confusing, so bear with me on this one. Originally the name was an alias coined by Daevid Allen for the *You* lineup in the songwriting credits (although written in French). But he also saw it as 'an international ideological/spiritual/aesthetic communications network for artists of all kinds who share the common vision of warm-hearted, pan-stylistic, inclusive art forms which serve the drive towards conscious evolution'. The name was also inspired by the sound of glissando guitar, which sometimes resembles a multitude of monks chanting or singing opera.

During his Australian exile he formed a band of the same name with Byron Bay musician Russell (sometimes Russel) Hibbs, also enlisting the help of Gilli on space-whisper, her then-husband Harry Williamson on piano and keys, Douglas Kerr on bass, Robert Calvert on sax and, on drums, an Irish wombat farmer called Neil Cairney. Harry was working at a studio with 24-track equipment and a vinyl record factory, and recorded and mixed the album in his spare time.

The results languished in the vaults for five years, although a single, 'Trial By Headline', was released in 1987. Recorded earlier, it was initially a completely separate project in defence of Lindy Chamberlain, who was convicted of murdering her child despite evidence from Aborigine trackers that the infant had been taken by a dingo. In 1991 the recordings were finally issued by Voiceprint (or Voice Print as they were briefly known) after Allen had returned to the UK and was beginning to become active again. Daevid wanted extra material on the album so Harry added classical Indian dance tracks he had recorded with dancer and choreographer Chandrabhanu, resulting in the rather unusual juxtaposition of folk-rock with South Indian dance music. The album is a somewhat disjointed collection of soundscapes and songs, with Hibbs's material faring particularly well. Out of Allen's two contributions, 'Trial By Headline' is a rap over a steady beat, while 'Away Away' is a folky song about French nuclear tests in the Pacific that was reused on the *Shapeshifter* album as 'La Bas La Bas'.

Invisible Opera Company Of Tibet (Tropical Version Brazil)
The Eternal Voice (No Label, 1991)
1. 'Inner Temple' 2. 'Raindrops On Banana Leaves' 3. 'Calm Lake & Autumn Moon' 4. 'Heart Song' 5. 'Inner Voice' 6. 'Numa Pessoa So' 7. 'Gliding' 8. 'Eternal Voice' (Song credits unspecified but probably Fabio Golfetti)

Glissando Spirit (Low-Life Records, 1993/Voiceprint, 1996)
1. 'Landing' 2. 'Uluwatu' 3. 'Electric Bird' 4. 'Baliman Energy' 5. 'Cosmic Dancer' 6. 'Inner Voice' 7. 'High Mountains Dance' 8. 'Dreaming' 9. 'Moon In The Sky' 10. 'Mirage' 11. 'Distant Shore' 12. 'Stars Can Frighten You' 13. '7 Keys' 14. 'The Wizard's Garden' 15. 'Eastside' (all tracks composed & played under universal influence of Compagnie d'Opera Invisible de Thibet)

Cosmic Dance Co [credited to Fabio Golfetti, Invisible Opera Of Tibet Tropical Version Brazil] (Invisivel, 1996)
1. 'Land Beneath The Earth' 2. 'Morning Star Rising With The Yellow Dawn' 3. 'The Eternal Voice (Late Night)' 4. 'Calm Lake & Autumn Moon' 5. 'Raindrops On Banana Leaves' 6. 'South Atlantic Wind' 7. 'Sound Inside The Flower Garden' 8. 'Dancing On The Earth'. (Song credits unspecified but probably Fabio Golfetti)

UFO Planante (Voiceprint, 2010)
1. 'First Contact' (C.O.I.T) 2. 'Sal Paradise' (Fernando Alge) 3. 'Stars' (Fabio Golfetti) 4. 'Spirits' (Fabio Golfetti) 5. 'Landing In Shambala' (C.O.I.T) 6. 'Moon In June' [live] (Robert Wyatt)

We've already learned that Fabio Golfetti of Brazilian progressive rock group Violetta De Outono was a big Gong fan and contacted Daevid Allen around

1988 with a view to collaborating with him. Allen encouraged Golfetti to create his own version of the Invisible Opera Company Of Tibet, and this band released a single, 'Numa Pessoa So' in 1989, followed two years later by *The Eternal Voice*, with May East on Tibetan singing bowls and bells. It's a collection of long, ambient instrumentals with lots of heady glissando and is available as a download from Bandcamp.

For 1993's Glissando Spirit Fabio put together a more stable lineup including Renato Mello on keyboards and sax and Claudio Souza on drums. This band also recorded and released *Live At The Britannia Cafe* (1994, Invisivel) and *Glissando Spirit Live* (2004, Invisivel). *Cosmic Dance Co*, also available as a Bandcamp download, is a collection of ambient soundscapes recorded just by Fabio, while *UFO Planante* is once again a proper band offering, this time with Fabio, Gabriel Costa on drums and Fred Barley on drums. Of particular interest on that album is 'Moon In June' with Robert Wyatt, recorded live in Sao Paulo in 2006.

Invisible Opera Company Of Tibet (UK Version)
The Jewel In The Lotus (GAS Records, 1995/Dakini Records, 2019)
1. 'Om Mani Padme Hum' (I.O.C.T./Trad) 2. 'All Coming True' (Jim Peters) 3. 'Bad Self' (Tim Hall) 4. 'The Size Of Minus One' (I.O.C.T.) 5. 'Bloody Engineers' (I.O.C.O.T.) 6. 'Goddess Dub' (I.O.C.O.T./Trad) 7. 'Bad Self Kipper' (I.O.C.O.T.) 8. 'Mysteries' (Hall) 9. 'Bad Bongos Meets The Great God Pan' (I.O.C.O.T.) 10. 'Om Tara' (I.O.C.O.T/Trad)

Songs From The Temple Of Now (Dakini Records, 2015)
1. 'Spirit Of Joy' [band version] (Arthur Brown, M. Oakey-Harris, Phil Curtis) 2. 'Tried So Hard' (Christian Tritsch, Daevid Allen) 3. 'Lilith' (Brian Abbott, Jackie Juno) 4. 'Temple Song' (Abbott, Juno) 5. 'Gateway To The Dead' (Abbott, Juno) 6. 'Tried So Hard' [band version] (Tritsch, Allen) 7. 'Now' (I.O.C.O.T.) 8. 'Spirit Of Joy' (Brown, Oakey-Harris, Curtis)

The Bardo Of Becoming (Dakini Records, 2020)
1. 'Dissolution' 2. 'Song Of The Bardo' 3. 'World Of The Living' 4. 'The Little Deaths' 5. 'The Collapsing Mountain (Earth)' 6. 'An Engulfing Ocean (Water)' 7. 'A Blazing Inferno (Fire)' 8. 'A Gusting Whirlwind (Air)' 9. 'The Three Abysses Pt1' 10. 'The Three Abysses Pt2' 11. 'The Approaching' (All tracks Brian Abbott)

We have touched on the origins of the UK Invisibles in the *Shapeshifter* section – you may recall it was the first band Daevid Allen put together in the UK when he returned from Australia in 1988. That lineup, including Didier Malherbe, Graham Clark and Shyamal Maitra, is represented on *Live in 1988 – The Return* (2005, Voiceprint) but fairly quickly morphed into Gongmaison and then Gong. One of the musicians who briefly played tablas during the ever-changing IOCT lineup was Devon-born musician

Brian Abbott, and a few years later he put together another group of Invisibles to support Allen and Russell Hibbs on tour, including Tim Hall on bass and vocals, Steve Hickeson on drums and Jim Peters on keyboards, flutes and vocals.

After a few cassette-only releases of live performances in 1993, the band offered *The Jewel In The Lotus* in 1995. The tracklisting above is from the 25th-anniversary release in 2019 – the original contained the first four tracks plus a live recording of 'Circle Around' with Allen and Hibbs guesting.

It took nine years before a second album saw the light of day. By this time there had been a personnel change, now with Phil Curtis on bass, Dan Barber drums, Clive Buckland-Bork on keyboards and Jackie Juno on lead vocals. This lineup recorded the *Live At Sonic Rock Solstice 2011* album, released a year later, followed by *Songs From The Temple Of Now*, aided and abetted by Allen and Arthur Brown of 'Fire!' fame. An early gig cassette recording, *Go Totally Bananas!: Live Spring 1994*, was re-released on CD by Dakini in 2006, and I can heartily recommend *Surfing The Wave Of The Mystery: Live At Kozfest 2018*, released by Dakini the following year.

A third studio album, *The Bardo Of Becoming*, appeared as this book went to press

The Magick Brothers
Live At The Witchwood 1991 (Voiceprint/Blueprint, 1992)
1. 'Zero Theme' (Daevid Allen) 2. 'Why Do We Treat Ourselves Like We Do?' (Allen) 3. 'I Am My Own Roadie' (Allen) 4. 'Herbaceous Border' (Mark Robson) 5. 'Have You Seen My Friend?' (Allen) 6. 'Wayland Smithy' (Trad/arr. Robson) 7. 'Trial By Headline' (Allen) 8. 'Isle Of Glass' (Robson) 9. 'Children Of The New World' (Allen) 10. 'Wise Man In Your Heart' (Allen, Mike Howlett, Pierre Moerlen) 11. 'Magick Brother' (Gilli Smyth).

Live In Glastonbury Town (Bananamoon Obscura, 2006)
1. 'Nowhere To Everywhere' (Daevid Allen, Mark Robson) 2. 'New Dreamtime' (Robson) 3. 'Ship Of Fools' (Allen) 4. 'Marks Intro' (Robson) 5. 'Tasmanian Road Song' (Robson) 6. 'Mullumbimby Mother' (Allen) 7. 'Sesame' (Joshi Chentrens) 8. 'Hours Gone' (Allen) 9. 'Herbaceous Border' (Robson) 10. 'Introd Heathens All Members' 11. 'Lady Dear Lady' (Allen) 12. 'Introd OAU' 13. 'Old As The Universe' 14. 'Happiest Coda' (Allen) 15. 'Magick Brother' (Allen).

Live In San Francisco (Gonzo Multimedia, 2012)
1. 'Audience Invocation' 2. 'Zero Theme' 3. 'Why Do We Treat Ourselves Like We Do?' 4. 'I Am My Own Roadie' 5. 'Herbaceous Border' 6. 'Have You Seen My Friend' 7. 'I Am…' 8. 'Wayland Smithy' 9. 'There Is No Death' 10. 'Wise Man In Your Heart' 11. 'Violin Interlude' 12. 'Magick Brother' 13. 'Om One' [instrumental] 14. 'Om Two With Friends' 15. 'The Finale – Back To Reality!' (No credits on album)

Not so much a band as an occasional touring trio consisting of Daevid Allen, violinist Graham Clark and Kangaroo Moon's Mark Robson on keyboards and didgeridoo. They never produced a studio album – their catalogue consists of the above entertaining live albums recorded between 1991 and 1998, and a limited-edition cassette. If you like Daevid's solo acoustic songs then you will love them augmented with keyboards and violin, and the occasional blast of didgeridoo. As you can tell from the tracklists, most of the songs are taken from Daevid's early solo albums, augmented by some very nice compositions from Robson.

Live At The Witchwood 1991 is the most freely available but *Live In Glastonbury Town* – No11 in Allen's Bananamoon Obscura series – contains some rarely-played tracks, such as 'Ship Of Fools' and 'Mullumbimby Mother', and the Gonzo Multimedia release includes a DVD.

Gongmaison

Gongmaison (Demi Monde, 1989/Voiceprint, 2005)

1. 'Flying Teacup' (Daevid Allen) 2. '1989' (Harry Williamson) 3. 'Titti-Caca' (Allen) 4. 'Tablas Logorhythmic' (Shyamal Maitra) 5. 'Negotiate' (Allen) 6. 'We Circle Around' (Trad)

Once again, the story of a Gong offshoot has been covered elsewhere in the book so we needn't go into it in too much detail here. This is the band that existed between the original UK Invisible Opera Company Of Tibet, and *Shapeshifter* Gong. The sole studio album, recorded in Wales, is a strange mixture – the name was supposed to suggest house music, and some of the tracks do indeed have repetitive electronically-programmed drumbeats courtesy of Harry Williamson. 'Flying Teacup' is a danceable re-imagining of 'Flying Teapot' – there is even an extended dance mix on the CD version! But '1989' is a jolly, knees-up ditty that reworks '1999' from Mother Gong's *Robot Woman 2,* while 'Titti-Caca' is almost folk music, with acoustic guitar and Graham Clark's violin to the fore. Those synth drums keep the rhythm going during parts of 'Negotiate' and 'We Circle Around' but by no stretch of the imagination can this be called 'house'! Neither one thing nor the other, *Gongmaison* is clearly a transition album on the way to *Shapeshifter*. To catch them at their best try *Live At The Glastonbury Festival 1989*, an altogether more successful collection.

Invisible Opera Company Of Oz

Melbourne Studio Tapes (Bananamoon Obscura, 2004)

1. 'Boperatica' 2. 'Magick Of The Circle' 3. 'Idealist' 4. 'Garden Song' 5. 'Trial By Headline' 6. 'Boperatico' 7. 'Lolli Song' 8. 'Never Too Late' 9. 'Here & Now I Allow' 10. 'I am My Own Roadie' (all titles Daevid Allen)

In 1990 Daevid Allen returned to Australia where a spontaneous demo recording took place at Harry Williamson's Spring Studio, with the help of Kangaroo Moon violinist Elliet Mackrell plus the then Mother Gong rhythm section. The demos were later released as part of Allen's limited edition Bananamoon Obscura series and, at the time of writing, this particular volume is still available from the Planet Gong website. These are mostly electrified versions of songs in Allen's acoustic collection and turned up later on various albums under various names.

Glo

Even As We (1995, GAS Records/1997, Gliss Records)
1. 'Deiea' (Gilli Smyth, Stephan Lewry) 2. 'I'm Your Gravity' (Smyth, Lewry) 3. 'Travellers Stargate' (Smyth, Lewry) 4. 'Crystal World' (Smyth, Lewry) 5. 'Doom Ghosts' (Smyth, Lewry) 6. 'AND' (Smyth, Lewry) 7. 'Pagii Herbus' (Smyth, Lewry) 8. 'Spirit Lover' (Smyth, Lewry) 9. 'Walk The Streets' (Smyth, Lewry, Taliesin Allen) 10. 'Goddesses Love Oranges' (Smyth, Lewry) 11. 'Let's GLO' (Smyth, Lewry) 12. 'Back To The Sea' (Smyth, Lewry) 13. 'Walk The Streets' [Excerpt]

What Gilli Smyth did after Mother Gong ... She teamed up with Here & Now and occasional Gong guitarist Stephan Lewry – aka Prof Steffe Sharpstrings – for an album of bubbly psychedelic soundscapes, described as 'ambient with beats', with vocals from Steffe and Gilli's space whisper. Chilled and tuneful, Glo is a little bit like a laidback System 7, quite gentle and contemplative in parts, and is well worth checking out. The band name stands for Goddesses Love Oranges.

Gongzilla

Suffer (Lolo Records, 1995)
1. 'Gongzilla' (Bon Lozaga) 2. 'Bad Habits' (Benoit Moerlen) 3. 'Sing' (Hansford Rowe) 4. 'Gongzilla's Dilemma' (Rowe) 5. 'Mr Sinister Minister' (Lozaga) 6. 'Almost You' (Lozaga) 7. 'Mezzanine' (Moerlen) 8. 'Hip-Hopnosis' (Lozaga) 9. 'Allan Qui?' (Rowe) 10. 'Senna' (Rowe) 11. 'Camel' (Moerlen)

Thrive (Lola Records, 1996)
1. 'Suffer' (Bon Lozaga) 2. 'Say It Loud' (Hansford Rowe) 3. 'Island' (Lozaga, Rowe) 4. 'Image' (Rowe) 5. 'Shaman' (Rowe) 6. 'Les Vosges' (Lozaga) 7. 'Listen To The Wind' (Rowe) 8. 'Image' [reprise] (Rowe) 9. 'Console Warmer' (Lozaga, Rowe, Gary Husband)

East Village Sessions (Lolo Records, 2003)
1. 'Haniface' 2. 'Aquila' 3. 'Lilly' 4. 'Ging Gong' 5. 'Thrive' 6. 'My Doctor Told Me So' 7. 'The News' 8. 'No Pennies Please'

Five Even (Lolo Records, 2008)
1. 'Say Hey' (Hansford Rowe) 2. 'French Grass' (Bon Lozaga) 3. 'Willy' (Bon Lozaga, Rowe) 4. 'American Dream' (Rowe) 5. 'Five Even' (Rowe) 6. 'When The Water's Gone' (Rowe) 7. 'Jersey Pines' (Rowe) 8. 'So High' (Rowe, Jameison Ledonia) 9. 'Jersey Pines' [Bis] (Rowe)

When Pierre Moerlen's Gong broke up in 1989, guitarist Bon Lozaga quit the music business to concentrate on running restaurants. But three years later he got itchy fingers and teamed up with PMG bassist Hansford Rowe to form a label, Lolo Records, and to release a number of solo albums under the name of Bon. This led to discussions with Pierre and his brother Benoit about reforming PMG, but the drummer decided to bow out. Instead, the remaining three pulled in guitarist Allan Holdsworth, US percussionist Bobby Thomas Jr and no fewer than three different drummers. The debut album, *Suffer*, was a powerful mix of heavy rock and jazz fusion, with Holdsworth's remarkable playing to the fore on four of the tracks and Benoit Moerlen's tuned percussion taking a bit of a back seat.

Celebrated British jazz drummer Gary Husband and experimental guitarist David Torn came in for follow-up *Thrive* – Husband stayed for *East Village Sessions*, then was replaced by Phil Kester for *Five Even*. While not as distinctive as PMG, Gongzilla nevertheless created some excellent jazz-rock and were a powerful live outfit, as evidenced on 2001 concert album recorded three years previously in Canada with the addition of David Fiuczynski on guitar.

Goddess Trance

Goddess Trance (GAS Records, 1996)

1. 'Bb In Trees' 2. 'Rocks And Fish' 3. 'Universal Mind' 4. 'Bird Wobble' 5. 'Doomerang Dreams' 6. 'Planet Eggs Crack' 7. '11th Of The 11th' 8. 'Distant Future' (all tracks improvised by Goddess Trance)

Electric Shiatsu (Voiceprint, 1999)

1. 'It's A Strange Place Here' (Orlando Allen) 2. 'Sugar Path' (Music: Daevid Allen, Dr Tone, O. Allen, Lyrics: Gilli Smyth) 3. 'Sirius Ma' (Dr Tone, Cleis Pearce) 4. 'Little Whale' (O. Allen) 5. 'Ali Baba' (O. Allen) 6. 'Strange Place' (Part 2) (O. Allen) 7. 'Triple Helix' (G. Smyth) 8. 'Journey Of The White Whale' (O. Allen)

After GLO Gilli Smyth worked with her son Orlando Allen, contributing the track 'Cyberwhale' to the *Gong Family Jewels* collection. He then took her lyrical ideas and set them to improvised music recorded mostly at a 1996 New Year's Eve party in Byron Bay along with Daevid Allen, Australian bassist Dr Tone – alias Tony Wandella – Nick Spacetree on keyboards, Orlando's brother Taliesin on congas and Kavi on flute, whistles, bells and things. The result is a laidback GLO, more trancey but still a bit dancey, particularly on the second album, recorded at local studios with contributions from Canterbury-connected guitarist Mark Hewins. By this time the band had shortened its name to Goddess T.

Daevid Allen's University Of Errors

Money Doesn't Make It (InnerSPACE Records, 1999)

1. 'Money Doesn't Make It' 2. 'Prince Of Sidewalk Scooter' 3. 'False Teacher' 4. 'Involve Me' 5. 'Mullumbimby Mother' 6. 'Submarine Of Salt' 7. 'Prof Impossible's

Preambule' 8. 'Cunning Style Construct' 9. 'Tailwind Upswerve' 10. 'Wedding Music' 11. 'Burn Your Money' 12. 'Can't Buy Me Sex' (all tracks music: University Of Errors, lyrics: Daevid Allen)

e2x10=Tenure (GAS Records, 2000)
1. 'Iced Tea Overture' 2. 'If You Are Changing' 3. 'Ocean Mutha' 4. 'Olde Guitar Body O' Mine' 5. 'Innisfree' 6. 'One Mother Of Pearl' 7. 'Pinky's Party Song' 8. 'Good Evening Ned Kelly' (all tracks music: University Of Errors, lyrics: Daevid Allen except 6 by WB Yeats)

Ugly Music 4 Monica (Weed, 2003)
1. 'Skulls Of Our Enemies' (Josh Pollock, Jason Mills) 2. 'Wage Slave' (Daevid Allen) 3. 'Mystico Fanatico' (Pollock, Allen) 4. 'Rich Men Eat My Voice' (Allen, University Of Errors) 5. 'So What?' (Allen, Miles Davis) 6. 'PHP 2032' (Allen) 7. 'Earthbound' (Pollock, Mills, Michael Clare) 8. 'Moo?' (Allen) 9. 'If You Die' (Allen, Clare) 10. 'Clarence In Wonderland' (Kevin Ayers) 11. 'Patapan' (Trad, Allen)

Jet Propelled Photographs (Cuneiform Records, 2004)
1. 'That's How Much I Need You Now' (Robert Wyatt) 2. 'Save Yourself' (Wyatt) 3. 'I Should've Known' (Hugh Hopper) 4. 'Shooting At The Moon' [aka Jet Propelled Photographs] (Kevin Ayers) 5. 'When I Don't Want You' (Hopper) 6. 'Memories' (Hopper) 7. 'You Don't Remember' (Wyatt, Daevid Allen) 8. 'She's Gone' (Ayers) 9. 'I'd Rather Be With You' (Ayers) 10. 'Love Makes Sweet Music' (Ayers) 11. 'Feelin' Reelin' Squeelin''(Ayers) 12. 'Hope For Happiness' (Brian Hopper) 13. 'We Know What You Mean [Soon Soon Soon]' (Ayers)

At the end of September 1998, after a short US tour, Daevid Allen jammed at Komotion Studios in San Francisco with members of a local psychedelic band, Mushroom (he had appeared on stage with them the previous night). He was so impressed with the results he wrote some lyrics and recorded them the following day, before flying home to Australia. Later, when he heard the final mixes from the sessions, he officially christened the lineup – Josh Pollock on guitar, Michael Clare bass and Pat Thomas drums – The University Of Errors (it made commercial sense to add Daevid Allen's name to it) and the first gigs took place in March the following year.

Dirty, grungy and anarchic, the albums are dominated by Pollock's crunchy, distorted guitar, while Allen sounds more excited and animated here than he has for a long time. Due to the nature of its recording process, *Money Doesn't Make It* is more a collection of formless jams with Allen doing a musical rap over the top. Later albums have more composed songs on them, culminating in 2004's *Jet Propelled Photographs*, on which the band rejuvenate the Soft Machine demos recorded with Giorgio Gomelsky in 1967, including the single 'Love Makes Sweet Music/Feelin' Reelin' Squeelin''.

Brainville
The Children's Crusade (Shimmy Disc, 1999)
1. 'March Of The Goodbyes' (Music: Brainville, Lyrics: Daevid Allen) 2. 'The Revenge Of Spartacus' (Music: Brainville, Lyrics: Daevid Allen) 3. 'The Children's Crusade' (Music: Brainville, Lyrics: Kramer) 4. 'Aphaville Beach' (Music: Brainville, Lyrics: Daevid Allen) 5. 'Goodbye Mother Night' (Music: Brainville, Lyrics: Daevid Allen) 6. 'The Killing' (Music: Brainville, Lyrics: Daevid Allen) 7. 'Useless By Moonlight' (Kramer) 8. 'The Fall Of Colonel Kong' (Music: Brainville, Lyrics: Daevid Allen) 9. 'The Revenge Of Clare Quilty' (Music: Brainville, Lyrics: Daevid Allen) 10. 'Brain Villa Collapse' (Music: Brainville, Lyrics: Daevid Allen) 11.'Merkin Mufley's Lament' (Allen)

One of the many questions you may be asking is, why no mention of the Daevid Allen Trio? Well, if we're being true to our principles here, then that band does not qualify because it pre-dates Gong (as do Allen's recordings with The Soft Machine). But we can celebrate this reunion of Daevid and Hugh Hopper some 36 years later, with Pip Pyle on drums. The original lineup was a quartet with New York musician and producer Mark Kramer (real name Stephen Michael Bonner) who was an occasional collaborator with Allen. They recorded Brainville's sole studio album, *The Children's Crusade*, at Kramer's New Jersey studio following a few gigs at around the same time Allen was exploring musical possibilities with Mushroom. Later, Brainville were reduced to a trio when Kramer left and became Brainville 3 when Henry Cow's Chris Cutler replaced Pip Pyle on drums.

As you can imagine, the result is musically challenging and uncompromising – avant-garde is probably the phrase, in that I 'avant-garde' a clue what's going on. But there's a certain wild, liberating charm to it all and occasional moments of psychedelic beauty. Sadly, Hopper died ten years later, aged 64, after being diagnosed with leukaemia.

Hadouk Trio/Quartet
Shamanimal (Celluloid 1999/Naïve, 2006)
1. 'Hadouk Blues' (Didier Malherbe, Loy Ehrlich) 2. 'Dragon De Lune' (Malherbe, Ehrlich) 3. 'La Course Des Nuages' (Malherbe, Ehrlich) 4. 'Shamanimal' (Malherbe, Ehrlich) 5. 'Gopi' (Malherbe, Ehrlich) 6. 'Salsa Movar' (Malherbe, Ehrlich) 7. 'Moussa' (Ehrlich) 8. 'Peau De Banane' (Malherbe, Ehrlich) 9. 'Vegetal Groove' (Malherbe, Ehrlich, Steve Shehan)

Now (Naive/Celluloid, 2002)
1. 'Alma Celesta' (Steve Shehan) 2. 'Theatre Des Singes' (Didier Malherbe, Loy Ehrlich, Shehan) 3. 'Barca Solaris' (Malherbe, Ehrlich) 4. 'Nacarat' (Malherbe, Ehrlich) 5. 'Le Petit Cheval Mopse' (Malherbe, Ehrlich) 6. 'Grand Large' (Malherbe, Ehrlich) 7. 'Polar Blues' (Malherbe, Ehrlich, Shehan) 8. 'O'Shehan Drum' (Shehan) 9. 'Bille En Tete' (Malherbe, Ehrlich, Shehan) 10. 'Echappade' (Ehrlich) 11. 'Echappee Belle' (Malherbe, Ehrlich, Shehan)

Utopies (Naïve, 2006)
1. 'Suave Corridor' (Ehrlich, Malherbe) 2. 'Baldamore' (Ehrlich, Malherbe) 3. 'Brasero Des Soucis' (Ehrlich, Malherbe) 4. 'Gardien De La Nuit' (Ehrlich, Malherbe, Shehan) 5. 'Idalie' (Ehrlich, Malherbe) 6. 'Centaurea' (Shehan) 7. 'Toupie Tambour' (Ehrlich, Malherbe, Shehan) 8. 'Clef Des Brumes' (Ehrlich, Malherbe) 9. 'Toupie Valse' (Ehrlich, Malherbe) 10. 'Hijaz' (Shehan) 11. 'Parasol Blanc 1' (Ehrlich, Malherbe, Hassell) 12. 'Parasol Blanc 2' (Ehrlich, Malherbe, Hassell)

Air Hadouk (Naïve, 2010)
1. 'Lomsha' (Loy Ehrlich, Didier Malherbe) 2. 'Aerozen' (Ehrlich, Malherbe) 3. 'Babbalanja' (Ehrlich, Malherbe, Steve Shehan) 4. 'Yillah' (Shehan) 5. 'Dididi' (Ehrlich, Malherbe) 6. 'Friday The 13th' (T. Monk) 7. 'Hang Around Me' (Shehan) 8. 'Hang2Hang' (Shehan) 9. 'Nambarai Gate' (Malherbe) 10. 'Nambarai' (Malherbe) 11. 'Ayel' (Ehrlich) 12. 'Taicotin' (Ehrlich, Malherbe) 13. 'Soft Landing' (Ehrlich, Malherbe, Shehan)

Hadoukly Yours (Naïve, 2013)
1. 'Chappak' (Didier Malherbe, Loy Ehrlich) 2. 'Ayur' (Ehrlich) 3. 'BORA Bollo' (Malherbe, Eric Lohrer, Ehrlich,) 4. 'Boro BOLLO' (Malherbe, Lohrer, Ehrlich) 5. 'Shadow Maker' (Ehrlich) 6. 'Bawu Call' (Malherbe) 7. 'Chaloupe De Chameau' (Malherbe) 8. 'Rouge Bambou' (Malherbe, Lohrer, Ehrlich, Jean-Luc Di Fraya) 9. 'Danse Des Lutins' (Malherbe) 10. 'Bittersweet Lullaby' (Malherbe, Lohrer) 11. 'Suite Cabaline 1' (Malherbe, Lohrer) 12. 'Suite Cabaline 2' (Malherbe, Lohrer) 13. 'Blueberry Hill' (Lewis, Stock, Rose)

Le Cinquieme Fruit (Naïve, 2017)
1. 'Matin Du Faune' (Eric Lohrer) 2. 'Tidzi' (Loy Ehrlich) 3. 'Dame de Coeur' (Ehrlich) 4. 'Le Jardin D'Hadouk' (Didier Malherbe, Ehrlich) 5. 'So Gong' (Malherbe, Ehrlich) 6. 'Tchoun' (Malherbe) 7. 'Les Fees D'Iris' (Lohrer) 8. 'Lila Et Lampion' (Ehrlich) 9. 'Valse Au Pays De Tendre' (Malherbe, arr Lohrer) 10. 'Le Cinquieme Fruit' (Malherbe, Lohrer, Jean-Luc Di Fraya, Ehrlich)

Le Concile des Oiseaux (Self-released, 2024)
1. 'Hadouk Song' 2. 'Dew Dance' 3. 'Soli Fugae' 4. 'Le Concile Des Oiseaux' 5. 'Le Hasard À Bretelles' 6. 'Less Gravity' 7. 'El Jazzouli' 8. 'Haj Bawu Blues' 9. 'Cellito & Doudouk, D'Amore' 10. 'Cellito & Doudouk, Rigodon'. All tracks by Didier Malherbe and Loy Ehrlich.

Ah, Hadouk. There is a special place in most Gong lovers' hearts for this gem of a band. Partly because it's Didier, the original Pot Head Pixie, and partly because it is such a warm, whimsical, ear-pleasing blend of jazz and ethnic folkiness, full of wonderful melodies drawn from French, African and Asian cultures.

It all began way back in 1995 when Didier and French multi-instrumentalist Loy Ehrlich recorded an album as a duo, naming it after their main instruments, the duduk and hajouj. So, Dujouj, then. No, only joking. It was, of course, Hadouk and, with the addition of percussionist Steve Shehan, this was adopted as the name of the trio, releasing their first album *Shamanimal* in 1999. In 2013, Hadouk lost Shehan but gained guitarist Eric Lohrer and percussionist Jean-Luc Di Freya, thus becoming a quartet for that year's album *Hadoukly Yours*, and its follow-up *Le Cinquieme Fruit*. *Live a FIP* (2004, Mélodie/Abeille Musique) captures the band live in the studio for a Radio France broadcast, while *Baldamore* (2007, Naive) is a concert at the Cabaret Sauvage in Paris.

House Of Thandoy

House Of Thandoy (No label, 2001)

1. 'Raga 99' (Higgins, Howlett, Sayer, Travis) 2. 'Dreamcatcher' (Higgins, Howlett, Sayer) 3. 'Fast 4 Word' (Higgins, Howlett, Sayer, Travis) 4. 'Deep Float' (Higgins, Howlett, Sayer) 5. 'Station pt1' (Higgins, Howlett, Sayer) 6. 'Station pt2' (Higgins, Howlett, Sayer) 7. 'Nightline' (Higgins, Howlett, Sayer)

Expanding Themes (No label, 2006)

1. 'Shake Yer Bizkit' 2. 'Rubber Jelly' 3. 'The Velvet Sofa' 4. 'Alternatum' 5. 'Gear Shift' 6. 'A Deeper Float' 7. 'Sketches Of Acton' (all tracks Cassidy, Higgins, Howlett)

In 2001 Mike Howlett was introduced to guitarist and synth-player Steve Higgins, formerly of Karmakanix, through producer John Leckie, and House Of Thandoy were formed after a jam at Mike's birthday party. They were later joined by drummer Eddy Sayer and made one (rather short) album with Theo Travis on flute and sax. In 2003 Steve Cassidy replaced Sayer for the second album.

Described as 'space-funk psychedelic grooves', it's a summing-up that may have to satisfy you as the CDs are rarer than Shergar's droppings, although some live recordings exist on the internet and reveal that, yes, this is a band that offers long, spacey, funky jams – a bit Here & Now, in fact – with Howlett's commanding bass very much to the fore. It would be nice to see these albums getting a proper release, so come on record companies!

Guru & Zero

Makoto Mango (Swordfish Records, 2004)

1. 'Kawabata Biodynamique' (Daevid Allen, Kawabata Makoto, Cotton Casino)

Beauty & The Basket Case (Bananamoon Obscura, 2006)

1. 'Coolbrow Cathartonica' (Boiled Egglake) 2. 'Thus Spake Lady Cottonade' (Fried Egglake) 3. 'Gentlemen Strolling On A Fine Line' (OM-Lette) 4. 'The Egg Dragon's Glittering Eyes' (Scrambled Egglake) 5. 'You Go OH YEAH' (Hemlocksfo Jesu Grill) 6. 'Vegan Feedback Smoothie Please' (Hsfo Muzzleman

Gridlock) 7. 'Psycho Delicate Hessianskin' (Hsfo Rabbihat Goldclampervan) 8. 'Elastic Beaverzip Cadenza' (Hsfo Sri Babaciao Siddhitrip) 9. 'Dread Lady Humanoid The Return' (Hsfo Goddex Crustica) 10. 'The Stranger In The Tights' (Hsfo Zoozen Boo) 11. 'Goodnight Nursery' (Hsfomigodquick)

The pedants amongst you may be saying, hang on Furbank, this is a collaboration, not a band and therefore disallowed under your own confused rules. And, to an extent, they would be right. Certainly, if these recordings had been credited to Allen, Makoto and Cotton they might not have got a look in – the fate that has befallen *I Am Your Egg*, credited to Gilli Smyth, Orlando Allen and Daevid Allen, for example. But Guru & Zero are more than just a collaboration – they are part of the Acid Motherhood story and a stepping stone to a new Gong. And who is Guru and who is Zero? Even Allen admitted he didn't know.

So what we have here are two albums released in the wrong order: *Beauty & The Basket Case* chronicles the early musical meeting of minds, recorded in 2002 at their second concert at the Egg Lake Festival on San Juan Island in Washington state and third gig at the Hemlock Tavern in San Francisco. Surprisingly, it opens with Allen on acoustic guitar, setting up a repetitive sequence of droning chords over which Makoto and Cotton provide strange noises and cries. Other tracks draw on Acid Mothers Temple compositions such as 'Pink Lady Lemonade', and synth and guitar improvisations with Allen gamely trying to inject some humour over the top.

Makoto Mango is a studio recording, made in early 2003 in Australia during the troubled and rain-sodden Acid Motherhood sessions. The single 46-minute track is built on Kawabata's guitar loops with Allen occasionally adding some melodic vocals. It's actually quite appealing in a hypnotic, minimalist way and would probably satisfy those Gong fans who consider most of the Acid Mothers Gong output to be a total racket.

Gong Matrices

Parade (Voiceprint, 2005)

1. 'Welcome To The Parade' 2. 'Annunaki' 3. 'Demon Barbie And The Super Computer Matrix' 4. 'Seas' 5. 'Battlefield/That's All Right George' 6. 'Email from The Most High' 7. 'The Driver's Seat' 8. 'Virtual Lover' 9. 'Mystery' (all tracks Gilli Smyth/Pierce McDowell except 'Battlefield' poem by Willibrordus S. Rendra)

In 1999 Gilli was involved in a spontaneous jam with multi-instrumentalist Pierce McDowell, Aryeth Frankfurter and Stephen Junca of local folk-prog band Azigza, and James Rotondi. They were so well-received that the lineup reconvened for additional gigs before entering a studio to recreate that original performance.

The result is surprisingly more organised than you might expect, with most of the tracks relying on McDowell's bass and Junca's percussion to provide rhythm and interest while Gilli recites poetry and provides her unique space whisper, and the delightfully-named Frankfurter decorates everything with tasteful flute and violin. The album, credited to Gong Matrices – Gilli Smyth, is both cosmic and funky and harks back to the best of Mother Gong.

Weird Biscuit Teatime/Daevid Allen Weird Quartet

DJDDAY (Voiceprint, 2005)

1. 'DJ Herbal Extract' (Daevid Allen, Michael Clare, Don Falcone, Trey Sabatelli) 2. 'Fashion Victim (Rubber Duck Dub)' (Allen, Clare, Falcone, Sabatelli, Michael Merrill) 3. 'Lavender' (Allen, Clare, Falcone) 4. 'O Dear (Save Me From The Social Security)' (Allen, Clare, Falcone, Sabatelli) 5. 'Beezlebabble Slush' (Allen, Clare, Falcone, Sabatelli) 6. 'Technicolour Tongue' (Allen, Clare, Falcone, Sabatelli) 7. 'Cathode Cathedral' (Allen, Clare, Falcone) 8. 'Trans Human Future' (Allen, Clare, Falcone, Sabatelli) 9. 'This Could Be The End' (Allen, Clare, Falcone, Sabatelli)

ELEVENSES (Purple Pyramid, 2016)

1. 'TransLoopThisMessage' (Daevid Allen, Michael Clare, Don Falcone, Paul Sears) 2. 'Imagicknation' (Allen, Clare, Falcone, Sears) 3. 'The Latest Curfew Craze' (Allen, Clare, Falcone, Trey Sabatelli) 4. 'Kick That Habit Man' (Allen, Clare, Falcone, Sears) 5. 'Secretary Of Lore' (Allen, Clare, Falcone, Sabatelli) 6. 'Alchemy' (Original song Falcone with new material Allen, Clare, Sabatelli) 7. 'The Cold Stuffings Of November' (Allen, Clare, Falcone, Sears) 8. 'Grasshopping' (Allen, Clare, Falcone, Sears) 9. 'God's New Deal' (Allen, Clare/Falcone/Radford) 10. 'Dim Sum In Alphabetical Order' [3.07] (Allen/Clare/Falcone/Sears) 11. 'Killer Honey' [3.15] (Allen/Clare/Falcone/Sears) 12. 'Under The Yum Yum Tree Café '[5.33] (Allen/Clare/Falcone/Sabatelli) 12. 'Banana Construction' [5.17] (Allen/Clare/Falcone/Sabatelli)

In 1998 American musician and producer Don Falcone invited a number of his progressive rock heroes to contribute to the first album by his band Spirits Burning. Among those who responded was Daevid Allen, who added guitar and vocals to some of the tracks, and went on to work with him on subsequent albums and a single, 'The Roadmap In Your Heart'. Some of the recordings also featured University of Errors bassist Michael Clare, and it was he who suggested the creation of a new band with Allen and Falcone.

Originally named ACF, then Inner Demons, it was Allen who came up with Weird Biscuit Teatime. Along with drummer Joey Sabatelli, the album was based on tracks initiated by Falcone before the others added their parts in San Francisco. The result is, indeed, weird – a bit University Of Errors with added glissando ambience and the occasional funky groove from Clare and Sabatelli. Allen's vocals are frequently creepy whispers or menacing snarls and his guitar work is, as you would expect, jagged and unpredictable.

The ACF trio recorded on and off over subsequent years, mostly remotely but about a third of the *Elevenses* album was put together in a studio in 2006.

When Sabatelli wasn't available, they pulled in Paul Sears on drums. In an interview with All About Jazz, Falcone said:

> In 2014, Michael and I decided to dedicate ourselves to finalising the album, and we spent almost a year doing that. In January of 2015, Daevid gave a thumbs up to the updates we had done. Additionally, Daevid wanted to add vocals to two songs, and gliss to three. He made a couple of attempts to record with his home set up in Australia, but was too weak, or unable to concentrate, to provide anything. Soon after, he left us.

The record label insisted on renaming the band Daevid Allen's Weird Quartet for *Elevenses*, and billed it as his last recording, although there is nothing here from him post-2008. Like *DJDDAY*, it's a fascinating and frequently entertaining melange of sounds and ideas ranging from the perky, Gong-ish 'Imagicknation' through frantic guitar workouts to the sheer madness of 'Banana Construction'. It's a bit of a mishmash, to be honest, but it's always good to hear Allen enjoying himself and he seems to be having a blast on these recordings.

Acid Mothers Gong
Live In Tokyo (Voiceprint, 2006)
1. 'Gnome' 11:11 2. 'Ooom Ba Wah!' 3. 'Crazy Invisible She' 4. 'The Unkilling Of Octave Docteur Da 4J' 5. 'Avahoot Klaxon Diamond Language Ritual' 6. 'Ritual: Umbrage Demon Stirfry & Its Upcum' 7. 'Jesu Ali Om Cruci-Fiction' 8. 'Ze Teapot Zat Exploded' 9. 'Eating Colonel Sanders Upside Down' 10. 'Vital Info That Should Never Be Spoken' 11. 'Parallel Tales Of Fred Circumspex' 12. 'The Isle Of Underwear' 13. 'Ohm Riff Voltage 245' 14. 'Total Atonal Farewell To The Innocents' (Mostly improvised so impossible to credit!)

Live In Nagoya (Vivo, 2006)
1. 'Hohoho! (Avahoot Klaxon's Acidological Report)' i 'Hohoho! 11 RDC (Raining Datsun Cogs)' iii 'RDC Over Tokyo' iv 'RDC Over Osaka v RDC Over Nagoya' vi 'Demon Starfry Flotilla' vii 'March Of The Wistful Wombat' viii 'Holi Yoli Echo ix Electroplasmic Barbecue x Breakfast For Freemale & 2 Dogs' 2. 'Makototen' i 'Makototen' ii 'Sacrodental Pornotheologist' iii 'Undone Melodies' iv 'Keeping Up With The Moments' v 'Melt Thy Teapot' vi 'Deconstructural Starpot' 3. 'Glissade Gillisade' i 'Glissade Gillisade 'ii 'Brainwatch Me' iii 'Alien Bananaply Species 04996C' iv 'Makotoply Series F1000 v Yoni Ululatio vi Codex Coda Glissade' 4. 'Lady Lemonade' i 'Hari Mascara Snake' ii 'A New & Very Unusual Philosophy/ Saying Nothing: Only Do' iii 'English Speaking People Meet Jesu Ali Om' iv 'Japanese Speaking People Meet Felix Falatio & Friend' v 'Lady Lemonade' 5. 'Bellyful Of Telephone/Why Do?' 6. 'Hari Balmy Bom Riff' 7. 'Virtual Lover' i 'Virtual Lover' ii 'The Park Dies For Porky' iii 'Some Enchanted Thieving' iv 'Armies Of The Legless' (Mostly improvised so impossible to credit!)

Acid Mothers Gong morphed out of the lineup that produced the *Acid Motherhood* album – indeed, the album wasn't even released when the name was being used at the end of 2003 for a loose conglomeration of Gong and Acid Mothers Temple members. A gig in October of that year is described on the Planet Gong website as a 'wild, one-off Gong band performance that splits the audience straight down the middle with one of the craziest and most challenging Gong gigs for years'. In April 2004 the lineup of Daevid Allen (guitar, vocals), Gilli Smyth (space whisper), Josh Pollock (guitar, megaphone), Yoshida Tatsuya (drums, sampler), Atsushi Tsuyama (bass), Kawabata Makoto (guitars), Cotton Casino (synth) and Hirishi Higashi (synth) did a small tour of Japan from which these recordings were drawn.

Mostly improvised on the night, the two live albums chronicle two gigs on Thursday, April 8 – the first at the Doors Club in Tokyo, the second some 350km away in Japan's fourth-largest city of Nagoya (the fast train takes 110 minutes). These are Marmite recordings, as shown by some of the reviews on Amazon, which range from 'Another fine live performance from one of the many offshoots' to 'Total racket'.

You certainly have to be open to the full-on audio onslaught of eight musicians seemingly playing eight different tunes with the volume knob up to 11. You may recognise a few things: the *Live in Nagoya* cut 'Makototen' bears some resemblance to the track of the same name on Acid Motherhood, while 'Bellyful Of Telephone' is the poem Allen recited on his third solo album *Now Is The Happiest Time Of Your Life.*

Personally, I prefer *Live In Tokyo* as a more successful blending of Gong and AMT – it includes an absolutely stonking version of 'Flying Teapot' plus a version of 'Master Builder' that takes the roof off and separates it into its constituent atoms. Acid Mothers Gong regrouped in 2006 for another short Japanese tour before its swansong at the Gong Family Unconventional in Amsterdam.

The Glissando Guitar Orchestra
Live At The Kozfest Festival (No label, 2014)
1. 'The Seven Drones'

The 7 Drones Live (No label, 2019)
1. 'Daevid's Introduction' 2. 'The 7 Drones Live'

Less a band, more an ad-hoc gathering of like-minded glissando enthusiasts. There had, apparently, been every intention of putting together some sort of glissando ensemble since 1974 but it didn't happen until the Gong Family Unconvention in 2006 when Daevid Allen was joined on stage by Steve Hillage, Fabio Golfetti, Brian Abbott, Steffe Sharpstrings, Josh Pollock, Kawabata Makoto, Harry Williamson, Jerry Bewley of Kangaroo Moon and Steve Higgins from House Of Thandoy. They played relaxing, meditational drones in seven different keys (later recreated for a Daevid solo album) that was released as a DVD. The two audio recordings listed above are only available as downloads from Bandcamp and were released in the wrong order – *The 7 Drones Live* is the earliest, capturing one of Allen's last performances in Birmingham in 2013, accompanied by Abbott, Shankara Andy Bole, Kev Hegan, Will Greenwood, Steve Pond, Dani Speakman and Steve Bemand. The following year Bole led another performance of the orchestra in aid of Allen's cancer fight fund.

Gong Expresso
Decadence (No label, 2018)
1. 'Decadence' (Hansford Rowe) 2. 'Zephyr' (Julien Sandiford) 3. 'Toumani' (Sandiford) 4. 'Talisman' (Sandiford) 5. 'The Importance Of Common Things' (Rowe) 6. 'Eastern Platinum' (Sandiford) 7. 'Frevo' (Sandiford) 8. 'God Knows' (Rowe)

When Gongzilla folded in 2010, Hansford Rowe formed HR3 with drummer Max Lazich and a young guitarist, Julien Sandiford, releasing one album in 2013. As they started work on the follow-up, they realised the new tunes they had demanded a more sensitive, cleaner approach. This resulted in Rowe replacing Lazich with Benoit Moerlen and Francoise Causse to provide low-key percussion, and having three old Gongsters in the lineup justified calling the new band Gong-Expresso, after the name Pierre Moerlen used for live shows in the 1970s.

Using crowdfunding to finance it, the result is an album that's surprisingly mellow, with the emphasis largely on melody rather than rhythm. To be honest, it doesn't sound much like Pierre Moerlen's Gong and even less like Gongzilla, which was a jam band at times, but it does have a gentle, contemplative appeal.

Would you like to write for Sonicbond Publishing?

We are mainly a music publisher, but we also occasionally publish in other genres including film and television. At Sonicbond Publishing we are always on the look-out for authors, particularly for our two main series, On Track and Decades.

Mixing fact with in depth analysis, the On Track series examines the entire recorded work of a particular musical artist or group. All genres are considered from easy listening and jazz to 60s soul to 90s pop, via rock and metal.

The Decades series singles out a particular decade in an artist or group's history and focuses on that decade in more detail than may be allowed in the On Track series.

While professional writing experience would, of course, be an advantage, the most important qualification is to have real enthusiasm and knowledge of your subject. First-time authors are welcomed, but the ability to write well in English is essential.

Sonicbond Publishing has distribution throughout Europe and North America, and all our books are also published in E-book form. Authors will be paid a royalty based on sales of their book. Further details about our books are available from www.sonicbondpublishing.com. To contact us, complete the contact form there or email info@sonicbondpublishing.co.uk